INTERNATIONAL EXPRESS

PRE-INTERMEDIATE
Student's Book

Liz Taylor

OXFORD
UNIVERSITY PRESS

OXFORD
UNIVERSITY PRESS

Great Clarendon Street, Oxford OX2 6DP

Oxford University Press is a department of the University of Oxford.
It furthers the University's objective of excellence in research, scholarship,
and education by publishing worldwide in

Oxford New York

Auckland Cape Town Dar es Salaam Hong Kong Karachi
Kuala Lumpur Madrid Melbourne Mexico City Nairobi
New Delhi Shanghai Taipei Toronto

With offices in

Argentina Austria Brazil Chile Czech Republic France Greece
Guatemala Hungary Italy Japan Poland Portugal Singapore
South Korea Switzerland Thailand Turkey Ukraine Vietnam

OXFORD and OXFORD ENGLISH are registered trade marks of
Oxford University Press in the UK and in certain other countries

ISBN-13: 978 0 19 457475 4
ISBN-10: 0 19 457475 X

Printed in China

ACKNOWLEDGEMENTS

*The authors and publisher are grateful to those who have given permission to reproduce
the following extracts and adaptations of copyright material:*

pp 24–7 Information about the Eden Project and adapted interview with Tim
Smit. Reproduced by kind permission of the Eden Project.

p 65 Interview with Harriet Lamb adapted from 'New style of global training
is on to a winner' by Harriet Lamb from *The Independent*, 9 March 2002.
Reproduced by permission of the Fairtrade Foundation which guarantees
producers a decent price for their produce.

p 80 Information on different culture types. Source: Lewis, Richard D, *When
Cultures Collide*, published 1999 by Nicholas Brealey Publishing www.nbrealey-
books.com. Reproduced by permission of Nicholas Brealey Publishing.

p 100 Extract from David Attenborough's script from the BBC's State of the
Planet series. Reproduced by permission of the BBC and David Attenborough.

p 103 Extract from 'Aspects of age' by Nick Ranking, BBC *On Air* magazine,
September 1998. Reproduced by kind permission of BBC *On Air* Magazine.

Sources:

p 20 Information about Electrolux from www.electrolux.co.uk

p 21 Information about Unilever from www.unilever.com

p 21 Information about Renault from
www.infocorporate.communication@renault.com

pp 52–3 Information about Slow Food from www.slowfood.com

pp 64–7 Information about the Fairtrade Foundation from
www.fairtrade.org.uk

pp 70–1 Information about Keymed, Maersk, and CMG from The Sunday
Times' *100 best companies to work for.*

Illustrations by: Adrian Barclay pp 11, 24, 49; Mark Duffin pp 20 (Electrolux
Group products), 36 (icons), 59, 101; Clive Goodyer pp 7, 47; Ian Jackson pp
108, 111; Kath Walker pp 73, 95, 118; Geoff Waterhouse pp 13, 28, 77, 117

Commissioned photography by: Philip Dunn pp 6, 8, 13, 22, 31, 40, 54, 72, 81;
Chris King p 52; Mark Mason Studios pp 21 (Unilever products), 64, 113

*We would also like to thank the following for permission to reproduce the following
photographs*: Alamy front cover (Image Source/woman on phone),
(J.Kase/Musée d'Orsay interior), back cover (Image100/woman on phone),
pp 12 (D.Copeman/camel), 18 (Image Source), 32 (Image100/Kirsten),
(BananaStock/Grady), 35 (ImageState/bridge with statues), (Jon Arnold
Images/street), (ImageState/spires), 43 (Brand X Pictures), 44 (View Stock/
Japanese man), (Stock Connection, Inc./two women), 46 (A.Segre/
underground), 50 (ImageState/sleep), 53 (N.Hanna/family meal), (Jon Arnold

Images/slow city), 60 (John Foxx/Tate exterior), (J.Kase/Musée d'Orsay
interior), 63 (Image100/woman), 67 (xela/coffee basket), 71
(BananaStock/doctor), 74 (Brand X Pictures/tribesmen), 92 & 93
(SCPhotos/Beijing), 93 (J.Bower/pollution), 94 (Image Source), 103 (John
Foxx/surfer), (D.Young-Wolff/man and camera), 104 (Image Source), 105
(Stock Italia/train), 106 (R.Richardson/Singapore), (Jon Arnold Images/Zurich),
109 (Robert Harding Picture Library Ltd/restaurants), 112 (P.Bowater/trees),
119 (Brand X Pictures/woman and two men), (Pixland/two men),
(Goodshoot/three men); Anthony Blake Photo Library pp 51, 52 (food & food
stand), 54 (restaurant), 121; Aviation-images.com pp 56, 105; By kind
permission of the Banca dei Monte Paschi di Siena p 86 (logo and
headquarters); By kind permission of Beretta p 86 (logo and gun); Corbis
front cover (D.G.Houser/clock), pp 12 (B.Krist/banners), (D.S.Robbins/post),
(W. Kaehler/hot dog), (W. Kaehler/park sign), (M.Everton/neon signs), 14
(R.Kaufman/Faria), (T.Wagner/Matsumara), 16 (G.Iundt/TempSport/kendo),
(T.Wagner/Matsumara), (J.Meech/Ecoscene/mountains), (R.Kaufman/Faria), 35
(D.G.Houser/clock), 60 (S.Bianchetti/Musée d'Orsay exterior), (Tate interior),
70 (R.Lewine), 71 (C.Gupton/class), (A.Skelley/crèche), 74 (W.Hodges/family),
74 (N.Benn/arabs), 76 (M.S.Yamashita/restaurant), 86 (M.Busselle/Chateau de
Goulaine), (Archivo Iconografico, S.A/Versailles), 90 (C.Aurness/contruction),
106 (O.Franken/cycle paths), 109 (V.Parys/Sygma/office buildings), 110
(J.Richardson/Vancouver), 112 (D.Bartruff/amphora), 115 (B.Krist/tree);
Reproduced by permission of the Eastman Kodak Company p 88 (three
modern cameras); The Eden Project/Apex/apexnewspix.com pp 24, 25, 26
(domes), 27 (all S.Burt), 26 (N.Gregory/frog); By kind permission of Electrolux
p 20 (logo, vacuum cleaner,1921 and fridge,1925); By kind permission of the
Fair Trade Foundation back cover (coffee grower), pp 64 (logo), 65, 66, 67
(Edgar & Blanca), 68; Getty Images pp 14 (Chabruken/Cresset), 17
(Chabruken/Cresset), 19 (T.Corney/couple), 32 (J.& K.Share/Bell), 44 (V C
L/C.Ryan/arab and man), 46 (B.Erlanson/office), 47 (L.D.Gordon/swimmer), 47
(D.Oliver/doctor), 50 (J.Cummins/tennis), 50 (E.Dreyer/dishwasher), 63
(E.Honowitz/man), 71 (D.Lo Tai Wai/fitness centre), 76 (D.Carrasco/Moscow),
84 (K.Chiba/man), 84 (P.Pacifica/woman), 90 (D.Smetzer/shopping mall), 90
(M.Rosenfeld/cars), 103 (B.Bailey/woman in helmet), 103 (R.Dahlquist/water-
skier), 110 (P.Adams/Sydney), 112 (W.Cocker/champagne), 115
(T.Bieber/tyres), 115 (D.Toase/wellies); Hulton Archive/Getty pp 17
(Keystone/soldiers), 46 (Picture Post/foundry), 46 (Fox Photos/haymakers), 89
(the Brownie), 89 (George Eastman House/Frederick Church/Archive
Photos/George Eastman with camera on ship), 115 (Edwin Levick/Archive
Photos/mackintosh); By kind permission of Kongo Gumi p 88 (Osaka Castle
top, Shitennoji Temple left, Aoyama College Museum right); By kind
permission of the Chateau de Goulaine p 88 (wine label); Crown copyright.
NMR p 61; Nature Picture Library/naturepl.com p 100; Press Association pp
19 (Ethno Images/father), 93 (EPA/M.Reynolds/cars), (EPA/TV); By kind
permission of RENAULT p 21 (logo and motorshow); Rex Features pp 19
(D.Hartley/job centre), (Sipa Press/stike), 29 (D.Crichlow/rowing),
(D.Crichlow/champagne), 30 (J.Jones), 97 (Wennstrom/smoke pollution), 98
(Action Press/town), (IJO/sign); By kind permission of Barone Ricasoli p 86
(wine label and vineyards); Robert Harding Picture Library p 52 (restaurant);
Royalty-free back cover (wine), pp 8, 62 & 81(wine), 14 (magazine cover), 32
(globe), 57, 96 (globe), 112 (rocket); Still Moving Picture Library p 106 (car
sharing); Still Pictures pp 96 (Z.Yi/UNEP), 97 (R.Giling/child with pot), 98
(A.Ishokon/UNEP/drought), 106 (J.Maier Jr./Curitiba); Veal Ventures Ltd p 29
(Andrew Veal), (C.Brandis/holding oar in air); Zefa front cover and p 74
(Westhill/businessmen), (H.Sitton/woman).

*The author and publisher would like to thank the following people for agreeing to be
interviewed for this book*: Geneviève Cresset, José Manuel Faría and Kensuke
Matsumura.

*The author and publisher would also like to thank the many teachers and institutions
who provided so much advice and assistance in the development of this new edition of
International Express, in particular*: Rick Baldwin, EF Executive Centre,
Cambridge; John Barnett and Paddy Mahoney, The Cambridge Academy of
English, Cambridge; Sarah Bickerdike; Tracy Byrne; Claire Giffen, Caledonian
School, Prague; Alison Gourd-Juillan; Mick Jeive, KS Kaderschulen, Zurich;
Philippa Skillman and the staff of King's College, Madrid; Jeremy Townend,
Infolangues, Lyon; Bruce Wade.

to International Express
Pre-Intermediate New Edition

Introduction	There are twelve units and three review units in this book. Each unit has four main parts: Language focus, Wordpower, Skills focus, and Focus on functions. The unit begins with an 'agenda'. This gives you the language contents of each unit.
Language focus	First, you learn new grammar, or revise grammar you studied before. You listen to a dialogue or read a text which presents the grammar in a real-life situation. Then you study examples of the grammar to understand how to use it correctly. You think about how the grammar works and you complete the rules.

Practice
You use the grammar in different practice situations: sometimes in speaking activities, sometimes in writing exercises. The exercises help you to learn the new language and use it with confidence. You do some of the practice activities with another student or in a group.

Pronunciation
These exercises help you with pronunciation problems. You listen to examples and practise the correct pronunciation.

Wordpower	In the second part of the unit you learn new vocabulary. You also learn ways to organize and remember useful words and phrases.
Skills focus	In the third part of each unit you improve your listening, speaking, and reading skills. You listen to interviews or read longer texts and you discuss topics in pairs or groups. You also practise writing.
Focus on functions	In the last part of each unit you learn the phrases you need for socializing with people at work or outside work. You also learn the phrases you need for telephoning in English.
Review units	There are three review units. You choose what to revise and complete the review exercises. You can use the self-check boxes to check your learning.
Pocket Book	In a pocket at the back of the *International Express* Student's Book there is a separate reference book with useful language from the Student's Book. You can use the Pocket Book in your lessons and take it with you when you travel. It has a Grammar section, with grammar tables and summaries for each unit; a Focus on functions section, with a summary of all the phrases for socializing and telephoning; and other useful information and reference material.
Listening scripts and Answer key	The scripts of all the listening material and the answers to the exercises are at the back of the Student's Book. You can study these after the lesson.
Workbook	There is an *International Express* Workbook which has extra exercises on grammar, vocabulary, and social English. It has a Student's cassette or CD with more pronunciation and social English exercises for further practice.

Good luck with learning English.

We hope you enjoy using *International Express*!

Contents

UNIT 1
First meetings

▼ AGENDA
▶ Present Simple, *Wh*- questions
▶ Frequency adverbs
▶ Personal information file. Learning
  vocabulary
▶ English in the world
▶ Introductions, greetings, and goodbyes

Language focus

1 Look at the pictures. What do you think happens at Vinexpo?

2 What information do the business cards give you?

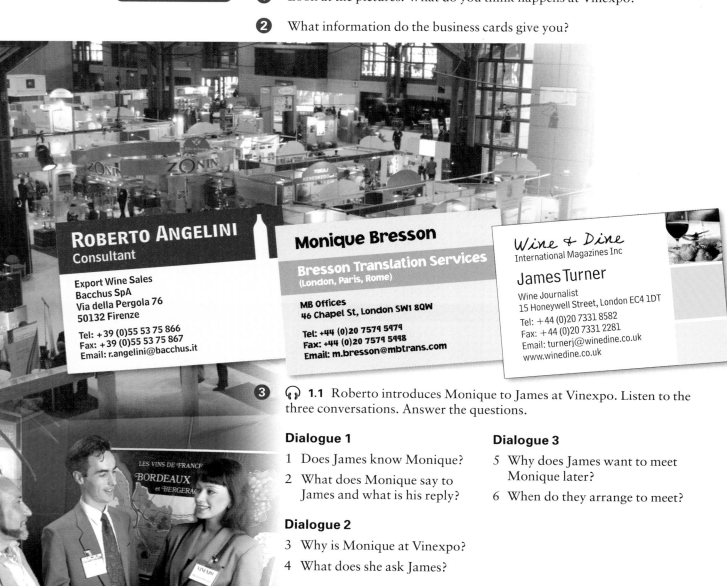

ROBERTO ANGELINI
Consultant

Export Wine Sales
Bacchus SpA
Via della Pergola 76
50132 Firenze

Tel: +39 (0)55 53 75 866
Fax: +39 (0)55 53 75 867
Email: r.angelini@bacchus.it

Monique Bresson

Bresson Translation Services
(London, Paris, Rome)

MB Offices
46 Chapel St, London SW1 8QW

Tel: +44 (0)20 7579 5979
Fax: +44 (0)20 7579 5998
Email: m.bresson@mbtrans.com

Wine & Dine
International Magazines Inc

James Turner

Wine Journalist
15 Honeywell Street, London EC4 1DT

Tel: +44 (0)20 7331 8582
Fax: +44 (0)20 7331 2281
Email: turnerj@winedine.co.uk
www.winedine.co.uk

3 🎧 **1.1** Roberto introduces Monique to James at Vinexpo. Listen to the three conversations. Answer the questions.

Dialogue 1

1 Does James know Monique?

2 What does Monique say to James and what is his reply?

Dialogue 2

3 Why is Monique at Vinexpo?

4 What does she ask James?

Dialogue 3

5 Why does James want to meet Monique later?

6 When do they arrange to meet?

4 🎧 **1.2** Listen to the conversation between Monique and James in a bar. Underline the correct answer.

Example What does James offer Monique?
He offers her a cup of coffee/a glass of red wine/<u>a glass of champagne</u>.

1 What does James do when he goes to the wine regions?

2 How often does James travel to Italy?

3 Where does Monique live?

He attends sales conferences/ interviews people/gives presentations.

He travels to Italy once a year/twice a year/two or three times a year.

She lives in London/Paris/Rome.

Present Simple

Read the examples. Complete the grammar rules.

Positive
- I **have** a translation business.
- He/She **lives** in London.
- We both **write** articles on wine.

Negative
- I **don't work** for *Wine & Dine* magazine.
- James **doesn't import** wines.
- The wine producers **don't speak** French.

Questions
- **Do** Roberto and James usually **visit** Vinexpo?
- What **do** James and Roberto **write** about?
- Where **does** Monique **live**?
- **Does** Roberto often **travel** to France?

Note *don't = do not, doesn't = does not*

Answers
- Yes, they **do**.

- They **write** about wine.
- She **lives** in London.
- Yes, he **does**.

- Use the _____ _____ to talk about long-term situations and routine activities.

I/you/we/they
- To make the positive, use the infinitive form.
- To make the negative, use *do + not (don't)* + infinitive.
- To make the question, use _____ + *I/you/we/they* + infinitive.

he/she/it
- The positive form always ends in _____ .
- To make the negative, use _____ + _____ *(doesn't)* + infinitive.
- To make the question, use _____ + *he/she/it* + infinitive.

How do we make questions and short answers in the Present Simple?

Pocket Book p. 12

Practice

1 Complete the sentences using the correct form of the verbs in brackets.

Example Roberto _____ wine. (export) *Roberto exports wine.*

1 Roberto _____ articles on wine. (write)

2 Monique _____ wine. (not import)

3 Roberto and James always _____ a lot of important people in the wine business at Vinexpo. (meet)

4 Monique _____ in France. (not live)

5 The Italian wine producers _____ French. (not speak)

6 James often _____ to France and Italy. (travel)

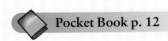

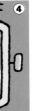

2 Write the correct question word for each picture.

When?   How often?   Which?   What? ✓   Where?   Who?

1 _____   3 _____   5 _____

2 *What?*   4 _____   6 _____

3 Write the questions for these answers. Use the question word in brackets.

Example He works for <u>*Wine & Dine* magazine</u>. (Which?)
Which magazine does he work for?

1 They live <u>in Dijon</u>. (Where?)

2 He goes there <u>three or four times a year</u>. (How often?)

3 They meet <u>at Vinexpo</u>. (Where?)

4 She visits them <u>in June</u>. (When?)

5 They meet <u>important people</u> at Vinexpo. (Who?)

6 He writes about <u>wine</u>. (What?)

Pronunciation

1 🎧 **1.3** Listen to the examples. We say the
questions in different ways.

a Do you speak Italian? ↗
b Which languages do you speak? ↘

2 🎧 **1.4** Listen to the questions. Write a ↗ or b ↘.

1 _____   4 _____   7 _____   10 _____

2 _____   5 _____   8 _____

3 _____   6 _____   9 _____

3 🎧 **1.4** Listen again and repeat.

4 Write *up* or *down*.

- In questions that begin with *do/does*, the voice
  goes _____ at the end.

- In questions that begin with question words,
  the voice goes _____ at the end.

4 Work in pairs. Practise asking and answering questions.

Example James/work for/magazine?
Does James work for a magazine? Yes, he does.

1 Monique/speak/Italian?

2 Where/she/work?

3 James and Roberto/write/about wine?

4 James/work for/*Wine & Dine?*

5 Roberto/know/Monique?

6 James/live in Italy?

7 he/love/his work?

8 James/go/France and Italy?

9 Where/Monique's parents/live?

10 she/travel/Paris?

5 Work in Group A or Group B.

Group A Read the Editor's letter and write five questions.
Group B Read the Visitor profile and write five questions.

James Turner

Monique Bresson

Editor's letter

Duncan Ross
Editor and publisher

Welcome back! Vinexpo opens this week for another meeting of old and new friends in the wine and spirits business. This is a special edition of our magazine to inform you of Vinexpo events. First we want to introduce James Turner. James works from our London office and specializes in French and Italian wines. He wants to write a book about Italian wines. He often travels to all the wine-producing countries in Europe and interviews the key people in our business. He tastes and rates wines for us every year. James enjoys photography and cooking; he likes French cuisine, and he plays golf and tennis when he has time between business trips. Come and meet James and all of us on Stand 49 and enter our competition.

Visitor profile

Monique Bresson

One of the special guests of the Vinexpo organizers this year is Monique Bresson. She is here as an interpreter and translator for our Italian colleagues and you can meet her on Stand 106. Ms Bresson runs a translation agency with offices in London, Paris, and Rome. She lives in London but commutes regularly to Paris. She knows a lot about the wine business because her parents have a vineyard near Dijon. Her father comes from Hungary and she speaks Hungarian and four other European languages. She enjoys skiing, horse-riding, and sailing at the weekends.

6 Read the other text and answer the other group's questions.

7 Work in pairs. Ask and answer three questions about other students.

Examples *Does Marco speak French?*   *Yes, he does.*
Where does he live?   *He lives in the city centre.*

Frequency adverbs

0%   never   rarely   sometimes   often   usually   always   **100%**

Read these examples and complete the grammar rule.

- I'm **always** very busy.
- He isn't **usually** late.
- They **never** visit us.
- I don't **always** get up early.
- We **usually** drive to work.
- They're **never** on time.

- We write words like *always/usually/never* after the verb *to be* but _____ other verbs.

8 Rewrite the sentences adding frequency adverbs to make true sentences. Add three more sentences about your daily routine.

1 I get up before 6 a.m.
2 My teacher goes to bed after midnight.
3 I drive to work.
4 I am late.
5 My friend uses a computer.
6 I speak English to colleagues.
7 My boss travels on business.
8 We are early for English classes.

9 Work in pairs. Ask your partner about his/her lifestyle. In the boxes below, tick (✔) the adverbs he/she uses. Add two more questions.

Example **Student A** *How often do you go to a disco?*
Student B *Sometimes.*

LEISURE SURVEY				
How often do you …	**never**	**rarely**	**sometimes**	**often**
1 play a sport at weekends?				
2 go to the theatre?				
3 eat at a restaurant?				
4 travel by plane?				
5 go out with friends?				
6 visit museums?				
7 walk in the country?				
8 read a newspaper?				
9 _____				
10 _____				

10 Your partner is a visitor at Vinexpo. Write a short Visitor profile about him/her for the *Wine & Dine* Vinexpo Special Edition, using the information in the Leisure survey.

Personal information file. Learning vocabulary

Organizing vocabulary

It is easier to learn and remember words if they are in groups. Here are some ways of organizing vocabulary.

1 Word groups

1 Add three more words to each topic group.

Work	Jobs	Family
employer	journalist	parents
colleague	interpreter	sister
_____	_____	_____
_____	_____	_____
_____	_____	_____

2 Complete the verb groups.

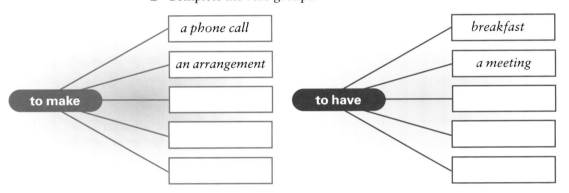

to make — a phone call / an arrangement / ____ / ____ / ____

to have — breakfast / a meeting / ____ / ____ / ____

3 Write the time expressions in the box in the correct group.

2001   10 a.m.   Tuesday morning   midday   5 July   the afternoon

at	in	on
the weekend	October	Sunday
_____	_____	_____
_____	_____	_____

2 Word maps

Add more vocabulary to complete the word map.

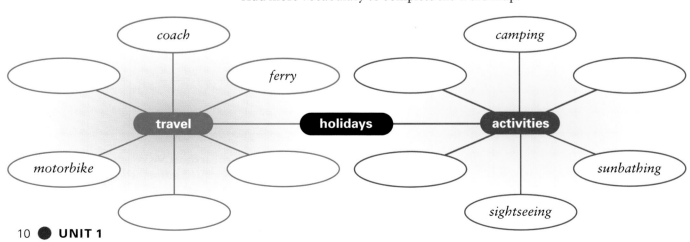

travel — coach, ferry, motorbike

holidays

activities — camping, sunbathing, sightseeing

3 **Word pairs**

Match the words that go together.

send   a business trip
meet   an email
make   a meeting
do   a visitor
attend   a job

4 **Opposites**

Write the opposite word.

cheap   _____   tall   _____

cold   _____   sad   _____

difficult   _____   hard-working   _____

Recording meaning

It is a good idea to write vocabulary that is useful to you in a vocabulary notebook or on cards, with information to help you remember the meaning and pronunciation.

1 Read these examples of ways to record meaning.

Write the word in a sentence to show its meaning.

earn – Top footballers earn a lot of money.

Write an explanation in English.

salary – the money you get for the work you do

Write the translation.

busy – ocupado

Add stress marks.

employment

Write the opposite word.

helpful – unhelpful

Draw a picture or diagram.

knife and fork

2 Work in pairs. Record the meaning of the words in the box. Use some of the ideas in **1**.

> flexitime   unemployed   quiet   to commute   suitcase

Asking for help

Here are some ways to ask for help.

- *Sorry, I don't understand.*
- *Can you repeat that, please?*
- *Could you speak slowly, please?*
- *What does … mean?*
- *I don't know what … means.*
- *Can you spell that, please?*

English in the world

1 Look at the list of the world's ten most important languages. The missing languages are Arabic, German, Japanese, Russian, and Spanish. Where do they go in the list?

The world's top ten languages	Spoken as a first language by
1 Mandarin Chinese	_____
2 English	_____
3 _____	266m*
4 Hindi	_____
5 _____	181m
6 Portuguese	_____
7 Bengali	_____
8 _____	158m
9 _____	124m
10 _____	121m

m = million

2 🎧 **1.5** Listen and check the missing languages.

3 🎧 **1.5** Listen again and complete the numbers of speakers.

4 How do we say these figures?

a 80%   b 69%   c 2bn   d 1.1bn   e ½   f ¾

5 Do the quiz in pairs. The answers are in **4**.

What do you know about English?

1 More than _____ people speak it as a second or foreign language.

2 Over _____ of the information on the Internet is in English.

3 _____ of the people who use the Internet communicate in English.

4 About _____ the population of the European Union speaks English.

5 _____ of the people in the European Union who don't speak English as a first language think it's the most important language to learn.

6 The estimated number of people in the world who are learning English at present is over _____.

6 🎧 **1.6** Listen to an interview with a language expert about English and check your answers to **5**.

7 There are about 20,000 English words in Japanese today. Can you say which English words these Japanese words come from?

Food and drink – *hambaagaa, chikin, biiru, jyusu*

Communication – *rajio, terebi, fakkusu, iimeeru*

8 Work in groups.

1 Which English words do you use in your language? Think about different topics, for example food and drink, communication, travel, and leisure activities. Make a list.

2 Present your list to the class.

9 Discuss your opinions.

1 Why do you think there are a lot of English words in other languages?

2 The governments of some countries are against the use of English words. What do you think? Are you for or against the use of English in your language?

Introductions, greetings, and goodbyes

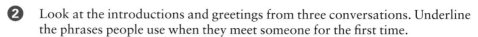

1 Work in pairs. Answer the questions.

1 When do people in your country shake hands?

2 What do you say in English when you don't hear a person's name?

3 When do you say *Good morning/Good afternoon/Good evening/Good night*?

2 Look at the introductions and greetings from three conversations. Underline the phrases people use when they meet someone for the first time.

1 Excuse me, are you …?
Hello, how are things?
May I introduce myself? I'm …
How do you do?

2 Nice to see you again.
How are you?
How's life?
How's the family?

3 Let me introduce you to …
I'd like to introduce you to …
Pleased to meet you.
Good to see you again.

3 🎧 **1.7** Listen to the three conversations. Look at **2** and tick (✓) the phrases you hear.

4 Match the phrases with the correct responses.

How are you?   Yes, that's right.
Pleased to meet you.   Then you must call me Luigi.
How do you do?   Very well, thank you. And you?
Please call me James.   How do you do?
How's life?   Pleased to meet you, too.
Hello, are you Roberto?   Not too bad, but very busy.

5 🎧 **1.8** Monique and James say goodbye at the airport after Vinexpo. Listen to their conversation and tick (✓) the phrases you hear.

Nice to see you again.   I really enjoyed meeting you, too.

I must go now.   Have a good trip back.

It was very nice meeting you.   Thank you, and the same to you.

I look forward to seeing you.   I hope to see you again.

6 You are in the wine business and you are at Vinexpo. Choose one of these business cards and decide why you are at the wine fair. Fill in your name in the gap on the card.

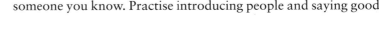

TRANS TALK

Translator
39, Wirral Avenue
London
SW1A 2AH

Tel/fax: + 44 (0)20 8122 2359
Email: transtalk@qtel.net.uk

NEWSWIDE REPORT
International

NEWS PHOTOGRAPHER
Vernon Mansions, Westway Drive
Croydon CR9 5TL

Tel/fax: +44 (0)20 8437 9215
Fax: +44 (0)20 7579 5998
Email: newsrep@ftl.net.uk

FIA Publications

Journalist
32 Belmont Square
London
W1 4TQ

Tel: +44 (0)20 7333 4656
Fax: +44 (0)20 7676 3654
Email: info@fia.co.uk

7 Walk around and introduce yourself to other people in the group. Greet someone you know. Practise introducing people and saying goodbye.

UNIT 2
The world of work

Language focus

1 🎧 **2.1** Listen to three extracts from interviews for a business magazine. Complete the information about the three people.

Business World Today
International edition
ISSUE 21

It's plain sailing for business the Australian way

Languages in the workplace

The clock is ticking for bonds

Extract 1
Name: José Manuel Faria
Job: _____, Food Division
Company: Unilever
Place of work: _____

Extract 2
Name: Geneviève Cresset
Job: Team Co-ordinator
Company: Téléimages
Place of work: _____

Extract 3
Name: Kensuke Matsumura
Job: _____, Professional Products
Company: Electrolux
Place of work: _____

2 🎧 **2.1** Listen to the interview extracts again. José Manuel, Geneviève, and Kensuke all need English for different activities at work. Which activities?

3 Work in groups. Answer the questions.
1 Do you need English for any of the activities you listed in **2**?
2 Make a list of needs for your group.

4 🎧 **2.2** Listen to three more extracts from the interviews. Answer the questions.

Extract 1
1 What very big change is Unilever making to its distribution system in Spain?
2 Why is José Manuel having a lot of meetings with consultants?

Extract 2
1 In what way is Téléimages changing?
2 What news is Téléimages hoping to get soon?

Extract 3
What is happening to Electrolux sales in Japan in
1 the Professional Products Division?
2 the Consumer Products Division?

5 Look at the verbs in **4**. They are all in the Present Continuous. Why?

Present Simple and Present Continuous

Read the examples. Complete the grammar rules and answer the question.

Present Simple

- I usually **stay** there for about a week.
- He **doesn't speak** Japanese.
- **Do** you **need** English in your job?
- How often **do** you **go** to international meetings?

Present Continuous

- We**'re changing** our distribution system.
- The Consumer Products Division **isn't having** this problem.
- **Are** companies like Electrolux **having** problems, too?
- What changes **is** Unilever **making**?

Write *the Present Continuous* or *the Present Simple*.
- Use _____ to talk about regular activities.
- Use _____ to talk about current activities.
- To make _____, use *am/is/are* + *-ing* form of the verb.

How do we make short answers with the Present Continuous?

 Pocket Book p. 11, 12

Pronunciation

1 🎧 **2.3** Listen to the examples. Notice the pronunciation of *do* and *does*.

	/də/ (weak)	/duː/ (strong)
Example 1	a Do you work in Paris?	b Yes, I do.

	/dəz/ (weak)	/dʌz/ (strong)
Example 2	a Does she live in Madrid?	b Yes, she does.

2 🎧 **2.4** Listen to the pronunciation of *do* and *does* in the sentences. Which sound do you hear? Tick (✓) a or b. The first one is done as an example.

	a (weak)	b (strong)
1 Where do they live?	✓	
2 Does she speak English?		
3 Yes, she does.		
4 What time do we arrive?		
5 Do you often travel abroad?		
6 Yes, I do.		

3 🎧 **2.4** Listen again and repeat the sentences.

4 When *do* or *does* is at the end of the sentence, do we pronounce it as the strong form or the weak form?

Practice Work in pairs, Student A with another Student A, Student B with another Student B.

Student A

1 Read about Kensuke Matsumura. Student B will ask you questions about him in ②.

Kensuke Matsumura works in Tokyo but he doesn't live there. He goes to work by underground and his journey takes one and a half hours. He works nine hours a day or more and usually takes work home at weekends. He spends about five hours a day on phone calls and emails. He doesn't get much time to relax but he enjoys watching TV, and once a month he does kendo. Like a lot of managers in Japan he has two weeks' holiday a year, and usually takes one week in the summer and the other in the winter.

2 Prepare questions about José Manuel Faria to ask Student B in ②. Use the words below and the Present Simple.

  a How many children/José Manuel Faria/have?
  b What language/he/speak at home?
  c What work/his wife/do?
  d Where/he/spend/most of his work time?
  e How often/he/travel to Bilbao?
  f Why/he/go/to Bilbao?
  g he/like/living in Barcelona?
  h What/he/enjoy doing/in his free time?

Student B

1 Read about José Manuel Faria. Student A will ask you questions about him in ②.

José Manuel Faria lives with his wife and two sons in Barcelona. After seven years in Spain they all speak Spanish, but at home their language is Portuguese, and his wife works as a translator in both languages. José Manuel spends most of his time working in Barcelona but every Monday he goes to Bilbao to visit his company's factory and have meetings with people there. He likes living in Barcelona and in his free time enjoys swimming with his sons and walking in the mountains.

2 Prepare questions about Kensuke Matsumura to ask Student A in ②. Use the words below and the Present Simple.

  a Where/Kensuke Matsumura/work?
  b he/live in Tokyo?
  c How long/his journey to work/take?
  d How many hours a day/he work?
  e How much time/he/spend on phone calls and emails?
  f What/he/do/to relax?
  g What/he/do/once a month?
  h How many weeks' holiday a year/he/have?

2 Work with a different partner, Student A with Student B. Ask your questions and answer your partner's questions.

3 Complete the article about Geneviève Cresset. Use the Present Simple or Present Continuous form of the verbs in brackets.

Geneviève Cresset _____¹ (start) work at 9 a.m. and _____² (finish) around 6 or 7 p.m. The company she _____³ (work) for, Téléimages, _____⁴ (produce) TV programmes and _____⁵ (sell) them to TV channels in France and other countries. About a hundred people _____⁶ (work) full-time in the company's Champs-Elysées office. Geneviève _____⁷ (not have) much time outside work but at present she _____⁸ (work) on an important project – she _____⁹ (write) a book. The book is about the wartime memories of two World War II soldiers. 'They were heroes,' she says, 'so right now I _____¹⁰ (record) their stories for the future. I think it _____¹¹ (be) important we _____¹² (not forget) the enormous courage of people like them.'

4 Prepare your answers to these questions.

What's happening in your life these days?

At work

Are there any changes or new developments in your
- organization?
- job?
- career plans?

Outside work

Is anything new happening in your
- family life?
- social life?

Are you
- making any plans for your next holiday?
- saving money for something important?
- making any changes to your home?

5 Work in pairs. Ask and answer the questions in **4**.

6 Tell the class three things about your partner's current activities.

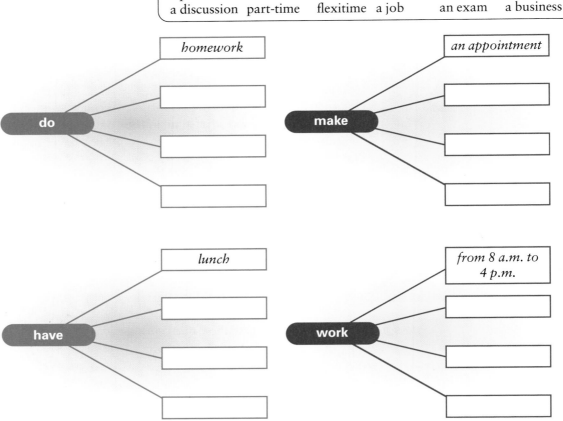

Work file. Verb groups

1 Complete the verb groups with words from the box.

| a phone call | some work | full-time | a meeting | a decision | a holiday |
| a discussion | part-time | flexitime | a job | an exam | a business trip |

homework

do

an appointment

make

lunch

have

from 8 a.m. to 4 p.m.

work

2 Prepare a question about each topic in the job description.

Examples *What hours do you work?*
Do you have discussions at work? Who with? What about?

JOB DESCRIPTION

Name _____

Job title _____

1 Working hours _____

2 Lunch _____

3 Phone calls _____

4 Meetings or
discussions _____

5 Business trips _____

6 Holidays _____

3 Work in pairs. Ask your partner your questions. Answer your partner's questions.

4 Match the words in the box with their meaning.

self-employed	in work ✓	unemployed	retired
a pensioner	out of work	on sick leave	on maternity leave
on paternity leave	on strike	in employment ✓	

A person who

1 has a job   *in work*   *in employment*

2 doesn't have a job _____ _____

3 works independently, not for an employer _____

4 doesn't work any more because of age _____ _____

5 is away from work because of illness _____

6 is away from work for the birth of a baby _____ _____

7 refuses to work because they want more money, better working conditions, etc. _____

5 Work in groups. Discuss the questions.

In your country

1 Do unemployed people get money from the state? If so, is it for a limited time only?

2 Is there an official retirement age? Is it the same for men and women?

3 Do many people retire early, before the official retirement age?

4 Are there many strikes? If so, which groups of people go on strike, and why?

5 How long is maternity leave?

6 Do you have paternity leave? If so, do many fathers take it?

Describing a company

1 The pictures show some of the products made by companies in the Electrolux Group. In pairs, match the names of the products with the pictures.

lawnmower _____   freezer _____   refrigerator _____

dishwasher _____   cooker _____   vacuum cleaner _____

washing machine _____

Electrolux

2 🎧 **2.5** A Swedish employee of Electrolux is welcoming a group of visitors. Listen to her presentation and complete the company datafile.

COMPANY DATAFILE

The Electrolux Group – the world's largest producer of powered appliances for kitchen, cleaning, and outdoor use.

Nationality _____
Head office _____
Started _____
World's first vacuum cleaner _____
First fridge _____
Employs _____ people
Sells its products in _____ countries
Worldwide turnover* € _____ million
Global divisions: Consumer Durables _____ % of sales
Professional Products

(Figures for 2002)

turnover = the total value of business done in a year

3 Read the phrases for describing a company.

Describing a company

(*Unilever/Renault*)	started in … dates from …	(*It*) has	companies subsidiaries	in …

(*Its*) head office is in …

(*It*)   produces …
manufactures …
sells …

(*It*)   employs …
has … employees

(*Its*) worldwide turnover is …

(*It*) has   (2) divisions
(5) business groups
(*many*) well-known brands

(*It*) spends (5%) of its revenue* on R + D*.
(50%) of its   revenue comes
sales come   from …   (*It*) has a (10%) market share in …

revenue = total amount of money received by a company in a period of time
R + D = Research and Development

4 Work in Group A or Group B.

Group A
Look at the information about Unilever. Prepare a short presentation about the company. Use suitable phrases from **3**.

Unilever

Nationality	British–Dutch
Started	1930
Head offices	Rotterdam and London
Employs	247,000 people in 57 countries
Worldwide turnover	€48,760m
Spending on R + D	2.3% of turnover
Global divisions:	Food – over 50% of sales
	Home and Personal Care
Business groups	10 regional groups, to meet needs of local markets
Sells its products in	150 countries to 150m customers

Unilever's well-known consumer brands include:

Food	Home and Personal Care
Knorr	Omo
Lipton's tea	Cif
Hellmann's mayonnaise	Domestos
Magnum ice cream	Dove
Flora	Lux

(Figures for 2002)

Group B
Look at the information about Renault. Prepare a short presentation about the company. Use suitable phrases from **3**.

RENAULT

Nationality	French
Head office	Paris
Started	1898
Employs	132,351 people in 36 countries
Spending on R + D	5.6% of revenue
Worldwide revenue	€36.336m
Global divisions:	Automotive – 93.1% of revenue
	Finance – 5% of revenue

The Automotive Division

The Renault Group	Renault, Samsung (South Korea), and Dacia (Romania)
	3rd largest company in France
	4.4% world market share
	top-selling cars – Mégane, Clio, Laguna
Renault–Nissan Group	world's 5th largest automobile manufacturer

(Figures for 2002)

5 Present your company to the other group. Listen to their presentation.

6 Write a short description of your own company or organization for a business magazine.

Making contact

1 🎧 **2.6** James Turner is telephoning Monique Bresson at her London office. Listen to the conversation and complete the receptionist's message pad.

> Message for   ....
> Caller's name   ....
> Company   ....
> Number   ....
> Please call   ☐
> Caller will phone back ☐

2 🎧 **2.6** Listen to the call again. Tick (✓) the phrases you hear.

Could I speak to Monique Bresson, please?
I'd like to speak to Monique Bresson, please.
Who's calling, please?
It's James Turner.
Hold the line, please.
I'm sorry, she's in a meeting.
I'm afraid she's busy at the moment.
Can you take a message?
Can I take a message?
Could you ask her to call me?
Could you tell her I called?

3 Work in pairs. Practise this telephone conversation. Use phrases from **2**. Then change roles and practise the conversation again.

Receptionist	**Caller**
Answer phone.	
	Ask to speak to Monique Bresson.
Ask who's calling.	
	Give your name and company.
Ask caller to hold the line.	
Say she's in a meeting.	
Offer to take a message.	
	Give the message.
Repeat the message.	
	Say thank you and goodbye.
Say goodbye.	

4 🎧 **2.7** James phones Monique later. Listen and complete the conversation.

R Bresson Translation Services.

J Can I _____ [1] to Monique Bresson, please?

R Who's _____ [2]?

J _____ [3] James Turner.

R Hold _____ [4], Mr Turner. (*phone rings*) Monique?

M Speaking.

R I have James Turner for you …

5 🎧 **2.8** James telephones Monique another day to arrange a meeting. Listen to the phone call and tick (✔) the correct answers.

1 The appointment is with
  a Mr Mikelore   b Mr Michelmore   c Mr Michinore

2 on
  a Friday   b Wednesday   c Tuesday

3 at
  a eleven o'clock   b ten o'clock   c three o'clock

4 His telephone number is
  a 020 7623 5469   b 020 7623 4459   c 020 7623 3409

6 Put the letters of the alphabet in the correct boxes below. Then practise saying them.

a b c d e f g h i j k l m n o p q r s t u v w x y z

/eɪ/ (as in *say*)	/iː/ (as in *she*)	/e/ (as in *ten*)	/aɪ/ (as in *fly*)	/əʊ/ (as in *go*)	/ɑː/ (as in *bar*)	/uː/ (as in *who*)
a	e	f	i	o	r	u

7 Work in pairs. Spell your name and the names of two people in your family to your partner. Your partner writes down the names. Check the spellings are correct.

8 Look at these ways of saying telephone numbers.

64459   six four four five nine   six double four five nine

01731   oh one seven three one (UK)   zero one seven three one (USA)

9 Practise saying these numbers.

56767   293401   334477   220499   020 8112 3665

10 Work in pairs. Choose one of the letter headings below, or your own company's letter heading. Ask and answer questions about your companies.

Examples   *What's the name of your company?*
                Can you spell that, please?
                Could you tell me your fax number, please?

PAPYRUS S.A.
rue des Grandes Filles 112
1050 Bruxelles
Tél: (+32) 2/534 93 67
Fax: (+32) 2/539 19 46
email: info@papyrus.be
www.papyrus.com

HUTTON NICHOLL GOOD
Architects and Landscape Planners
The Barn House, Chippenham
Wiltshire, SN14 8EZ
Tel: (+44) 01249 374226   Fax: (+44) 01249 372107
email: info@hng.co.uk   www.huttonnichollgood.co.uk

AGUASAN
Calle Castelló 75
Madrid, 28006
Tel: +34 91 5624857
Fax: +34 91 5629834
email: aguasan@ag.es
www.aguasan.com

UNIT 3
Challenges

▼ AGENDA
▶ Past Simple
▶ Regular and irregular verbs
▶ Sports and leisure file. Verb groups
▶ Solo achievements
▶ Welcoming a visitor

Language focus

1 Read the information about the Eden Project, one of the UK's top visitor attractions. Would you like to go there?

eden project

The Eden Project shows the importance of plants and how we depend on them for the air we breathe, the clothes we wear, and for our food and medicines.

In the biomes there are 80,000 plants from around the world.

The Humid Tropics Biome is the world's largest greenhouse, 50 metres high and 240 metres long, with giant rainforest trees and a 25-metre-high waterfall. It has plants and products from the Amazon, West Africa, Malaysia, and Oceania.

The Warm Temperate Biome has plants from three different areas of the world with the same climate: South Africa, the Mediterranean, and California. There are also olive groves, grapevines, and orange and lemon trees.

The Roofless Biome outside has plants from Chile, the Himalayas, Australasia, and Cornwall. Works of art tell the story of the plants and their use in food, medicine, and construction.

Humid Tropics Biome

Warm Temperate Biome

LONDON
Bristol
CORNWALL
The Eden Project

The Arena is an outdoor amphitheatre for musical and theatrical events.

2 🎧 **3.1** Listen to an interview with Tim Smit, the man who first had the idea of the Eden Project. Complete the datafile.

Eden Project datafile

- The idea of the Eden Project began with a discussion in a *pub*.
- The idea became a reality _____ [1] years later.
- The project cost £_____ [2].
- The Millennium Commission gave £_____ [3].
- When work began in _____ [4], it rained every day for _____ [5] days.
- In its first year, Eden had _____ [6] visitors.

3 🎧 **3.1** Listen to the interview again. Answer the questions.

1 What did Tim Smit and his friend want to do for Cornwall?
2 Where did the idea of a rainforest in a greenhouse come from?
3 Did they expect to have so many visitors in the first year?
4 In Tim Smit's opinion, what was the reason for Eden's success?

4 Look at the verbs in **2** and **3**. They are all in the Past Simple. Why?

Tim Smit

Past Simple

Read the examples. Complete the grammar rules.

Positive
- We **wanted** to bring more visitors to the area.
- We **had** a wonderful team of people.

Negative
- The weather certainly **didn't help** us.
- The workers **didn't make** any progress for three months.

Questions
- **Did** you **find** it?
- **Did** you **expect** so many visitors?
- How much **did** the project **cost**?
- Where **did** you **get** the money from?

Short answers
- Yes, we **did**.
- No, we **didn't**.

- Use the Past Simple for finished actions and situations in the past.
- To make the Past Simple of regular verbs, add _____ to the end of the verb.
- For the Past Simple of irregular verbs, see Pocket Book p. 6.
- To make the negative, use *did not* or _____ + infinitive.
- To make the question, use _____ + subject + _____.
- To make short answers, use _____ (positive) and _____ (negative).

Pocket Book p. 10

Practice **1** Past Simple quick test. Complete the table.

INFINITIVE	become	begin	come		do			give	have		think
PAST SIMPLE				cost		found	got			made	

Pronunciation **1** 🎧 3.2 Listen to the examples. Notice the pronunciation of the *-ed* endings of the verbs.

/d/	/t/	/ɪd/
a lived	b helped	c visited

2 🎧 3.3 Listen to the verbs and tick (✓) the sound you hear at the end of each word. The first one is done as an example.

	arrived	started	worked	wanted	rained	increased	expected	watched	received	needed
/d/	✓									
/t/										
/ɪd/										

3 🎧 3.3 Listen to the verbs again and repeat them.

4 How do we pronounce the *-ed* ending when the infinitive form of the verb ends in *-t* or *-d*, e.g. *start*, *need*?

---

2 Complete the article. Use the Past Simple form of the verbs in brackets.

The man behind the Eden Project

Tim Smit was born in 1955 in the Netherlands of an English mother and a Dutch father. Because his father _____ ¹ (work) for KLM airlines his parents _____ ² (live) abroad. Tim _____ ³ (not live) with them but _____ ⁴ (go) to an English boarding school, which he _____ ⁵ (hate). On holidays in Turkey he _____ ⁶ (become) interested in archaeology and _____ ⁷ (study) it at university. After university he _____ ⁸ (get) a job as an archaeologist at a museum in the north of England.

He _____ ⁹ (love) the job but he _____ ¹⁰ (not earn) a good salary so instead he _____ ¹¹ (begin) a career as a rock musician in London and _____ ¹² (start) a band. In 1982 the band _____ ¹³ (have) a number one hit in thirteen countries. Five years later he _____ ¹⁴ (move) to Cornwall with his wife and three young children, and this move _____ ¹⁵ (bring) the biggest change in his life.

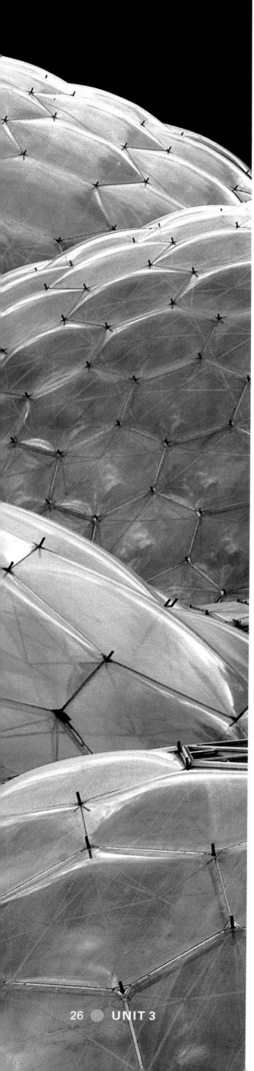

3 The journalist who interviewed Tim Smit for the article in **2** asked him questions like the ones below. Think of more questions and add them to the list.

Early years
Where were you born?
Where did you grow up?

School years
Where did you go to school?
What subjects were you good at?

Hobbies/sports
What hobbies did you have when
   you were younger?

Travel/holidays
How did you spend your holidays?

After school
What did you do after leaving school?

Work
What was your first job?
What did you do after that?

4 Work in pairs. Ask your partner the questions in the list in **3**. Answer your partner's questions. Tell each other more about past events in your lives.

5 Work in pairs, Student A with another Student A, Student B with another Student B.

Student A

1 Read *Eden – key dates*. Student B will ask you questions about it in **6**.

Eden – key dates

- November 1994   The Eden Project received its first grant* of £25,000.
- May 1997   The Millennium Commission gave Eden a grant of £37.5m.
- May 2000   Thousands of people watched the construction of the biomes.
- October 2000   The 'green team' planted the first trees in the Humid Tropics Biome.
- March 2001   7,000 visitors arrived at Eden for the official opening.
- June 2001   Eden welcomed its one millionth visitor.

grant = money that is given, e.g. by the government, for a particular purpose

2 Prepare questions to ask Student B in **6** to complete *2001 – Eden's first year*. The first one is done as an example.

2001 – Eden's first year

a The Eden Project brought _____ to the local economy. (How much …?)
  (*How much did the Eden Project bring to the local economy?*)

b The Project created _____ jobs. (How many …?)

c 94% of local business people said _____ . (What …?)

d Local people complained* because _____ . (Why …?)

e On an average day Eden had _____ visitors. (How many …?)

f On _____ 2001 the number of visitors went up to 14,000. (When …?)

complain = say you are unhappy

Student B

1 Read *2001– Eden's first year*. Student B will ask you questions about it in **6**.

2001 – Eden's first year

- The Eden Project brought £1 million to the local economy.
- The Project created 400 jobs.
- 94% of local business people said Eden was very good for business.
- Local people complained* because traffic problems in the area increased.
- On an average day Eden had 10,000 visitors.
- On 28 July 2001 the number of visitors went up to 14,000.

complain = say you are unhappy

2 Prepare questions to ask Student A in **6** to complete *Eden – key dates*. The first one is done as an example.

Eden – key dates

a	_____	The Eden Project received its first grant* of £25,000. (When …?) *(When did Eden receive its first grant of £25,000?)*
b	May 1997	The Millennium Commission gave Eden _____ (How much …?)
c	May 2000	Thousands of people watched _____. (What … ?)
d	October 2000	The 'green team' planted the first trees in _____. (Where …?)
e	March 2001	7,000 visitors arrived at Eden _____. (Why …?)
f	In _____	Eden welcomed its one millionth visitor. (When …?)

grant = money that is given, e.g. by the government, for a particular purpose

6 Work with a different partner, Student A with Student B. Ask your questions and answer your partner's questions. Write the missing information.

7 Discuss the questions.

1 What do you think of the Eden Project?

2 Did your country get any new buildings or special projects in the year 2000, to celebrate the millennium? If so, what is your opinion of them?

8 Choose one of the topics below. Prepare to talk about it for one minute.

- A holiday I remember
- A recent business trip
- My first trip abroad
- A childhood memory

9 Work in groups. Take turns to talk about the topic you prepared in **8**. Answer questions about it from your group.

Sports and leisure file. Verb groups

1 What are the most popular sports and leisure activities in your country?

2 Complete the verb groups with vocabulary from the box.

> football   windsurfing   exercises   tennis   skiing
> sailing   yoga   weight training   volleyball

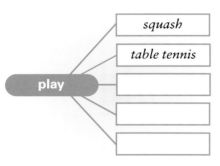
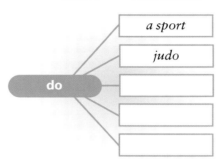
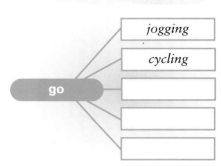

play	squash
	table tennis

do	a sport
	judo

go	jogging
	cycling

3 Add other sports to the verb groups in **2**.

4 Work in groups. Discuss the questions.

1 Do you do any of the sports in **2** and **3**? If so, how often?
2 Do you watch any of the sports in **2** and **3**? If so, which do you enjoy watching most?

5 Match the verbs in A with the words and phrases in B.

A

go to   watch   play   listen to   read

B

the radio	a restaurant	music	TV	a computer game
the theatre	magazines	books	chess	a musical instrument
the cinema	a nightclub	cards	a video	newspapers
a concert				

6 Work in pairs. Write eight questions about the activities in **5**. Use the Present Simple and the Past Simple.

Examples *Do you usually read a newspaper every day?*
Did you watch TV yesterday evening?
What kind of music do you like?

7 Work with a different partner. Ask your partner the questions you wrote in **6**. Answer your partner's questions.

8 Tell the class three things about your partner's leisure activities.

Skills focus

Solo achievements

1 Look at the pictures and headlines. What do you think happened?

One woman wonder

A life of ups and downs for Debra Veal

Heroine who survived sharks, tankers, and hurricanes

I'm going to carry on without you

2 Match the words in A with their meaning in B.

A		B	
1	panic	a	small electric light that you can carry
2	supertanker	b	large dangerous fish with sharp teeth
3	hurricane	c	sudden feeling of fear
4	shark	d	very large ship that transports oil, petrol, etc.
5	loneliness	e	violent storm with very strong winds
6	torch	f	feeling of unhappiness because you are alone

3 Read the article *Going it alone*. Complete the section on the left of the chart with information about Debra Veal and her journey.

Going it alone

On 7 October 2001 Debra and Andrew Veal left Tenerife to row across the Atlantic Ocean. One hundred and thirteen days later, on 26 January 2002, after a journey of 4,768 kilometres, Debra arrived in Barbados – alone. The Veals trained for the race for four years but after eight days at sea her husband, a top rower with fifteen years' experience, began to have panic attacks and couldn't sleep at night. Six days later a safety yacht arrived to take Andrew home and 27-year-old Debra made the difficult decision to continue the journey alone. She started rowing at 5.30 every morning and rested for short periods in the day. During the night she woke every hour to check for supertankers. She survived hurricanes, sharks, and loneliness.

One night a wave six metres high turned her boat over and damaged her navigation light. She repaired it in the dark, with no torch.

Debra talked to her husband every day by satellite phone, often in tears at the terrible conditions. In the first six weeks the telephone bill was £4,000! After arriving in Barbados she said 'I can't think, I'm too excited,' then added, 'I'm looking forward to proper meals instead of packaged food, the company of humans instead of birds and fish, and sleeping in a bed that doesn't move around.' Later on she wrote a book about her journey called *Rowing It Alone*.

	Debra Veal	Polly Vacher
age	_____	_____
travelled in	_____	_____
left	Tenerife on _____ 2001	_____ on _____ 2002
arrived	in _____ on _____ 2002	at_____ on 17 May 2002
length of journey	_____ km	_____ km
number of days	_____	_____
problems	hurricanes, _____ _____	tropical thunderstorms, _____ _____

4 Read the article *Going it alone* on p. 29 again. What do these phrases refer to?

1 four years   3 fifteen years   5 every hour   7 £4,000

2 eight days   4 5.30   6 six metres

5 Work in pairs. The words and phrases below are from a radio news report about the solo journey of another woman, Polly Vacher. Use them to describe what you think happened on her journey.

round-the-world trip   one-engine aeroplane   deserts and oceans

tropical thunderstorms   ran out of fuel   £150,000 for a charity

disabled people

6 🎧 **3.4** Listen to the news report. Were you right?

7 🎧 **3.4** Listen again. In the chart in **3** on p. 29, complete the section on the right with information about Polly Vacher's journey.

8 Work in pairs. How many similarities can you find between the two women and their journeys? How many differences? Continue the lists.

Similarities	Differences
Debra and Polly both made solo journeys.	*Debra's didn't start as a solo journey.*
They are both married.	*Polly has three children.*
…	…

9 Work in groups. Discuss the questions.

1 Do you know of other people who took on big challenges like Debra and Polly?

2 What do you think makes people want to do things like row across the Atlantic and fly around the world alone?

3 Would you like to do something very adventurous or challenging in your life? If so, what?

Welcoming a visitor

1 🎧 **3.5** James is in California to visit a local wine business. Listen to his conversation with the receptionist and answer the questions.

1 Who does James want to see?

2 What does the receptionist ask him to do?

2 James is meeting Wayne Brown for the first time. Which of these topics do people often talk about when they meet professionally for the first time? Underline your choices.

the visitor's journey   the town/place they are in
the weather   other towns/cities/countries
sport   their salaries
their jobs   politics
holidays   work/jobs in general

3 🎧 **3.6** Listen to their conversation. Tick (✓) the questions Wayne asks James.

How did you get here?   How was your flight?
Did you have any problems finding us?   Did you have a good journey?
What was the weather like in London?   Is this your first visit to California?

4 🎧 **3.7** Wayne and James have lunch together and get to know each other better. What does James say about

1 his first trip to California?   2 his career in wine journalism?

5 Which of the following do you think are important to make a good conversation? Tick (✓) your choices and add suggestions.

To be good at conversation you need to

1 listen carefully.
2 give only 'yes' or 'no' answers.
3 show interest and ask questions.
4 both listen and talk.
5 answer questions and add extra information.
6 only ask questions if you are the host.
7 _____
8 _____

6 🎧 **3.7** Listen to James and Wayne again. Look at **5** and underline what they do in their conversation. Why is this a good conversation?

7 Here are some topics people often talk about in the first five minutes in a professional situation. Work in groups. Think of a few questions for each topic.

CONVERSATION TOPICS	
The weather	(home and away)
The visit	(travel, reason for visit)
The visitor	(family, home life, leisure, interests)
First impressions	(likes and dislikes, food and drink)
Places, travel, and holidays	(city you are in, other places)
Work	(general, current projects, future plans)
Sports and leisure	(interests)
News	(local or global)

8 Now check Pocket Book p. 23 for a list of useful questions.

9 Work in pairs. One student is the host and the other is the visitor. Choose from the topics in **7** and talk together for three minutes. Then change partners and roles.

UNIT 4
Plans and arrangements

▼ **AGENDA**

▷ **Futures: Present Continuous, *going to* + infinitive**

▷ **Hotel file. Words and symbols**

▷ **Emails, faxes, and letters**

▷ **Staying at a hotel**

Language focus

1 Look at the information about a company called Global Training. Answer the questions.

1 What kind of training does Global Training provide?
2 What training materials do they produce?
3 Who founded the company?

As more and more companies become part of the global market and employ international teams, cultural awareness is vital for success. Global Training provides cross-cultural training courses and consultation worldwide, and produces a wide range of training materials, including videos, online self-access courses, country briefings, and *Cross-culture Journal*.

Global Training was founded by Mark Grady, Jan Kirsten, and Vana Bell in 1997. They have extensive experience of living and working in different cultures, and of working closely with companies to identify and meet their training needs.

Examples of topics on some recent seminars:
• Understanding cultural differences
• Intercultural communication
• Negotiating worldwide
• Body language
• Building multicultural teams
• Culture shock

GLOBAL TRAINING

Jan Kirsten

Mark Grady

Vana Bell

2 Read Mark's email to Jan.

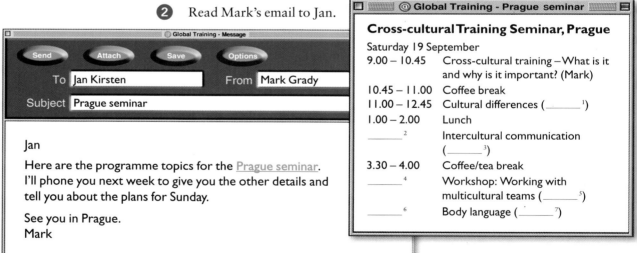

Global Training - Message

Send   Attach   Save   Options

To Jan Kirsten   From Mark Grady

Subject Prague seminar

Jan

Here are the programme topics for the Prague seminar.
I'll phone you next week to give you the other details and tell you about the plans for Sunday.

See you in Prague.
Mark

@ Global Training - Prague seminar

Cross-cultural Training Seminar, Prague

Saturday 19 September

9.00 – 10.45	Cross-cultural training – What is it and why is it important? (Mark)
10.45 – 11.00	Coffee break
11.00 – 12.45	Cultural differences (_____¹)
1.00 – 2.00	Lunch
_____²	Intercultural communication (_____³)
3.30 – 4.00	Coffee/tea break
_____⁴	Workshop: Working with multicultural teams (_____⁵)
_____⁶	Body language (_____⁷)

3 🎧 **4.1** Listen to the first part of the phone conversation between Mark and Jan. Complete the seminar programme in **2** with the information about times and speakers which Mark gives.

4 🎧 **4.2** Listen to the second part of the phone conversation. Answer the questions.

1 Are they going to have a fixed programme on Sunday?
2 What are they going to show?
3 What are they going to do after 12.30?

Futures: Present Continuous, *going to* + infinitive

Read the examples. Complete the grammar rules.

Present Continuous

- **I'm giving** the first presentation on Saturday, from 9.00 to 10.45.
- **You're not doing** anything on Saturday morning.
- **Is** Vana **doing** the workshop on working with multicultural teams?
- What **are** we **doing** in the evening?

going to + infinitive

- **We're going to show** our training videos and our online courses.
- **We're not going to have** a fixed programme on Sunday.
- **Are** we **going to demonstrate** any of our materials?
- How much time **are** we **going to spend** on the videos and online courses?

Write *going to + infinitive* or *the Present Continuous*.
- Use _____ for fixed future arrangements.
- Use _____ for future plans, intentions, and decisions.

When we use the Present Continuous for future arrangements, we usually give the future time.

Look at Listening scripts 4.1 and 4.2 on p. 127. Find more examples of the Present Continuous and *going to* + infinitive and underline them. Do all the examples of the Present Continuous refer to future arrangements?

Do we normally use *going to* with the verbs *to come* and *to go*?

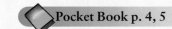 Pocket Book p. 4, 5

Practice Look at Jon's diary for next week and complete the sentences. Use the Present Continuous form of the verbs in brackets. The first one is done as an example.

May		May
3 *Monday*		*Thursday* **6**
11.00 Andy Parr – discuss sales figures.		BM604 Brussels dep. 8.50
interviews – 3.15 Marie Nicolle		pm – European managers' meeting
4.30 Thomas Hesen		
4 *Tuesday*		*Friday* **7**
new factory – whole day		back from Brussels BM607
12.45 lunch with Chris Hunt		arr. 11.10
		La Trattoria 8.30
5 *Wednesday*		*Saturday* **8**
9.15 dentist		tennis – sports centre
pm – prepare Brussels		10.00–11.30
presentation		*Sunday* **9**
		lunch – parents

1 Jon *is meeting* _____ Andy Parr at 11.00 on Monday. (meet)

2 He _____ all Tuesday at the new factory. (spend)

3 At 9.15 on Wednesday he _____ to the dentist. (go)

4 He _____ to Brussels on Thursday morning. (fly)

5 The European managers _____ a meeting on Thursday afternoon. (have)

6 Jon _____ back from Brussels at 11.10 on Friday morning. (arrive)

7 Jon's parents _____ to lunch on Sunday. (come)

2 Complete the questions about Jon's other arrangements. Use the Present Continuous form of the verbs in the box. The first one is done as an example.

> discuss ✓   eat   get   have   interview   play   prepare

1 What _is he discussing_ at the meeting with Andy Parr? The sales figures.
2 When _____ Marie Nicolle? At 3.15 on Monday.
3 Who _____ lunch with on Tuesday? Chris Hunt.
4 What _____ on Wednesday afternoon? His Brussels presentation.
5 Which flight _____ on Thursday morning? BM604 to Brussels.
6 Where _____ on Friday evening? At La Trattoria.
7 What time _____ tennis on Saturday? From 10.00 to 11.30.

Pronunciation

1 🎧 **4.3** Listen to the two questions. Notice the pronunciation of *to*. Which is the strong form?

　　　　　　/tuː/　　　　　　　　　　　/tə/
a Who are you writing to?　　b Are you writing to Mark?

2 🎧 **4.4** Listen to the pronunciation of *to* in the sentences. Which sound do you hear? Tick (✓) a or b. The first one is done as an example.

	a (strong)	b (weak)		a (strong)	b (weak)
1 Is he going to Japan?	___	✓	5 Which companies is he writing to?	___	___
2 He's going to change his job.	___	___	6 Where are you going to stay?	___	___
3 Which country is he travelling to?	___	___	7 Which airport are you flying to?	___	___
4 Are they coming to see us?	___	___			

3 🎧 **4.4** Listen again and repeat the sentences.

When *to* is at the end of the sentence, do we pronounce it as the strong form or the weak form?

4 Match the questions with the answers. Then practise the pronunciation in pairs.

1 Who did you talk to?　　　　　　　a I drove to work.
2 What did you listen to?　　　　　　b I talked to Maria.
3 Where did you drive to?　　　　　　c I went to Brazil.
4 Which country did you go to?　　　d I listened to the news.

---

3 Match words and phrases from A, B, and C to make seven questions. Use the *going to* + infinitive form as in the example.

Example *Are you going to take up a new sport next year?*

A	B	C
study	any business trips	soon
have	anything expensive	in the next few weeks
change	abroad	in the next three months
buy	a big family	next year ✓
travel	a new sport	in the near future
take up ✓	a holiday	
make	your job	
	another foreign language	
	a new sport or hobby ✓	

4 Work in pairs. Ask your partner the questions you prepared in **3**. Answer your partner's questions. Give reasons for your answers.

5 Work in different pairs. Every year your company offers its most successful employees a four-day holiday. This year the destination is Prague and you and your partner are the winners! Look at the information on Prague. Make a detailed plan of what you are going to do each day. Then present your plan to another pair.

Congratulations!

We have pleasure in enclosing details of your flights and hotel, and information on Prague.

Flights				Hotel
Sunday 12 June	OK 0649	dep. 09.00	arr. 11.55	Half-board accommodation at the Four
Thursday 16 June	OK 0651	dep. 15.50	arr. 18.40	Seasons Hotel, Prague, from Sunday 12 June until Thursday 16 June.

WHAT TO SEE AND DO IN PRAGUE

Prague is an easy city to explore on foot. Three districts popular with tourists are Hradčany, the Castle District, high above the rest of the city; Malá Strana, the Little Quarter, dating from the 13th century; and Staré Město, the Old Town, with beautiful renaissance, gothic, and baroque buildings.

THE CASTLE DISTRICT
Not a castle but a group of buildings – houses, palaces, and churches, dating from different centuries. Today the historical and political centre of the Czech Republic.

St Vitus' Cathedral
Largest cathedral in the Czech Republic, started in 1340, finished in 1929. Daily 9 a.m. to 4/5 p.m.

Golden Lane
Picturesque row of little 16th-century houses. Franz Kafka worked at no. 22. Walking tour of Prague Castle daily at 11 a.m. Duration 90 minutes.

THE LITTLE QUARTER
18th-century baroque palaces, houses, and gardens, used today as embassies and consulates.

Wallenstein Palace and Gardens
17th-century palace created by Italian architects and artists.

Petřín Hill
Observation Tower – copy of Eiffel Tower. Great views of Prague.

Charles Bridge
Prague's most famous landmark. Wonderful views of river and castle – illuminated at night.

THE OLD TOWN
The heart of Prague – markets, shops, restaurants, and pubs.

Old Town Hall
Superb views from 14th-century clock tower. Mechanical figures of the Astronomical Clock come to life every hour.

Tyn Church
Famous 14th-century Prague church with eighteen spires.

Nightlife

Drinking
Traditional beer halls, wine cellars, cafés and romantic terraces on the river.

Eating
Klášterní Restaurace – in-house brewery, Bohemian specialities in 12th-century monastery.

Le Café Colonial – French brasserie, popular with locals.

Jazz and rock
AghaRTA Jazz Centrum – Prague's best jazz club. Open until 1 a.m.

Classical, opera, ballet
Rudolfinum – classical music.
(Czech Philharmonic)

Estates Theatre – plays, opera, and ballet.

Classical concerts at Prague Castle, and in churches and palaces.

Hotel file. Words and symbols

1 Work in pairs. Do the hotel quiz.

Hotel quiz
What is the difference between

1 a double room and a twin room?
2 a bath and a shower?
3 a suitcase and luggage?
4 half-board and full-board?
5 a key and a keycard?
6 a bill and a receipt?
7 a lift and an elevator?

2 What do the symbols show? Find the words in the lists.

Hotel facilities	Guest rooms
restaurant	satellite TV
cocktail bar	multi-line phone
lounge	computer/fax point
nightclub	air-conditioning
swimming pool	minibar
sauna	tea- and coffee-making facilities
fitness room	24-hour room service
car park	safe
business centre	hairdryer
conference facilities	

3 🎧 **4.5** Listen to a telephone conversation between a secretary and the receptionist at the Meridiana Hotel. Tick (✓) the hotel's facilities in the list in **2**.

4 Which of the hotel facilities in **2** are important for you

a on a short city-break holiday?   b on a business trip?

5 Where in a hotel do you see these signs and notices? Explain in your own words what they mean.

1 Please vacate your room by 12 noon.

2 FIRE EXIT

3 In case of fire break glass and press bell.

4 Please clean my room

5 Please DO NOT DISTURB

6 Dial 5 for a wake-up call.

7 Dial 9 for an outside line.

Emails, faxes, and letters

1 Do you write emails, faxes, or letters in English? If so

1 what do you write about?

2 do you have problems writing in English? If so, what problems?

2 Do the quiz in pairs.

CORRESPONDENCE QUIZ

1 What are these dates in British English and American English?
 a 11/4/03 b 12/8/02 c 3/5/04

2 Which is correct?
 a Dear Mr John Hunter
 b Dear Mr Hunter

3 In correspondence with a woman, when do we use
 a Miss? b Ms? c Mrs?

4 What do these abbreviations mean?
 a info. b nos. c attn d asap e enc.

5 Match the beginnings and endings.
 a Dear Mrs Marzan   i Best wishes/Best regards
 b Dear Sir/Madam   ii See you soon.
 c Dear Marco   iii Yours sincerely/Yours/Best regards
 d Hi   iv Yours faithfully

3 Read the emails and the letter. Which is

1 an apology and a request for information?

2 a message to a friend?

3 a reply to a colleague?

4 a hotel booking?

A

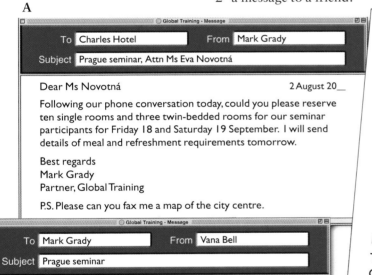

To [Charles Hotel] From [Mark Grady]

Subject [Prague seminar, Attn Ms Eva Novotná]

Dear Ms Novotná   2 August 20__

Following our phone conversation today, could you please reserve ten single rooms and three twin-bedded rooms for our seminar participants for Friday 18 and Saturday 19 September. I will send details of meal and refreshment requirements tomorrow.

Best regards
Mark Grady
Partner, Global Training

P.S. Please can you fax me a map of the city centre.

B

To [Mark Grady] From [Vana Bell]

Subject [Prague seminar]

Attachments: <u>Presentation summaries</u> & <u>Workshop</u>   12 August 20__

Hi Mark

Thanks for your email and all the programme details. Sorry I didn't get back to you yesterday – too much work!
I attach two files with everything you asked for. Let me know if you need anything else – I'm away for the next two days.

See you in Prague.
Vana

C

KOH-I-NOOR A.S.
F. A. Gerstnera 3
CZ 703 00 Ostrava
Ceská Republika

tel. +420 69 000 200
fax +420 69 000 808
e-mail sovakp@koh-i-noor.cz
www.koh-i-noor.cz

Mr Mark Grady
Partner, Global Training   28 July 20__
17 Barley Road, Chiswick
London W4 4GH

Dear Mr Grady

This letter is to thank you for the invitation to your Cross-cultural Training Seminar in Prague on 19 and 20 September. Unfortunately I will not be able to attend as I will be away on business. Would you please tell me if you are planning to repeat the seminar at a later date as I would be very interested to attend.

Yours sincerely

Petr Sovák
Personnel Manager

D

To [Barry West] From [Marie Sirová]

Subject [Hello]

Hi Barry   30 August 20__

This email is to get in touch again after a long time. How are you? Are you enjoying your new job in Prague? I'm going to be in Prague soon, attending a seminar and staying at the Charles Hotel 18–21 September. I'd love to see you. Any chance of meeting on Sunday 20 after 1 p.m., or any time on Monday 21?

Hoping to see you soon.
Marie

4 Complete the table with phrases from the correspondence in **3**.

1 **Starting**

_____ (_our phone conversation today ..._)

In reply to (_your fax received ..._)

Thank you for (_your fax of ..._)

_____ (_your email ..._)

2 **Saying why you're writing**

I am writing (_to enquire about ..._)

I am pleased (_to confirm ..._)

_____ (_to thank you ..._)

This fax is (_to give you details of ..._)

_____ (_to get in touch ..._)

3 **Requesting**

_____ (_reserve ..._)

_____ (_tell me ..._)

Please fax/email me (_your mobile phone no._)

4 **Attaching documents (email)**

_____ (_two files ..._)

5 **Enclosing documents (letter)**

I enclose (_a copy of ..._)

6 **Giving bad news**

I am sorry (_to inform you ..._)

_____ (_I will not be able to ..._)

7 **Apologizing**

I apologize for (_the delay ..._)

I'm sorry about (_the mistake ..._)

_____ (_I didn't get back to you earlier ..._)

8 **Ending**

Please contact me again (_if you need any more information_).

_____ (_if you need anything else_).

I look forward to (_welcoming you ..._).

_____ (_to see you soon_).

_____ (_in Prague_).

5 Complete the fax, letter, and email on p. 39 with suitable phrases from the table in **4**.

6 Work in pairs. Look at the phrases in the table in **4**. Think of alternatives to the phrases in brackets.

Examples _Following (our meeting last week ...)_
I am pleased (to inform you that ...)
I attach (a translation).

7 Work with a different partner.

1 Write a fax to Mark Grady. Request a copy of Global Training's brochure and information about cross-cultural seminars in your country.

2 Write Barry's email reply to Marie. Answer the questions in her email and say you'd love to meet her in Prague. Suggest a time and place to meet.

E

17 Barley Road, Chiswick
London W4 4GH
Tel: +44 (0)20 8735 6654
Fax: +44 (0)20 8735 4420
Email: info@globaltraining.co.uk

GLOBAL
TRAINING

Mr P. Sovák
Personnel Manager
Koh-i-noor a.s.
F.A. Gerstnera 3
CZ 703 00 Ostrava
Czech Republic   29 July 20___

Dear Mr Sovák

_____ ¹ your letter of 28 July. I was sorry to hear you
will not be able to attend our seminar in September but I hope we can
welcome you at a later date. _____ ² a copy of our
company brochure and our programme of future seminars in Central
European countries. _____ ³ if you need any more
information.

Yours sincerely

Mark Grady

Mark Grady
Partner, Global Training

enc.

F

FAX MESSAGE
Charles Hotel, Jungmannovo na'městí 30, 110 00 Praha 1
Tel: +420 222 333 444   Fax: +420 222 333 445
www.charleshotel.com   email: info@charleshotel.com

To	Global Training	From	Eva Novotná
Attn	Mark Grady	Date	4 August
Subject	Room reservations	No. of pages	2

Dear Mr Grady

_____ ¹ your email received today.
_____ ² the delay in replying.
_____ ³ to confirm we have reserved ten
single rooms and three twin-bedded rooms as requested, for
Friday 18 and Saturday 19 September.
_____ ⁴ welcoming you to our hotel.

Best regards
Eva Novotná

PS I hope the map on page 2 of this fax is clear.

G

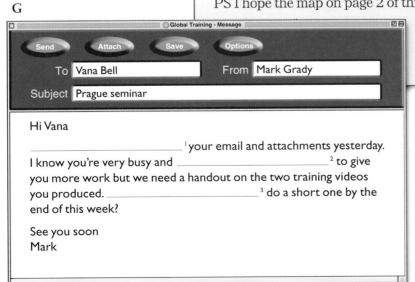

Global Training - Message

Send   Attach   Save   Options

To Vana Bell   From Mark Grady

Subject Prague seminar

Hi Vana

_____ ¹ your email and attachments yesterday.
I know you're very busy and _____ ² to give
you more work but we need a handout on the two training videos
you produced. _____ ³ do a short one by the
end of this week?

See you soon
Mark

Staying at a hotel

1 ⌒ **4.6** Read the emails. Then listen to the phone call James makes to the hotel. Answer the questions below.

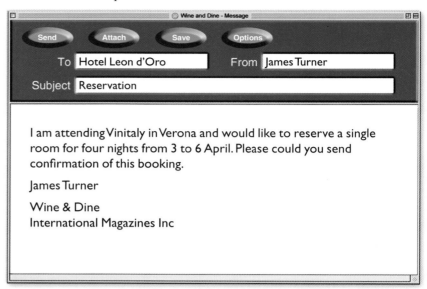

Wine and Dine - Message

To Hotel Leon d'Oro   From James Turner

Subject Reservation

I am attending Vinitaly in Verona and would like to reserve a single room for four nights from 3 to 6 April. Please could you send confirmation of this booking.

James Turner

Wine & Dine
International Magazines Inc

Leon d'Oro - Message

To James Turner .   From Hotel Leon d'Oro

Subject Re: Reservation

Dear Mr Turner

Thank you for your email. We have reserved a single room for you for four nights from 3 to 6 April.

We look forward to welcoming you on 3 April.
Luisa Bianchi

Reservations, Hotel Leon d'Oro
34, Piazza Rasso, 80057 Verona
Tel: + 39 (0) 45 596378, Fax: + 39 (0) 45 597878

1 What does James want to do?

2 What is the problem?

2 ⌒ **4.6** Listen again and complete this part of the conversation.

R Oh, yes, Mr Turner. I remember.

J I'd like to book a _____[1], for a colleague, for the 4th of April.

R Let me see. Oh, _____[2], Mr Turner, but we're fully booked on the 4th of April, because of Vinitaly.

J Oh, _____[3].

R You could try the Hotel Europa.

J Yes, I'll do that. _____[4]. Goodbye.

3 🎧 **4.7** James checks in at the hotel. Listen to his conversation with the receptionist and tick (✓) the phrases you hear.

I'd like a room, please.

I have a reservation.

Could you fill in this form, please, and sign here?

Here's your key.

Here's your keycard.

Have you got a suitcase?

The porter will take your luggage.

Could I have an early morning call, at 6.30?

Do you need anything else?

4 🎧 **4.8** James checks out of the hotel. Listen to the conversation and tick (✓) T (true) or F (false).

	T	F
1 The hotel doesn't accept credit cards.	___	___
2 James wants to stay at the hotel again.	___	___

5 🎧 **4.8** Listen again and complete this part of the conversation.

J _____¹ my bill, please? _____² by credit card?

R Yes, _____³.

J Good.

R I hope _____⁴ your stay here.

J Oh, yes, _____⁵.

6 Work in pairs. Role-play these situations.

Student A
- You are a wine importer and want to go to Vinitaly.

Situation 1

Telephone the Hotel Due Torri in Verona to book a single room for 4 and 5 April.

Situation 2

You want to bring two colleagues with you so you need two more rooms. Telephone the hotel again and try to change the booking.

- You are now the receptionist at the hotel.

Situation 3

Welcome your guest. Check the reservation is for a single room for two nights. Ask the guest to complete and sign the registration form. The guest's room is number 43 on the second floor.

Situation 4

Check out your guest. The hotel accepts credit cards. Wish your guest a good trip back.

Student B
- You are a receptionist at the hotel.

Answer the telephone. Accept the booking.

Answer the telephone again. One guest cancelled this morning. You have one room available on 4 and 5 April.

- You are now a guest at the hotel.

Arrive and check in at the Hotel Due Torri in Verona. Ask for an early morning call. Ask about breakfast.

Check out of the hotel. Ask if you can pay by credit card.

REVIEW UNIT A

▼ **AGENDA**
▶ Grammar ❶ – ❼
▶ Focus on functions ❽ – ⓫
▶ Vocabulary ⓬ – ⓭

This unit reviews all the main language points from Units 1–4. Complete the exercises. Check your learning with the self-check box at the end.

❶ **Present Simple and frequency adverbs**

Make true sentences about your lifestyle. Add four more sentences. Use the frequency adverbs in the box.

> always   usually   often   sometimes   rarely   never

Example *I often go out in the evening.*

1 go out in the evening
2 travel by plane
3 read English newspapers or magazines
4 watch the news on TV
5 do yoga
6 eat at restaurants
7 go to the cinema
8 play tennis

❷ **Present Simple questions and short answers**

Work in pairs. Match A and B below. Then prepare questions in the Present Simple to ask your partner. Use short answers.

A	B
meet	English on the phone
make	international meetings
speak	business trips
attend	to work by car
write	flexitime
work	foreign visitors at work
go	emails in English

Example   **Student A** *Do you meet foreign visitors at work?*

Student B *Yes, I do./No, I don't.*

❸ **Present Simple and Present Continuous, frequency adverbs**

Each of the sentences below has a grammar mistake. Find the mistakes, then write the correct sentences.

1 They travel often on business.
2 At present our business do very well.
3 He's having meetings with customers every week.
4 They always are early for work.
5 How often are you visiting them?
6 She talks to some clients right now.
7 When do you finish usually work?
8 I'm having five weeks' holiday every year.
9 He studies for an exam at the moment.
10 Are you always travelling to work by car?

4 Past Simple

Write the Past Simple forms of these verbs.

1 become _____ 6 fly _____

2 begin _____ 7 give _____

3 bring _____ 8 grow _____

4 cost _____ 9 say _____

5 find _____ 10 think _____

5 Present Simple, Present Continuous, and Past Simple

Complete the text with the correct form of the verbs in brackets.

Manuel González _____ [1](come) from Spain. He usually
_____ [2] (live) in Madrid and _____ [3] (work) as a journalist
for a Spanish newspaper, but two years ago he _____ [4] (decide) to
take a year off work to live in different countries in Europe and write a book
about Europeans. He _____ [5] (spend) the first two months in
Scandinavia and then _____ [6] (move) to Germany for a month. At
present he _____ [7] (stay) in Paris, where he _____ [8] (rent)
a flat for five weeks. Four years ago he _____ [9] (write) a best-selling
travel guide to Spain and now he _____ [10] (work) hard to have the
same success with his book about Europeans.

6 Past Simple questions

You asked a colleague about his last business trip. He gave you these answers.
What were your questions?

Example I flew with KLM. (Which … ?)
   Which airline did you fly with?

1 I went to New York. (Where … ?)
2 I was there for three days. (How long … ?)
3 I stayed at the Sheraton Hotel. (Where … ?)
4 I met some senior managers. (Who … ?)
5 I attended four meetings. (How many … ?)
6 I got back yesterday evening. (When … ?)

7 Futures: Present Continuous, *going to* + infinitive

Work in pairs. Tell your partner about your plans and arrangements for next week.
Use the Present Continuous and *going to* + infinitive.

Examples *On Monday at 11 a.m. I'm giving a presentation at work.*
   On Wednesday evening I'm going to play tennis with a friend.

8 Introductions and greetings

Work in pairs. Give a suitable response to these introductions and greetings.

1 How do you do?   5 How are you?
2 Pleased to meet you.   6 How are things?
3 Please call me John.   7 It was very nice meeting you.
4 How's the family?   8 Have a good trip back.

9 **Welcoming a visitor**

You are welcoming a visitor from another country. Think of five questions to ask the visitor. Ask about their journey, the reason for their visit, their job, their home town, and their first impressions.

1 _____

2 _____

3 _____

4 _____

5 _____

10 **Telephoning: making contact**

Complete this telephone conversation.

R Good morning. *Wine & Dine* magazine.

J Good morning. _____ ¹ Duncan Ross, please?

R Who _____ ², please?

J _____ ³ James Turner.

R Hold _____ ⁴ please, Mr Turner. I'm sorry, Mr Ross _____ ⁵. Can I _____ ⁶?

J Yes. _____ ⁷ to call me? My number is 020 1986 5053.

R Yes, Mr Turner. _____ ⁸.

J Thank you. Goodbye.

11 Telephoning: leaving messages

Work in pairs. Practise these telephone calls. Make up two more calls.
Change roles.

Student A

> **Situation 1**
> Phone Ian Bell. Your number is
> 556767.

> **Situation 2**
> Phone the Sales Director of
> Whole Foods Ltd. Your number is
> 774884.

Student B

> **Situation 1**
> Ian Bell is in a meeting. Take a
> message.

> **Situation 2**
> You work for Whole Foods Ltd.
> The Sales Director is on holiday.
> Take a message.

12 Vocabulary

Work in Group A or Group B. Write a vocabulary test to give to the other group.
Choose ten of the words below. Write a sentence or phrase to help the other group
guess each word.

Example Word *receipt*

Clue *You get this after you pay a bill or pay for something you buy.*

salary	pensioner	fridge	expensive	receipt ✓
magazine	keycard	abroad	skiing	flight
unemployed	journalist	suitcase	busy	sightseeing
Swedish	on strike	elevator	swimming pool	hard-working

13 Vocabulary test

Give your vocabulary test to the other group. Do the other group's test. Return
your answers for checking.

Look at the self-check box below. Tick the areas you need to review again.

SELF-CHECK BOX	Yes	No	Pocket Book
• Present Simple			12
• Frequency adverbs			12
• Present Continuous			11
• Futures: Present Continuous, *going to* + infinitive			4, 5
• Introductions and greetings			18
• Welcoming a visitor			23
• Telephoning: making contact			22
• Telephoning: leaving messages			23
• Vocabulary			

UNIT 5
How healthy is your lifestyle?

Language focus

1 Work in groups. Discuss your opinions.
In what ways are people's lifestyles today
a healthier than 100 years ago?
b less healthy than 100 years ago?

2 Read *Top tips for a healthier you* from Dr Dawes' website.
1 What advice does he give about
a working at a computer?
b reducing stress?
c eating and drinking?
d sleep?
e relaxation?
2 What do you think of his advice? Is any of it useful for you?

TOP TIPS
for a healthier you

Your work

1 How many hours a day do you work at a computer?

If, like a lot of people, you spend most of your day working at a computer, make sure you get some regular breaks during the day. Leave your desk and go for a short walk, or do a few exercises at your desk.

2 How much time do you have for lunch?

Do you leave your office for lunch or, like many people, just eat a sandwich at your desk? It's important to get out of the office for at least 30 minutes a day and find some time to relax and sit down for a meal.

3 Are there any parks or green areas near your office?

If so, you don't have any excuses! Go out at lunchtime for some exercise and relaxation.

4 Does your job make you stressed?

When you feel stressed, stop what you're doing and take some long, slow breaths. One of the best ways to reduce stress is to do lots of physical exercise, for example running, or playing tennis or football. It also helps to get a little fun and relaxation every day.

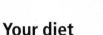

Your diet

1 Do you drink any alcohol?

A lot of alcohol is, of course, bad for your health, but a little wine with meals, especially red wine, is good for your heart, so enjoy it!

2 Do you eat lots of fruit and vegetables?

To stay healthy you need to eat a lot of fruit and vegetables. Experts recommend at least five servings a day.

3 How much cheese and butter do you eat?

Many people love cheese, so if you don't want to give it up, try to give up butter instead. A diet that doesn't have any butter is much healthier.

4 Do you drink a lot of coffee?

Like alcohol, a lot of coffee isn't good for you, but caffeine is a good painkiller so if you have a headache, a cup of coffee may be better than an aspirin!

Your leisure time

1 How many hours do you usually sleep?

Most people need seven or eight hours' sleep each night. Research suggests people who get less sleep are more likely to get ill and grow old more quickly.

2 How much time do you spend on sport or exercise?

Try to spend at least a little time on sport or exercise every day and, if you can, more time at weekends.

3 How many days' holiday do you have a year?

There aren't many people who would say 'no' to more holidays. The important thing is to spend your holidays doing something you really enjoy. That way you can get the most benefit.

4 How much relaxation do you usually get in a day?

Most people don't find much time to relax but relaxation is very important – to get your energy back and reduce the problem of stress.

Mass and count nouns

Complete the table with mass and count nouns from *Top tips for a healthier you* in ❷.
Then complete the grammar rules.

Mass	Count	Mass and count*
relaxation	hours	exercise/exercises
stress	computer	time/times
a _ _ _ _ _ _ l	o _ _ _ _ e	wine/wines
c_ f _ _ e	s _ _ _ w _ _ h	fruit/fruits
b _ _ _ _ r	p _ _ _ s	cheese/cheeses
r _ s _ _ _ _ h	v _ _ _ t _ _ _ _ s	sport/sports
e _ _ _ _ y	h _ _ _ _ _ y	

Write *singular* or *plural*.
- Count nouns have a _____ and _____ form. We can count them.
- Mass nouns do not have a _____ form. We cannot count them.
- Some nouns are both mass and count.*
- With mass nouns we do not use *a* or *an*.

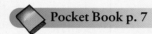 Pocket Book p. 7

some/any, a lot of/lots of, much/many, a little/a few

Read the examples. Put ticks (✓) in the table to show when we use *any*,
a lot of/lots of, *much/many*, and *a little/a few*, as in the examples for *some*.

some/any
- Make sure you get **some** regular breaks during the day.
- Go out at lunchtime for **some** exercise.
- You don't have **any** excuses!
- A diet that doesn't have **any** butter is much healthier.
- Are there **any** parks or green areas near your office?
- Do you drink **any** alcohol?

a lot of/lots of, much/many
- **A lot of** alcohol is bad for your health.
- Do you eat **lots of** fruit and vegetables?
- **Many** people love cheese.
- There aren't **many** people who would say 'no' to more holidays.
- Most people don't find **much** time to relax.
- How **many** hours do you usually sleep?
- How **much** time do you have for lunch?

a little/a few
- **A little** wine with meals is good for your heart.
- Do **a few** exercises at your desk.

We use with	some	any	a lot of/lots of	much	many	a little	a few
count nouns	✓						
mass nouns	✓						
positive sentences	✓						
negative sentences							
questions	✓						

Note We also use *some* in questions which are offers or requests.
Would you like some wine?
Can I have some water?

Look at *Top tips for a healthier you* in ❷. Find more examples of mass
and count nouns with *some/any*, *a lot of/lots of*, *much/many*, and *a little/a few*, and underline them.

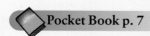 Pocket Book p. 7

Practice

❶ Complete the conversations with *some/any*, or *a little/a few*.

1 **A** Have we got _____ coffee?

   B Only _____. Shall I buy _____?

2 **A** Did you buy _____ vegetables?

   B Only _____. There wasn't a very good choice.

3 **A** Would you like _____ wine?

   B Yes, but just _____. I have to drive later.

4 **A** Have _____ chocolates. They're delicious.

   B Thanks, but only _____. I'm trying to lose
_____ weight.

❷ Which of these words are mass nouns and which are count nouns?
Write M (mass) or C (count) next to the words.

traffic _____   information _____   meeting _____   news _____

money _____   business trip _____   article _____   advice _____

❸ Complete the dialogues with *a lot of/lots of*, *much*, or *many*.

1 **A** Hello, Jim, you're early!

   B Yes, there wasn't _____ traffic this morning. How
_____ people are coming to my presentation?

2 **A** Have you got _____ information about the new company?

   B No, but a colleague gave me _____ advice on where to find it.

3 **A** Sue, how _____ business trips did you make last month,
and how _____ money did you spend on meals with
customers?

   B I need to work it out. Can I tell you tomorrow?

4 **A** Did you have _____ meetings last week?

   B Yes, every day. I didn't have _____ time for anything else!

5 **A** Was there _____ news about the economic crisis in the
paper today?

   B Not really, but there were _____ articles about the changes
the government is introducing.

Pronunciation

1 🎧 **5.1** Listen to the examples. Notice the different stress patterns.

● ●   ● ●   ● ● ●

a coffee   b champagne   c exercise

2 🎧 **5.2** Listen to these words. What is the stress pattern? Tick (✓) a, b, or c. The first one is done as an example.

	a ● ●	b ● ●	c ● ● ●
1 vegetable			✓
2 problem			
3 alcohol			
4 research			
5 sandwich			
6 advice			

3 🎧 **5.2** Listen to the words again and repeat them.

4 Look at these words. What is the stress pattern? Write a, b, or c.

1 butter _____
2 holiday _____
3 colleague _____
4 weekend _____
5 headache _____
6 energy _____

5 🎧 **5.3** Listen to the words and repeat them.

4 Work in pairs. Write a question about each topic in the table below.

Examples   *How many hours a day do you work?*
           How much time do you spend on English?

Time survey	You	Your partner
1 work		
2 English		
3 sport or exercise		
4 sleep		
5 relax		
6 cooking		
7 housework		
8 watch TV		

5 Work in different pairs. Interview your partner and answer your partner's questions. Make a note of both your answers in the *You* and *Your partner* columns.

6 Tell the class what your partner spends

a a lot of time on.

b only a little time on.

Food file. Word groups

1 Work in pairs. Look at this menu from Claret's Restaurant. Write the different kinds of meat, fish, vegetables, and fruit under the correct headings.

Claret's Restaurant

Starters
Tuna and red pepper salad
Cold cucumber soup with prawns
Smoked salmon pâté
Duck and red cabbage salad

Main courses
Beef in red wine with onions
Lamb cutlets with roast potatoes
    and courgettes
Grilled Dover sole with boiled new
    potatoes
Pork with cider and apples
Lemon grilled chicken breasts with
    fried aubergines

Desserts
Pears in Marsala wine
Fruit brûlée with strawberries,
    grapes, and peaches
Frozen yoghurt with cherries
Selection of cheeses

Meat	Fish/Seafood
duck	tuna
beef	

Vegetables	Fruit
red pepper	apples

2 Think of other foods you know and add them to the list.

3 Look at the menu again. Underline any methods of cooking.

Example <u>roast</u> potatoes

4 Which of these methods of cooking do the pictures show? Write *roast*, *grilled*, *fried*, or *boiled*.

1 _____ 2 _____ 3 _____ 4 _____

5 Work in groups. Think of your favourite dish but don't say the name. In turn, ask questions to find out about each person's dish. Guess the name.

Examples *Is it a main course?*
What are the ingredients?
How do you cook it?

6 Work in groups. Prepare a menu for a celebration dinner at the end of your English course. Suggest two starters, two main courses, and two desserts. Then present your menu to the class.

Slow down and enjoy life

① Read the information about Slow Food. Answer the questions.

1 When did the Slow Food movement begin, and why?
2 Can any city become a 'Slow City'?
3 What festivals does Slow Food organize?
4 What does Slow Food Editore publish?

Slow Food

In 1986 the Italian journalist and food writer Carlo Petrini was horrified when McDonald's opened its first fast food outlet in Italy in one of Rome's most famous squares, the Piazza di Spagna. In protest, he started the Slow Food movement. In a short time it had 10,000 members. Today, it has over 66,000 members in 50 countries and is continuing to grow.

Slow Cities

The Slow Cities movement came from the philosophy of Slow Food. It started in 1999 with four Italian cities. Today eighteen Italian cities are 'Slow Cities' and many more want to join the movement. Only cities with a maximum of 50,000 inhabitants can join.

Slow Food festivals

Slow Food organizes the world's largest food and wine event and the world's largest cheese festival, both in Italy.

Slow Food Editore

Slow Food Editore publishes guides on Italian food, wine, and culture, and the international magazine *Slow* published in six languages (Italian, English, French, Spanish, German, and Japanese).

2 Work in Group A or Group B.

Group A read about Slow Food and write five questions.
Group B read about Slow Cities and write five questions.

Slow Food

Members of Slow Food meet regularly to enjoy long slow sociable meals. But Slow Food isn't just about enjoying good food. It's about improving the quality of our lives. It believes a slower pace of life is healthier and better for us and that fast food and the fast life is destroying an important part of our culture. 'Each culture has its own language, music, art, and it also has its food culture', says Carlo Petrini, the founder of Slow Food. Psychologists agree. They tell us it's important for human beings to enjoy a good meal together around a table, and that it's especially important in families. The Slow Food movement wants to make sure we don't lose our food culture and our regional cooking. Slow Food also works with teachers in schools to teach children about food and how to enjoy it. The number of fast food outlets continues to grow, but 6,000 of Slow Food's 66,000 members are in America, the home of fast food. Perhaps things are changing?

Slow Cities

Slow Cities are cities of 'good living'. They promise to work to improve the quality of life of their citizens and protect local businesses, skills, and traditions. They promise to reduce traffic and noise, create cycle paths, protect parks and green areas, and ban* car alarms and neon-lit advertisements. They promote local food production, small shops that sell local speciality foods, and restaurants that serve traditional dishes. For example, in Bra there are no cars in the town square, and the fruit and vegetables in school meals are organic. The food and wine festivals that Slow Food organizes attract thousands of tourists every year. Paolo Saturnini, founder of the Slow Cities movement, believes this is the way to protect the unique character of our towns and cities, and stop the invasion of fast food and the American way of life. And he's pleased about the long list of towns in Italy and abroad which want to join the Slow Cities movement. It shows that a lot of people agree with him.

ban = not allow

3 Read the other article and answer the other group's questions.

4 🎧 **5.4** Listen to the opinions of four members of Slow Food. Number the statements 1, 2, 3, or 4 to show which speaker's opinion they express.

Speaker

a Slow food isn't only for the rich.   _____

b Town squares should be for people.   _____

c Discovering different food is one of the pleasures of travelling.   _____

d The traditional way of eating together around a table is disappearing.   _____

5 Work in groups. Say what you think and explain why.

1 How popular is fast food in your country?

2 Is fast food destroying your country's food culture?

3 Is discovering different food one of the pleasures of travelling for you?

4 Do you agree that 'families that eat together stay together'?

5 Would you like to live in a Slow City?

At a restaurant

Claret's Restaurant

White Wines
Sancerre
Frascati
Muscadet
Chablis
Chardonnay

Red Wines
Rioja
Chianti
Beaujolais
Burgundy
Corbières
Pinot Noir

1 🎧 **5.5** Monique and James are in Claret's Restaurant. Listen to their conversation. Tick (✓) what they order on the menu on p. 51 and the wine list above.

2 🎧 **5.6** Listen to the next part of their conversation. Who do you think pays the bill?

3 🎧 **5.7** Listen to the final part of their conversation. Why do you think James asks Monique about her birthday?

4 🎧 **5.5, 5.6, 5.7** Listen to the conversations again. Tick (✓) the phrases you hear.

Recommending

What do you recommend?

The … is usually excellent here.

I recommend …

Ordering

I'll/We'll have …

I'd/We'd like …

Could we have …?

Offering

Do have some more …

What about …?

How about …?

Would you like …?

Declining

Thank you, but I couldn't eat any
    more.

No, thank you.

No, but thanks all the same.

Thanking and responding

Thank you for a really excellent meal.

Thank you for a lovely evening.

I'm glad you enjoyed it.

Accepting

Yes. I'd like that.

Yes. That would be very nice.

5 Complete the conversation in Claret's Restaurant. Use the menu on p. 51 and the wine list opposite, and the phrases in **4**. Pat is the host and Steve is the guest.

Pat   Right. Let's order.

Steve   Hmm … . It all looks good. What _____ [1]?

Pat   Well, for a starter _____ [2], and for the main course _____ [3]?

Steve   Yes, _____ [4].

Pat   And _____ [5] to drink?

Steve   _____ [6]?

Pat   Yes, _____ [7].

(*Later*)

Pat   Now, _____ [8] a dessert?

Steve   Thank you, but _____ [9].

Pat   _____ [10] sure? _____ [11] a coffee or a cognac?

Steve   _____ [12].

(*At the end of the meal*)

Steve   Thank you _____ [13], Pat.

Pat   _____ [14].

6 Work in pairs. You are in a restaurant.

Student A   You are the host/hostess.

Student B   You are the guest.

Practise the conversation. Then change roles.

Student A	Student B
Ask B what he/she would like.	
	Ask for a recommendation.
Recommend a starter/main dish.	
	Say what you would like.
Offer a drink: wine/beer.	
	Say what you would like.
(*Later*)	
Offer a dessert/coffee/cognac.	
	Reply. Thank A.
Reply to thanks.	

7 Work in groups of three or more. You are in a restaurant. One person is the waiter/waitress, another is the host/hostess, and the others are guests. Use the menu on p. 51. Ask the waiter/waitress and the host/hostess to recommend and describe dishes on the menu.

UNIT 6
Flying gets cheaper

▼ AGENDA

▸ Comparative and superlative adjectives
▸ Air travel file. Word groups
▸ Transformations
▸ Making arrangements

Language focus

Special offers:

Only $29 each way
Los Angeles   to/from   Phoenix (Arizona)

Only $59 each way
Indianapolis   to/from   Orlando (Florida)

Only $79 each way
Washington   to/from   Orlando (Florida)

Only $89 each way
Chicago   to/from   Phoenix (Arizona)

Some current fares in Europe:

Amsterdam – Geneva	from €45.49
Paris – London	from €56.99
London – Prague	from €31.99
Milan – Paris	from €57.49

Lowest-ever fares!

London Stansted to:

Frankfurt (Hahn)	£2.99
Barcelona (Girona)	£4.99
Rome (Ciampino)	£7.99
Biarritz	£9.99

Dublin to:

Edinburgh	€5.00
Brussels	€9.99
Paris (Beauvais)	€15.00
Malaga	€29.99

all fares are one-way

---

① Look at the names of some airlines and examples of their fares.

1 Do you know the nationalities of these airlines?

2 What do you think of the fares?

3 These airlines are called 'no-frills' airlines. What do you think that means?

② 🎧 **6.1** Listen to an interview with a travel industry consultant. She describes six ways no-frills airlines save money. What does she say about

1 method of selling?

2 tickets?

3 number of flight attendants?

4 type of aircraft?

5 turnaround time?

6 airports?

③ Work in pairs. Compare your answers for **②**.

④ 🎧 **6.1** Listen to the interview again. Check your answers for **②**.

⑤ Complete the table. If you are not sure of the form, check Listening script 6.1 on p. 128–9.

	Adjective	Comparative		Superlative
Regular (1 syllable)	big	bigger		_____
	cheap	_____		_____
	few			fewest
	long	longer	(the)	_____
	low	_____		lowest
	near	nearer		_____
	quick	_____		quickest
	small			smallest
(2 syllables ending in -y)	easy	_____	(the)	easiest
(2 or more syllables)	crowded	less/ _____	(the) least/ most	crowded
	efficient	more _____		efficient
	expensive	more _____		_____
Irregular	far	farther/further		_____
	little	_____	(the)	least
	many	_____		most

Comparative and superlative adjectives

Complete the grammar rules, using the table in ❺, and answer the questions.

One-syllable adjectives

- To make the comparative, add *-er* to the end of the adjective.
- To make the superlative, add _____ to the end of the adjective.

When does the consonant usually double in a one-syllable adjective?

 Pocket Book p. 2

Two-syllable adjectives ending in *-y*

- To make the comparative, change the *-y* to *-i* and add _____.
- To make the superlative, change the *-y* to *-i* and add _____.

Other adjectives with two or more syllables

- To make the comparative, put *more* or *less* before the adjective.
- To make the superlative, put _____ or _____ before the adjective.

Look at Listening script 6.1 on p. 128–9. Which words do we use before a comparative adjective to show a bigger difference?

as ... as

- Do they have **as** many flight attendants **as** on traditional airlines?
- Smaller airports are usually **not as** busy **as** the big ones.

- We use *as ... as* to show something is the same or equal and *not as ... as* to show it isn't.

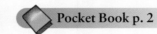 Pocket Book p. 2

Practice ❶ Complete the article. Use the comparative or superlative form of the adjectives in brackets. Check Pocket Book p. 2 if necessary.

No-frills airlines

How do they rate?*

In a recent *Which Airlines?* survey of 61 airlines, the low-cost airline easyJet was voted one of the *best*[1] (good) airlines, along with famous names like Singapore Airlines, Emirates, SAS, and Thai Airways. Ryanair had a _____ [2] (low) rating than easyJet but, not surprisingly, all the no-frills airlines got the _____ [3] (high) ratings for value for money and the _____ [4] (bad) ratings for leg room and seat comfort.

How to find the cheapest flight

The _____ [5] (important) thing to remember is to book as early as possible and to be flexible about dates. Travelling at weekends and on Fridays and Mondays is _____ [6] (expensive) than on the other days of the week because flights on those days are _____ [7] (crowded). To get the _____ [8] (cheap) fare, fly on the _____ [9] (early) or the _____ [10] (late) flights on Tuesdays, Wednesdays, or Thursdays. It is _____ [11] (good) to book online than on the phone because all the airlines give a discount for online bookings.

Delays

In general, no-frills airlines have a _____ [12] (bad) record for punctuality than the traditional airlines and there are _____ [13] (many) complaints about delays from customers of low-cost airlines than from other airlines. If there is a technical problem it usually means a _____ [14] (long) delay than with other airlines because low-cost airlines don't usually have extra aircraft they can use.

Changing a booking

If you need to change a passenger name or flight booking it's _____ [15] (easy) with some airlines than with others. For example with easyJet you pay £10 to make any change, plus the extra money if the fare for the new booking is _____ [16] (high). Ryanair has a much _____ [17] (complicated) system, with seven different types of fare. As a general guide, the _____ [18] (high) fares are the _____ [19] (flexible).

How do they rate? = How good are they?

2 Work in pairs. Look at the information about four no-frills airlines in 2002. Write six questions in the Past Simple. Use adjectives from the box in the comparative or superlative form.

Example *Which airline carried the highest number of passengers?*

many/few   high/low   big/small   young/old

No-frills airlines 2002 profile	Southwest	Ryanair	SkyEurope	AirAsia
Country	USA	Ireland	Slovakia	Malaysia
Date started	1971	1985	2002	2001
No. of passengers	64m	11.1m	60,117	2.2m
No. of routes	58	76	11	20
No. of employees	27,000	1,500	100	948
Percentage of online sales	30%	94%	25%	25%

3 Work with a different partner and exchange questions. Read your partner's questions and prepare the answers. When you are ready, tell your partner the answers.

4 🎧 **6.4** Listen to two people talking about the methods of travel they use. Complete the table.

Travel by	Speaker 1	Speaker 2
plane	*business trips, holidays*	*holidays*
train		
underground		
car		
bus		
motorbike		
bike		

5 🎧 **6.4** Listen again. Make a note of the comparative and superlative adjectives they use.

Examples *faster, most enjoyable*

6 Work in groups. Talk about which of the methods of travel in **4** you use and why, and any other methods you use.

Think about travel
   • to work
   • for business trips
   • to your English lesson
   • for holidays
   • for evening activities
   • at weekends

7 Work in groups. Tell your colleagues about your best or worst travel experience. Then answer their questions about it.

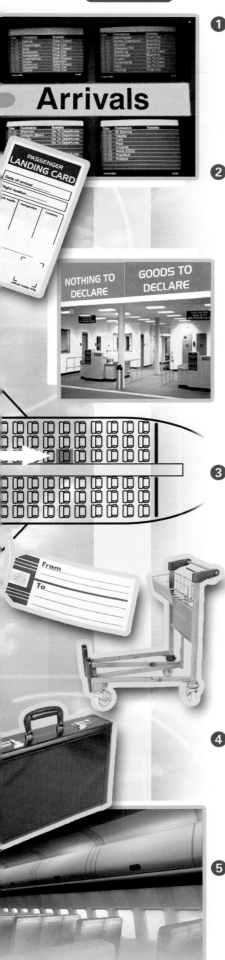

Air travel file. Word groups

1 Look at the pictures. What do they show? Find the words in the box.

overhead locker	window seat	check-in desk	ticket
information desk	arrivals screen	security check	trolley
passport control	landing card	passport	seat-belt
safety instructions	hand-luggage	suitcase	label
flight attendant	duty-free shop	briefcase	aisle seat
customs			

2 Work in pairs. Write the words and phrases in the box in **1** under the correct heading.

Documents	Terminal	On board	Luggage
boarding card	*departures screen*	*life-jacket*	*baggage claim*

3 Do you normally hear the sentences below at the check-in desk (C) or on the plane (P)? Tick (✓) C or P.

                                                      C   P

1 How much hand-luggage do you have? ____ ____
2 Do you prefer an aisle or a window seat? ____ ____
3 Could you put your bag in the overhead locker, please? ____ ____
4 Did you pack your bags yourself? ____ ____
5 Please make sure you turn off all mobile phones. ____ ____
6 We suggest you keep your seat-belt fastened during the flight. ____ ____
7 Have you left your bags unattended at any time? ____ ____
8 Non-EU passengers are required to fill in a landing card. ____ ____
9 Please remain seated until the aircraft has come to a complete standstill. ____ ____

4 🎧 **6.5** Listen to some airport announcements. Number the descriptions below 1 to 4 in the order you hear the announcements.

a an announcement for passengers waiting to get on the plane _____

b a security announcement to all passengers _____

c a request to a passenger _____

d a last call to two passengers _____

5 Work in groups. Choose a topic. Talk about the topic for one minute.

1 My most recent flight
2 Why I fly/don't fly
3 Airports I like/dislike

Transformations

1 Look at the photos. Tell the class anything you know about these two museums.

Musée d'Orsay

Tate Modern

Musée d'Orsay

Tate Modern

2 Work in pairs, Student A and Student B.

Student A

1 Read about the Musée d'Orsay.

2 Tell Student B about the Musée d'Orsay. Include information about
a the year 1900.   c after the war.   e 1977.
b during World War II.   d 1973.   f 1986.

3 Student B will tell you about Tate Modern. Ask questions if you don't understand anything.

The Musée d'Orsay

Today, the Musée d'Orsay is one of Paris's most famous art museums, and it has over two million visitors a year. Yet it began life not as a museum but as a train station and hotel. Like the Eiffel Tower, it was built for the World Exhibition of 1900, and until 1939 was one of the city's main stations. Then trains started to get longer and more powerful, and the platforms at the Orsay Station were too short, so after 1939 it was used only for local trains. During World War II it became a mailing centre for sending packages to prisoners of war. After the war it served as a welcome centre for prisoners returning home. It was then used in several film sets, including Orson Welles' film of Kafka's *The Trial*.

In 1973 the hotel closed its doors for the last time. There were plans to demolish the old hotel and station, and build a large modern hotel in their place. Fortunately a new interest in 19th-century architecture saved it from destruction and in 1977 the French government decided to convert the building into a museum of art. The Musée d'Orsay welcomed its first visitors on 9 December 1986.

Student B

1 Read about Tate Modern.

2 Student A will tell you about the Musée d'Orsay. Ask questions if you don't understand anything.

3 Tell Student A about Tate Modern. Include information about
  a what the building was before it became an art museum.
  b 1981.
  c the architect of the power station.
  d two Swiss architects.
  e 1995.
  f 12 May 2000.

Tate Modern

In the year 2000 London got its first modern art museum, Tate Modern. It was a project to celebrate the Millennium and is now one of London's most popular museums. It is, however, very different from other modern art museums like the spectacular Guggenheim Museum in Bilbao or the Pompidou Centre in Paris. Both of these are contemporary buildings, designed to be museums of art. Tate Modern started life not as a museum but as a power station, producing electricity for London. Construction began in 1947 and it was used as a power station until 1981 when the price of oil increased and it became more efficient to produce electricity in other ways. The architect of the power station also designed the famous British red telephone box!

Seventy architects, including some of the best-known in the world, entered the competition to design the museum. Two young Swiss architects were the winners. Work began in 1995 and Tate Modern opened to the public on 12 May 2000.

3 The phrases below are from an interview about the two museums. What do the underlined words mean?

1 … the exterior is very <u>ugly</u>.

2 … an <u>enormous amount of space</u>.

3 … that huge area was the <u>turbine hall</u> …

4 … ideal as an <u>exhibition space</u> …

5 … the museums <u>are similar</u> in other ways …

4 🎧 **6.6** Listen to an interview with a tourist guide about the Musée d'Orsay and Tate Modern. What does she say about

1 people's opinions of the buildings?

2 the space inside the museums?

3 their locations?

5 Work in groups. Choose a topic from the list and tell your colleagues about it.

- a museum you know
- museums you would like to visit in the future
- art you like/dislike
- a building you like/dislike

6 Answer questions from your colleagues about your topic.

Making arrangements

1 Read the letter and answer the question.
Why is Duncan Ross writing to Monique Bresson?

Wine & Dine

International Magazines Inc
15 Honeywell Street
London
EC4 1DT

Tel: +44 (0)20 7331 8579
Fax: +44 (0)20 7331 2280

email: rossd@winedine.co.uk
www.winedine.co.uk

Dear Ms Bresson

I hope you remember me from last year. James Turner introduced us at Vinexpo, and you gave me your business card. I am writing to you because I want to publish a French edition of *Wine & Dine* Magazine and would like to form a long-term business relationship with a translation agency.

Do you have time to join me for lunch one day, to discuss the possibility of doing business together? I will telephone you next week and, if you are interested, we can arrange a meeting.

Yours sincerely

Duncan Ross

Duncan Ross
Editor and Publisher

June

14 Monday

15 Tuesday

16 Wednesday

17 Thursday

18 Friday

2 🎧 **6.7** Duncan Ross calls Monique a week later. Listen to their conversation and write down the appointment (day, time, name of restaurant) in Monique's diary.

3 🎧 **6.7** Listen to the conversation again and tick (✓) the phrases you hear.

Making an appointment

When would be convenient for you?

When are you free?

Is ... possible for you?

Shall we say ...?

What time would suit you?

How about ...?

What about ...?

Saying 'yes'

Yes, ... suits me fine.

Yes, that's fine.

Yes, I can make it on ...

I look forward to meeting you ...

See you on ...

Changing an appointment

I'm very sorry.

I have to cancel the appointment on ...

I'm afraid I can't manage our meeting on ...

Could we arrange another time?

Saying 'no'

No, I'm afraid I'm busy then.

No, I'm afraid I've got another appointment ...

4 🎧 **6.8** Monique phones Duncan Ross a few days later. Listen to their conversation and answer the questions.

1 What is Monique's problem?

2 Is Duncan free on Thursday 17th?

3 Which day suits both of them?

5 🎧 **6.8** Listen to their conversation again and tick (✓) the phrases in **3** you hear.

6 Complete the conversation. Use phrases from **3**.

Andrew	Hello. Is that _____ ¹?
Chris	Yes, speaking.
Andrew	This is _____ ². Could we arrange a meeting to discuss our trip to the UK?
Chris	Of course. _____ ³ for you?
Andrew	_____ ⁴ next Tuesday morning?
Chris	No, _____ ⁵ then.
	_____ ⁶ on Wednesday afternoon?
Andrew	Yes, _____ ⁷.
Chris	_____ ⁸ 2.30?
Andrew	_____ ⁹. See you on Wednesday, then. Goodbye.

7 Work in pairs. Practise making an appointment. Change roles and make an appointment for another meeting.

8 Complete the conversation. Use phrases from **3**.

Armand	Hello. Is that _____ ¹?
Jan	Yes, _____ ².
Armand	This is _____ ³. I'm very sorry. _____ ⁴. Could we _____ ⁵?
Jan	Yes, _____ ⁶. When _____ ⁷?
Armand	Is _____ ⁸ for you?
Jan	No, _____ ⁹. How about _____ ¹⁰?
Armand	Yes, _____ ¹¹.
Jan	Good. _____ ¹².

9 Work in pairs. Change the appointments you made in **7** above.

10 Work in pairs. Role-play two more phone calls. Telephone your colleague and make an appointment for next week. Ring again and change the appointment.

UNIT 7
Changing lives

Language focus

1 Look at the pictures and answer the questions.

1 These products all have one thing in common. What do you think it is?

2 When you buy products like these do you know
   a which countries they come from?
   b how much of the price goes to the growers?

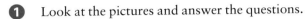

Fairtrade – Guarantees a better deal for Third World producers

Simply buying a Fairtrade product can help a village get clean water or children to go to school. Four and a half million farmers and their families, in 36 countries, benefit from Fairtrade.

The Fairtrade Foundation permits companies whose products meet the international standards of Fairtrade to put the name 'Fairtrade' on their products. These products include coffee, tea, cocoa, and fresh fruit. Under the Fairtrade system the producers receive a fair price which includes extra money, called a 'social premium', to help them improve their living and working conditions. Fairtrade gives them advance payments to help with production costs and long-term contracts so they can plan for the future.

In general, global trade has made people in the rich developed countries richer and people in the poor developing countries poorer.

2 Read the information about the Fairtrade Foundation. Find words and phrases which mean

1 promises

2 business agreement

3 poor countries that are trying to improve their economy (two expressions)

4 receive an advantage

5 countries with advanced economies

3 Answer the questions.

1 What does Fairtrade guarantee to the people it helps?

2 Who does Fairtrade help?

3 Which countries has global trade helped most?

4 The underlined words in A are from an interview about Fairtrade. Match them with their meaning in B.

A	B
1 Since 1988 Fairtrade has <u>expanded</u> …	a event that causes a lot of damage and problems
2 This has been a <u>disaster</u> …	b being very poor
3 They've built <u>wells</u> …	c got bigger
4 … people are <u>willing</u> to pay a bit more …	d happy, ready
5 … to help people escape <u>poverty</u>.	e deep holes in the ground from which you get water

5 🎧 **7.1** Listen to an interview with Harriet Lamb, the Executive Director of the Fairtrade Foundation in the UK. Complete the datafile.

FAIRTRADE DATAFILE

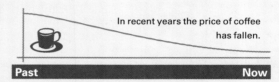

- Fairtrade started in _____ ¹ in the UK and in _____ ² in the Netherlands.
- At present it is in _____ ³ countries, mostly in western Europe, but also the USA, _____ ⁴, Australia, New Zealand, and _____ ⁵.
- The first country in eastern Europe to have Fairtrade is _____ ⁶.
- Producers can use the social premium to improve their _____ ⁷ and _____ ⁸ conditions.
- In the UK sales went up by _____ ⁹ % in _____ ¹⁰.
- Usually the price of a Fairtrade product is about _____ ¹¹ to _____ ¹² % more than the average price.

6 🎧 **7.1** Listen again and check your answers.

Past Simple and Present Perfect Simple

Read the examples and answer the questions.

Past Simple

- Fairtrade **started** in the Netherlands in 1988.
- In the UK sales **went up** by 50% in 2001.
- When **did** the idea of Fairtrade **start**?

1992

Fairtrade started in the
UK in 1992.

| Past | Now |

Present Perfect Simple

- Since 1988 Fairtrade **has expanded** into many other countries.
- In recent years the price of coffee, cocoa, and bananas **has fallen**.
- Fairtrade **has** just **started** in eastern Europe.
- **Have** sales **increased**?   Yes, they **have**.
                                     No, they **haven't**.
- What kind of improvements **have** they **made**?

In recent years the price of coffee has fallen.

| Past | Now |

- To make the Present Perfect Simple, use *has* or *have* + the past participle of the verb.

1 Which tense do we use for situations and actions that happened
   a at a definite time in the past?
   b in a period of time from the past to the present?

2 Which tense do we use with expressions like
   a *in 2001, when*?
   b *since 1988, in recent years, just*?

Look at Listening script 7.1 on p. 130. Find more examples of verbs in the Present Perfect Simple. What period of time do they refer to?

📔 Pocket Book p. 6 (irregular verbs), 10, 13

Practice **1** Quick test. Complete the table.

Infinitive	Past Simple	Past Participle
be		
come		
cost		
fall		
get		
go		gone/been*
grow		
make		

* See Pocket Book p. 13

2 Work in pairs. Complete the sentences with the correct time expression, a or b.

1 I made a research trip to Africa _____.
  a a year ago   b in the last six months

2 The price of coffee has fallen _____.
  a in 1992   b every year since 1992

3 Rich countries have got richer and poor countries have got poorer
  _____.
  a in the 1990s   b in the last decade

4 Did sales of Fairtrade products increase _____?
  a recently   b last year

5 How many producers has Fairtrade helped _____?
  a since 1988   b between 1988 and 2000

3 Complete the extracts from a newspaper article about Fairtrade. Put the verbs in brackets in the correct tense, Past Simple or Present Perfect Simple.

Since 1992 the price of cocoa beans _____ [1] (fall) by 50%. In the same period the price of a bar of chocolate _____ [2] (increase) by 65%, but the farmers who grow cocoa _____ [3] (not receive) a higher price for their crop.

In the last decade the wages of workers on many banana plantations _____ [4] (decrease). In 1993 workers in Costa Rica _____ [5] (earn) $250 a month. In 1997 their wages _____ [6] (fall) to $187 and in 2001 they _____ [7] (go down) again – to only $160.

In recent years global trade _____ [8] (make) it possible for the rich developed countries to buy their coffee, tea, cocoa, bananas, etc. from the country with the cheapest price, changing from one country to another. This _____ [9] (be) a disaster for whole communities in the developing world who _____ [10] (grow) the same crop for generations.

Pronunciation

1 🎧 **7.2** Listen to the examples. What do you notice about the underlined words?

Example 1   a Carla hasn't left.   b I think she has.

Example 2   a Have sales increased?   b No, they haven't.

2 🎧 **7.3** Listen to the sentences. Underline the words that are stressed.

1 The company has expanded.

2 Has it made a lot of changes?

3 No, it hasn't.

4 Their prices have increased.

5 I'm sure they haven't.

6 I think they have.

3 When are *have/haven't* and *has/hasn't* stressed? When are they not stressed?

4 Underline the words you think are stressed.

1 Has she made any progress?

2 I'm sure she has.

3 I hope they haven't forgotten the meeting.

4 Do you think they have?

5 Have they finished the work?

6 They haven't started it yet!

5 🎧 **7.4** Listen and check your answers.

6 Work in pairs. Practise saying the sentences in **4**. Emphasize the stressed words.

4 Work in pairs, Student A with another Student A, Student B with another Student B.

Student A

1 Read about two coffee growers in Costa Rica. Student B will ask you questions about them in **5**.

Edgar and Blanca grow coffee and vegetables in Costa Rica. When they got married, 32 years ago, they had no land. They worked long hours for other people and earned very little, but after sixteen years they had enough money to buy some land. They decided to grow coffee. They borrowed the money they needed and Edgar joined the local cooperative. But three years later, just when his crop was ready, the price of coffee fell to its lowest point ever. For most coffee producers this was a disaster, but Edgar was one of the very few lucky ones because his cooperative sells most of its coffee to the Fairtrade market in Europe. Fairtrade's price covered the cost of production and this saved the cooperative producers from disaster.

2 Prepare questions using these words to ask Student B more about Fairtrade and Edgar and Blanca in **5**. Use the Present Perfect in all your questions.

    Example   Who/Fairtrade/help?
                    Who has Fairtrade helped?

  a What/Fairtrade give/people in the Third World?
  b What/producers/improve?
  c What/they/stop using?
  d How/communities/use/the social premium?
  e What/Edgar and Blanca/build?
  f What/their children/receive?
  g What/Edgar/do/all his life?

Student B

1 Read about Fairtrade, and Edgar and Blanca. Student A will ask you questions about them in **5**.

Fairtrade has helped millions of people in the Third World. It has given them hope for the future. For example producers have improved their lives and the quality of their crops, and many of them have stopped using dangerous chemicals. Communities have used the social premium to make wells to get clean water, and to build schools and hospitals. The story of Edgar and Blanca, who grow coffee and vegetables in Costa Rica, is typical. After many years of hard work they have built a bigger house and their children have received an education. 'All I have ever done is work, work, work,' says Edgar. 'I had no choice, but now my children can choose what they want to do.'

2 Prepare questions using these words to ask Student A more about Edgar and Blanca in **5**. Use the Past Simple in all your questions.

    Example   How long ago/they/get married?
                    How long ago did they get married?

  a Who/Edgar and Blanca/work for?
  b They/earn a lot of money?
  c What/they/buy?
  d What/they/decide to grow?
  e What/Edgar/join?
  f When/the price of coffee/fall?
  g Why/be/Edgar lucky?

5 Work with a different partner, Student A with Student B. Ask your questions and answer your partner's questions.

6 Work in groups. Discuss the questions.

1 Have you seen or bought Fairtrade products in your country? If so, where?

2 Do you think Fairtrade is a good way to help people in the Third World escape poverty? Why? Why not?

7 Work in pairs. Ask your partner five questions using the words below. Tick (✔) the things your partner has done. If the answer is 'Yes, I have', ask for more details. Answer your partner's questions.

Example   **Student A** *Have you travelled abroad this year?*

                Student B *Yes, I have.*

                Student A *Where did you go? What did you do?*

Student A

1 travel/abroad this year?

2 meet/any foreign visitors this month?

3 see/any good films recently?

4 do/any sport this week?

5 have/a birthday in the last four months?

Student B

1 have/a holiday this year?

2 buy/anything expensive this month?

3 use/English at work this week?

4 make/a long journey in the last two months?

5 read/any good books recently?

8 Work with a different partner. Imagine your partner is a friend you haven't seen for a long time. Tell him/her about what you've done in the last six months. Ask questions to get more information.

Begin

Student A *Hi, I haven't seen you for ages! How are you?*

Student B *Fine thanks, but I've been very busy.*

Student A *Have you? What's happened?*

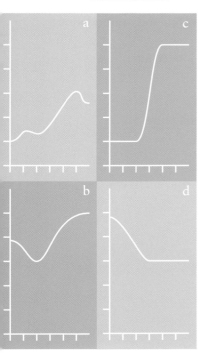

Trends file. The language of graphs

1 Match the descriptions with the correct graphs.

1 Exports fell slightly, then improved. _____
2 Unemployment decreased steadily, then remained stable. _____
3 Sales rose sharply and reached a peak in the summer. _____
4 Production costs went up dramatically, then levelled off. _____

2 Complete the table.

Verb		Noun
Infinitive	Past Simple	
▲ go up	_____	
▲ improve	_____	an _____
▲ increase	_____	an _____
▲ rise	_____	a _____
▼ decrease	_____	a _____
▼ fall	_____	a _____
▼ go down	_____	

3 Write *slightly*, *steadily*, *sharply*, or *dramatically* under each diagram.

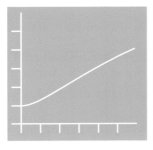 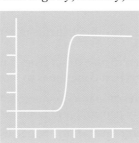 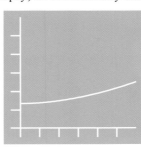 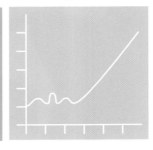

1 _____ 2 _____ 3 _____ 4 _____

4 Read the examples. Complete the sentences with the correct preposition.

Examples *Sales rose **by** 2% …*
*There was a slight increase **in** the rate of inflation.*
*There was a fall of 2.5% **in** exports …*
*Unemployment remained stable **at** 2.5 million …*
*Production went down **from** 5,000 **to** 4,400 units a month …*
*Prices increased **by** €5 per item …*

1 Sales went up _____ 9%.
2 Inflation remained stable _____ 2.5%.
3 There was a steady decrease _____ production costs.
4 Exports fell _____ 1,000 units _____ 870 units a month.
5 Production costs rose _____ €3 per unit.
6 There was a rise _____ 3% _____ salaries.

5 🎧 **7.5** Listen to a sales manager describing his company's sales figures. Complete the graph.

6 Work in pairs. Choose a product you know and draw a graph to show sales of the product in a six-month period. Write a description of your graph.

7 Work with a different partner. Describe your graph to your partner. Draw the graph your partner describes. Do not show each other your graphs until you have finished.

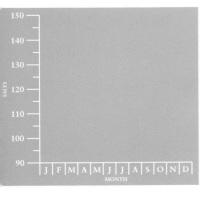

The best companies to work for

1 From the list of eleven company benefits below, find the word or phrase that means

1 place where babies and young children are looked after. _g_
2 flexible working hours. _____
3 extra money for doing your job well. _____
4 money you get from your company when you retire. _____
5 making progress in your job. _____

a good pay and holidays
b bonus for good performance
c flexitime
d executive dining room
e free meals
f career development
g crèche
h fitness centre
i company pension
j private health care
k social and sports club

2 Discuss the questions.

1 Which three benefits in **1** are the most important ones for you as an employee?
2 Are there any other benefits not in the list which are important to you?

3 🎧 **7.6** Listen to an extract from a radio programme called *Working Week*. It is about the best companies to work for in the UK. Answer the questions.

1 In the best companies, who gets benefits like private health care, a company pension, and bonuses?
2 Is it difficult for staff to change from full-time to part-time work in the best companies?
3 How many of the companies in the survey have their own crèche?
4 What do you not find in companies with a very open democratic structure?

4 Read about three companies in *The best companies to work for* survey: CMG, Keymed, and Maersk. Prepare your answers for the group discussion in **5**.

5 Work in groups. Discuss the questions. Give reasons for your opinions.

1 Do you think it is a good idea for a company to help the local community and schools like Keymed? Do you know any other companies that do this?
2 What do you think of CMG's open company culture?
3 What do you think of Maersk's holidays for staff?
4 Which of the three companies would you prefer to work for?

Keymed

(Japanese-owned UK medical equipment maker)

Keymed was one of the first companies in Britain to set up a high-quality in-company crèche. The company pays most of the cost, with parents paying just £15.50 a day. There's a company pension and private healthcare, and staff get a bonus for perfect attendance. In the first half of 1999, 250 workers received £150 for never missing a day. Keymed managers are active in community organizations and schools, and the company also supports local charities*.

charity = organization that helps people who are poor, sick, etc.

CMG

(UK information technology company)

What CMG's employees like most about their company is its culture of openness. There are no private offices and managers sit among the rest of the staff. Anyone in the company can find out a colleague's salary and performance details. CMG also believes in good management. If anyone is unhappy with their manager, the company wants them to say so.
CMG gives its staff good holidays, a company pension, private healthcare, and opportunities for career development.

Maersk

(Danish shipping company with offices in the UK)

Maersk has offices in 80 countries. Trainees can join a two-year programme in which they work in different countries before taking a management position. During that time they must study two foreign languages at evening school. Staff get private healthcare and dental treatment. At Christmas the company gives them presents of wine, chocolates, biscuits, and a £100 voucher. In summer they can have a free holiday with their family at one of the cottages the company rents in Devon, Yorkshire, and Scotland.

Opinions and suggestions. Agreeing and disagreeing

1 🎧 **7.7** Listen to the first part of a conversation between Duncan Ross and James Turner. Answer the questions.

1 What celebration does Duncan want to discuss with James?
2 Why does Duncan want to charter a plane?
3 What other event does Duncan suggest they celebrate?
4 What does James think about this idea?

2 🎧 **7.7** Listen again and tick (✓) the phrases you hear.

Asking for opinions

What do you think about … ?
What's your opinion of … ?
How do you feel about … ?

Giving opinions

In my opinion …
I think …

Agreeing

I agree.
I certainly agree with that.
I agree completely.

Disagreeing

I'm afraid I don't agree.
I'm sorry, but I disagree.

3 🎧 **7.8** Listen to the second part of their conversation. Tick (✓) T (true) or F (false).

	T	F
1 There is a busy programme on the first day.	___	___
2 James thinks the treasure hunt is a good idea.	___	___
3 The last event on the programme is a dinner.	___	___
4 Duncan wants to make sure they've invited everyone.	___	___

4 🎧 **7.8** Listen again and tick (✓) the phrases you hear.

Making suggestions

I suggest …
How about … ?
What about … ?
Why don't we … ?
Why not … ?
We could …

Asking for suggestions

Do you have any suggestions for … ?
Any ideas on … ?

Accepting suggestions

Yes, that's a good idea.
Yes, let's do that.

Rejecting suggestions

Yes, but …
I'm not sure about that.
I'm afraid I don't like that idea.

5 Match A with B to make suggestions.

A	B
I suggest we	invite some friends for dinner?
How about	spend next Sunday in the country?
What about	going away for a few days?
Why don't we	go to a restaurant in the evening.
Why not	go skiing next weekend.
We could	buying tickets for the music festival?

6 Work in groups. Choose two or three of these statements and discuss them. Use the phrases in **2** to ask for and give opinions, and agree or disagree with your colleagues.

1 Flexitime at work is a good idea.

2 Violence on TV is dangerous.

3 Fast food is necessary nowadays.

4 Video games are bad for children.

5 Mobile phones – you love them or hate them.

7 Discuss one of these topics in groups. Use the phrases in **4** to suggest solutions, and accept or reject the ideas of your colleagues.

1 At present your company pays for your English course. Next year, it wants employees to pay 50% of the cost. What can you do to stop this change?

2 It's your company's 50th anniversary next year. Suggest ways of celebrating the occasion.

3 Your town wants to improve its leisure facilities. Suggest changes and improvements.

UNIT 8
Crossing cultures

▼ AGENDA

▸ Modal verbs: *should/shouldn't, may, might*

▸ *have to/don't have to*

▸ *it's important to/not to*

▸ Descriptions file. Using a dictionary and word building

▸ Across cultures

▸ Invitations

Language focus

1 Read the questions. Talk about what happens in your country and describe any differences with other countries you know.

What happens in your country?

1 How do people greet
   a family members?
   b close friends?
   c colleagues at work?
   d visitors to their company/organization?

2 Do colleagues at work call each other by their
   a first names?
   b family names?

3 How punctual are people for
   a business meetings?
   b social events?

4 How separate are work and private life? Do employees
   a take work home?
   b invite colleagues or business visitors to their home?
   c give their company their phone number when they're on holiday?

5 What presents do people take when they are invited to a person's home?

2 The words in A are in the extracts in **3**. Match them with their meaning in B.

A	B
1 schedule	a opposite of 'polite'
2 agenda	b programme of work to do
3 interrupt	c without words
4 rude	d how someone looks
5 non-verbal	e say something is very good
6 appearance	f speak when another person is speaking
7 compliment	g list of subjects to discuss at a meeting

3 Read these extracts from *Understanding Cultural Differences*, a book that gives advice about working in other countries. Then discuss with a partner which country you think the author is describing.

Extract 1

… It's important to be serious in a work situation. They don't mix work and play so you shouldn't make jokes as you do in the UK and USA when you first meet people. They work in a very organized way and prefer to do one thing at a time. They don't like interruptions or sudden changes of schedule. Punctuality is very important so you should arrive on time for appointments. At meetings it's important to follow the agenda and not interrupt another speaker. If you give a presentation, you should focus on facts and technical information and the quality of your company's products. You should also prepare well, as they may ask a lot of questions. Colleagues normally use family names, and titles – for example 'Doctor' or 'Professor', so you shouldn't use first names unless a person asks you to.

Sweden _____   France _____   Germany _____

4 Were your answers in **3** correct? Do you think the descriptions of the nationalities are accurate? Do you disagree with any of the advice?

5 Look at the extracts in **3** again. What verbs and phrases does the author use to give advice?

Modal verbs

Modal verbs are special auxiliary verbs which add extra meaning to the main verb. For example, modals can express advice, necessity, and possibility.

Read the examples and complete the grammar rules. Then answer the questions.

should/shouldn't

- You **should** arrive on time for appointments.
- You **shouldn't** make jokes as you do in the UK and USA.

- Use *should* to say *it's a good idea*.
- Use _____ to say *it's a bad idea*.

have to/don't have to

- They **have to** ask everyone in the company.
- You **don't have to** be formal.

- Use _____ to say *it's necessary or obligatory*.
- Use _____ to say *it's not necessary or obligatory*.

Note To say *it's necessary* we also use *it's important to/not to*.

may/might

- They **may** ask a lot of questions.
- They **might** think you're rude if you don't.

- Use _____ to say *it's about 50% possible*.
- Use *might* to say *it's less than 50% possible*.

Do *should*, *may*, and *might* have -*s* in the *he/she/it* form?
Do we use *to* after *should/shouldn't*, *may*, and *might*?
How do we make questions with *should*?
How do we make questions with *have to*?

 Pocket Book p. 8

Find other examples of these modal verbs in the book extracts in **3**.

Understanding Cultural Differences

Extract 2

... Politeness and good manners are very important and business meetings are very formal. Business cards are also important and they exchange these at the beginning of a meeting. They always look at them carefully, so you should do the same as they might think you're rude if you don't. A lot of communication is non-verbal. They are very good listeners and may ask a lot of questions to check they understand everything. In a conversation they wait longer before they reply than westerners do, so it's important not to speak in those long pauses but to wait for their reply. In their culture it's rude to ask direct questions or to say 'No' or 'I disagree'. In business it takes a long time to make a decision because they have to ask everyone in the company. When they say 'Yes' it may mean 'I understand', not 'I agree', and when they smile it might be because they don't know what to say.

Japan _____ India _____ China _____

Extract 3

... People and personal relationships are more important than time and schedules, which are flexible. People may be late for an appointment, although they are more punctual in the north of the country than in the south. To north Europeans their way of working may seem disorganized and inefficient. In meetings they don't feel they have to follow the agenda or speak only in turn. They interrupt each other a lot and often all talk at the same time. They are excellent communicators and are very expressive in their use of body language. Appearance and good manners are important, so you should dress well and be polite, but you don't have to be formal. Food is a very important part of life, and is very good, so remember to compliment them on their cuisine.

France _____ Italy _____ Spain _____

Practice

1 Complete the sentences. Use a modal verb which adds the meaning in brackets.

1 In California you _____ be 21 to drink alcohol. (It's obligatory.)

2 In the Netherlands you _____ be 18 to buy beer, but you do to buy wine. (It's not necessary.)

3 In Hong Kong you _____ get a fine if you eat or drink on the subway system. (It's possible.)

4 In Thailand you _____ get permission before you take photos of images of Buddha. (It's a good idea.)

5 In Turkey and Japan you _____ blow your nose in public. (It's a bad idea.)

2 Work in pairs. Can you suggest reasons for these cultural dos and don'ts? Discuss your ideas.

In Russia

1 Why is it important not to give an even number of flowers (e.g. 8, 10, 12) as a present?

2 Why shouldn't you smoke in Red Square, Moscow?

3 Why do you have to leave your coat in the cloakroom when you go to a restaurant or a theatre?

4 If you visit someone in their home in winter, why should you take a pair of indoor shoes with you?

In Japan

1 Why shouldn't you speak loudly or show you're angry when speaking to Japanese people?

2 Why is it important not to pour your own drink when you are with friends or people you know?

3 Why should westerners stand further away than is normal for them when they are in conversation with Japanese people?

4 Why do you have to take a shower before you get into a Japanese communal bath?

3 🎧 **8.1** Listen to the answers. Were you right?

Pronunciation

1 🎧 **8.2** Listen to the example. Which two words have the main stress? Underline them. Why are they stressed?

Example *You might have a few problems, but you won't have many.*

2 🎧 **8.3** Listen to the sentences below. Underline the two words in each sentence that have the main stress.

1 You should always be punctual, but you don't have to be formal.

2 You don't have to wear a suit, but you must wear a tie.

3 You have to get permission first, but the managers don't.

4 The Japanese may think you rude, but the Italians won't.

5 It's important to be serious at work, but not when you're at a party.

3 🎧 **8.3** Listen again. Repeat the sentences.

4 Work in pairs. Practise the sentences in **2**. Change the meaning by changing the stress.

4 A foreign visitor who is going to work in your company/organization for a year needs your advice. What reply would you give to the visitor's questions below? Use *should/shouldn't*, *have to/don't have to*, *may/might*, *it's important to/not to* in your answers.

Examples *You don't have to use a person's title when you're talking to them, but of course it's important to use it when you write the name on a letter or a formal list.*

At a meeting you should keep to the agenda and not interrupt people because they may think you're rude. You should wait until a person has finished speaking before you say anything.

1 How should I greet people in the morning? Should I shake hands with colleagues or just say 'hello'?

2 Should I use a person's title if they have one?

3 At a meeting, is it important to keep to the agenda? Is it OK to interrupt or do I have to wait my turn to speak?

4 Should I dress formally for work? Do I have to wear a suit and tie every day?

5 Are people usually serious at work or is it OK to make jokes?

6 At a business lunch is it OK to discuss business during the meal or should I wait until after the meal?

7 To talk to more senior people do I have to make an appointment or can I just knock on their door?

8 Do people usually exchange business cards at first meetings? If so, should I do it at the beginning of the meeting?

5 Work in groups. Brainstorm your ideas for this competition. Then make a list of your eight best ideas. Use *should/shouldn't*, *have to/don't have to*, *may/might*, *it's important to/not to*.

COMPETITION

Win a three-month intensive English course in the country of your choice! All you have to do is answer this question.

What is the secret of successful language learning?

Here are some suggestions for topics. Add other topics.

- motivation
- course length
- learning vocabulary
- reading newspapers, books, magazines in English

Examples *It's very important to be motivated and to enjoy speaking the language.*

You have to be patient. It takes a long time to learn a language well.

6 Present your ideas to the class.

Descriptions file. Using a dictionary and word building

1 A good dictionary gives you information that helps you learn vocabulary more easily. Read the dictionary extracts. Use the information to complete the table.

* **efficient** /ɪ'fɪʃnt/ **adj** able to work well without making mistakes or wasting time and energy: *Our secretary is very efficient.* • *You must find a more efficient way of organizing your time.* ⇢ opposite **inefficient** -efficiency /ɪ'fɪʃnsi/ **noun** [U] -efficiently **adv**

* **honest** /'ɒnɪst/ **adj 1** (used about a person) telling the truth; not deceiving people or stealing: *Just be honest – do you like this skirt or not?* • **To be honest**, *I don't think that's a very good idea.* **2** showing honest qualities: *an honest face* • *I'd like your honest opinion, please.* ⇢ opposite for both senses **dishonest** -honesty **noun** [U] ⇢ opposite **dishonesty**

* **polite** /pə'laɪt/ **adj** having good manners and showing respect for others. *The assistants in that shop are always very helpful and polite.* • *He gave me a polite smile.* ⇢ Opposite **impolite** or **impertinent** -politely **adv** -politeness **noun** [U]

* **punctual** /'pʌŋktʃuəl/ **adj** doing sth or happening at the right time; not late: *It is important to be punctual for your classes.* ➤ We say the train, bus, etc was **on time** not punctual. -punctuality /ˌpʌŋktʃu'æləti/ **noun** [U]: *Japanese trains are famous for their punctuality.* -punctually **adv**

* **reliable** /rɪ'laɪəbl/ **adj** that you can trust: *Japanese cars are usually very reliable.* • *Is he a reliable witness?* ⇢ opposite **unreliable** ⇢ verb rely -reliability /rɪˌlaɪə'bɪləti/ **noun** [U] -reliably /·əbli/ **adv**: *I have been reliably informed that there will be no trains tomorrow.*

Definition taken from the *Oxford Wordpower Dictionary* © Oxford University Press 2002

Adjective	Opposite adjective	Noun
efficient	_____	_____
honest	_____	_____
polite	_____	_____
punctual	*unpunctual**___	_____
reliable	_____	_____

*A dictionary does not usually give the opposite adjective when it begins with the prefix *un-* .

2 We add a prefix to the beginning of a word, and a suffix to the end, e.g *unpunctual*, *punctuality*. Look at the table in **1**. Which other prefixes make an opposite adjective? Which other suffixes make a noun from an adjective?

3 Match the adjectives in the box with the definitions.

ambitious	adaptable	creative	easy-going	hard-working
organized	outgoing	patient	sensitive	sociable

A person who ...   **Adjective**

1 enjoys being with other people   _____

2 waits and doesn't get angry   _____

3 works with energy and effort   _____

4 is calm and relaxed   _____

5 wants to be successful   _____

6 plans their work and life   _____

7 adapts easily in different situations   _____

8 uses their imagination to make and do new things   _____

9 is interested in other people and new experiences _____

10 shows understanding of other people's feelings,   _____
    problems, etc.

4 Complete the table. Use the correct prefix (*dis-*, *im-*, *in-*, *un-*) and suffix *-ation*, *-ity*, *-n*, *-ce*).

Adjective	Opposite adjective	Noun
ambitious	_____	_____
organized	_____	_____
patient	_____	_____
sensitive	_____	_____

5 Which three adjectives in **1** and **3** best describe your character? Would you like to be different in any way?

6 Work in groups. We often use particular adjectives to describe national characteristics, e.g. *Italians are very sociable, Brazilians are easy-going, Japanese are very polite*, etc. Choose four adjectives from **1** and **3** which you think describe four different nationalities.

7 Tell the class which adjectives you chose in **6**, and which nationalities you think they describe and why.

8 Do you think descriptions of national characteristics help us to understand other nationalities better, or are they too general to be helpful?

Across cultures

1 In his book, *When Cultures Collide*, about working with different nationalities, Richard D. Lewis divides countries into three cultural groups: 'Linear-active', 'Multi-active', and 'Reactive'. In his opinion, each group of countries in A has one of the cultures in B. Match the countries with the cultures.

A
- south-east Asia and Finland
- southern Europe and Latin America
- the USA and northern Europe

B

Linear-active	**Multi-active**	**Reactive**
• do one thing at a time	• do several things at the same time	• are punctual
• are punctual	• are unpunctual	• follow the timetable of the person they are doing business with
• follow timetables and schedules	• prefer flexibility to fixed timetables and schedules	• do not express individual opinions or disagreement
• rarely interrupt	• often interrupt	• listen very carefully and do not interrupt
• focus first on the job and finishing it in time	• think personal relationships are as important as the job	• do not speak first and pause before replying

2 🎧 **8.4** Listen to the first part of a talk about Linear-active, Multi-active, and Reactive cultures. Check your answers for **1**.

3 🎧 **8.5** Listen to the second part of the talk. Complete the table to show the differences between the three groups. Write L (Linear-active), M (Multi-active) and R (Reactive) at appropriate points on the lines, as in the example.

punctual	*LR* _____ *M*	unpunctual
long pauses in conversation	_____	no long pauses in conversation
a lot of eye contact	_____	very little eye contact
stand close together	_____	stand further away
use gestures a lot	_____	use gestures very little

4 What do you think of Richard Lewis's analysis of different cultures? How useful is it in helping to avoid cultural misunderstandings?

5 Work in groups. Compare your answers to the questions.

In your country

1 how much eye contact is there between
  - people talking to each other?
  - strangers passing in the street?

2 do people
  - stand close enough to touch each other when they are speaking?
  - show affection in public (e.g. holding hands, kissing)?

3 what gestures do people use to
  - indicate 'Yes' and 'No'?
  - attract the attention of someone in a group?
  - call a waiter?
  - indicate they don't understand?
  - show surprise?

6 Describe any differences you have heard about or noticed in other nationalities. Do you think any of the differences could cause a cultural misunderstanding?

Invitations

1 🎧 **8.6** Read the invitation. Listen to the telephone conversation between Monique Bresson and Duncan Ross. Answer the questions.

1 What invitation does Duncan make on the phone?

2 What is Monique's response?

Wine & Dine

Monique Bresson is invited to the 10th anniversary celebration of *Wine & Dine* magazine, to take place on Saturday 14 and Sunday 15 June at Glencross Castle, Scotland.

Return flight London–Edinburgh by charter aircraft is included in this invitation.

Duncan Ross
Editor and Publisher *Wine & Dine* magazine

RSVP, 15 Honeywell Street, London EC4 1DT
Tel: +44 (0)20 7331 8579, Fax: +44 (0)20 7331 2280
Email: rossd@winedine.co.uk   www.winedine.co.uk

2 🎧 **8.7** After talking to Monique, Duncan phones James Turner. Listen to their conversation. Answer the questions.

1 Why doesn't James accept Duncan's invitation?

2 What makes him change his mind?

3 🎧 **8.6, 8.7** Listen to both telephone conversations again. Tick (✓) the phrases you hear.

Inviting	**Accepting**
I'd like to invite you to …	Thank you. I'd be delighted to accept.
Would you join us … ?	Thank you. I'd love to.
Would you like to … ?	Thank you. I'd enjoy that.
Why don't you … ?	
How about … ?	

Declining

I'd love to, but (*I'm afraid I can't*).

Thanks a lot, but (*I've made another arrangement*).

4 Work in pairs. Use the phrases in ❸ to make and respond to invitations. Think of two more situations and practise them.

Student A

Situation 1

Invite your colleague to join you for lunch tomorrow.

Suggest another day next week.

Situation 2

Decline and give a reason.
Suggest lunch another day.

Student B

Decline and give a reason.

Accept.

Invite your colleague for a drink after work.

Accept.

REVIEW
UNIT B

This unit reviews all the main language points from Units 5–8. Complete the exercises. Check your learning with the self-check box at the end.

1 **Mass and count nouns, *some/any, a lot of, much/many, a little/a few***

Five of the sentences below have a grammatical mistake. Find the mistakes, then write the correct sentences.

1 I do a lot of sport at weekends.

2 There wasn't much traffic this morning.

3 Could you give me an information, please?

4 We didn't have many problems with the new system.

5 The news are not very good.

6 Would you like a little wine?

7 Did she give you a good advice?

8 How many money did you spend?

9 Only a few people came to the meeting.

10 I didn't buy some coffee.

2 ***some/any, a lot of/lots of, much/many***

1 Work in pairs. Use the words in A and B to make eight questions with *much ... ?* and *many ... ?*

Examples *Do you get much stress in your job?*
How many hours a day do you spend at a computer?
How much relaxation do you get on weekdays?

A	B
do	relaxation
drink	holidays
eat	sport or exercise
get	hours at a computer
have	cups of coffee
spend	alcohol
	vegetables
	fruit
	hours of sleep
	stress
	cheese and butter

2 Work with a different partner. Ask your partner your questions and answer his/her questions. Use *some, any, a lot of/lots of, much,* and *many* in your answers.

3 **Comparative and superlative adjectives: quick test**

What are the comparative and superlative forms of these adjectives? Add four more examples.

1 big _____ _____

2 easy _____ _____

3 near _____ _____

4 good _____ _____

5 efficient _____ _____

6 much/many _____ _____

7 bad _____ _____

8 far _____ _____

9 early _____ _____

10 crowded _____ _____

11 flexible _____ _____

12 little _____ _____

4 Past Simple and Present Perfect Simple

Complete the sentences. Put the verbs in brackets in the correct tense, Past Simple or Present Perfect Simple.

1 In 1998 prices _____ by 2%. (increase)

2 The economic situation _____ a lot since 2001. (improve)

3 How long ago _____ university? (you, finish)

4 He _____ to Japan twice last month. (go)

5 How many countries _____ in the last two years? (they, visit)

6 The company _____ a lot in recent years. (grow)

7 Where _____ your last holiday? (you, spend)

8 She _____ her new job two weeks ago. (start)

9 Sales _____ every year since 1999. (go up)

10 I _____ a lot of problems recently. (have)

5 Present Perfect Simple questions

Work in pairs, Student A and Student B. Ask your partner questions in the Present Perfect Simple. If your partner answers *Yes, I have*, ask for more details. Add two more questions.

Example (have) a birthday in the last three months?

        Student A *Have you had a birthday in the last three months?*

        Student B *Yes, I have.*

        Student A *When was your birthday? What did you do?*

Student A

Ask Student B

1 (see) any good films this month?

2 (write) any emails in English this week?

3 (have) a holiday in the last six months?

4 (buy) anything expensive recently?

5 _____

6 _____

Student B

Ask Student A

1 (visit) any interesting places recently?

2 (eat) any foreign food in the last two weeks?

3 (speak) English at work this week?

4 (do) any sport in the last five days?

5 _____

6 _____

6 Modal verbs: giving advice

Use *should*, *shouldn't*, and *it's important to/not to*, to give advice to someone who wants to

1 learn another language in a short time.

2 get good results in an exam but hates studying.

3 become fit and healthy but does no sport.

4 stop smoking.

5 lose weight.

6 relax more but is a workaholic.

7 Modal verbs: possibility

Work in pairs. Tell your partner what you *may* or *might* do

1 one evening next week.

2 next weekend.

3 next summer.

4 in two or three years' time.

8 Modal verbs: necessity

Say which of these things you *have to* do in your job and which things you *don't have to* do.

1 start work at a fixed time
2 wear a uniform
3 use English on the phone
4 talk to customers
5 write emails in English

6 work overtime
7 travel abroad on business
8 attend meetings
9 write reports
10 spend time with foreign visitors

9 Making and changing arrangements

Work in pairs, Student A and Student B. Practise making and changing arrangements.

Student A

Phone B and ask for a meeting.

Suggest a day.

Say 'yes'.

Student B

Say 'yes'. Ask when.

Apologize and say 'no'. Suggest another day.

End the conversation.

Student B

Phone A to change the meeting date.

Suggest two dates.

Say 'yes'. End the conversation.

Student A

Ask when B is free.

Choose a date.

10 Inviting

Work in pairs. Write a short conversation for each of the following situations. Practise the conversations with a partner.

Situation 1
Sue phones Mike to invite him to a party. Mike declines and gives the reason.

Situation 2
Mike phones Sue to invite her to the theatre. Sue accepts.

Situation 3
James Turner phones Monique Bresson. He invites her to travel to Scotland with him to Duncan Ross's anniversary celebration. (You decide on Monique's answer.)

11 Making suggestions

Work in pairs, Student A and Student B. Plan some activities for next week. Suggest, then accept or reject, the following activities. If you don't like the suggestion, give an alternative activity. Add two more suggestions.

Student A

1 a walk in the country
2 a visit to an exhibition
3 a boat trip on the river
4 a game of tennis
5 _____

Student B

1 a concert
2 a party for a friend's birthday
3 dinner at a good restaurant
4 a theatre visit
5 _____

Example Student A *How about going to a museum on Monday afternoon?*

Student B *Yes, fine. What about having an Italian meal in the evening?*

12 Giving opinions, agreeing, and disagreeing

Work in pairs. Practise asking and giving opinions. Agree or disagree with your partner's opinion. Ask about

1 a famous film star
2 a sport
3 a holiday destination
4 a capital city
5 a national cuisine
6 a famous politician

13 Restaurant language

Work in groups. Write out a simple local menu. Practise describing the dishes, and asking for and making recommendations.

14 Vocabulary

Work in Group A or Group B. Write a vocabulary test to give to the other group. Choose ten of the words below. Write a sentence or phrase to help the other group guess each word.

Example Word *improvement*   Clue *the noun of 'to improve'*

inhabitant	traffic	passenger	airline	rude
disorganized	company pension	improvement ✓	headache	crowded
briefcase	schedule	cycle path	relaxation	ambitious
delay	fare	disaster	seat-belt	staff

15 Vocabulary test

Give your vocabulary test to the other group. Do the other group's test. Return your answers for checking.

Look at the self-check box below. Tick the areas you need to review again.

SELF-CHECK BOX	Yes	No	Pocket Book
• Mass and count nouns			7
• *some/any, a lot of, much/many, a little/a few*			7
• Comparative and superlative adjectives			2
• Past Simple and Present Perfect Simple			10, 13
• Modal verbs			8
• Making/changing arrangements			18
• Inviting			18
• Making suggestions			20
• Opinions/agreeing/disagreeing			20
• Vocabulary			

UNIT 9
For over a century

▼ AGENDA

▶ Present Perfect Simple and Continuous, *since* and *for*

▶ Business headlines file. Word families and collocation

▶ Changing China

▶ Offers and requests

Language focus

1 How much do you know about the history of your company/organization/institution?

Do you know

- how old it is?
- who founded it?
- what its first product/service was?
- in what ways it has changed or developed since it began?

2 The pictures show products of some of the oldest companies in the world. In pairs, try to complete the sentences about the companies with the figures in the box.

> a 1472   b 1665   c 850   d 1000   e 500

1 The Château de Goulaine has been in the same family since the year _____ .

2 Barone Ricasoli has been producing wine for more than _____ years.

3 The Banca Monte dei Paschi di Siena was founded in _____ .

4 Beretta has been making guns for nearly _____ years.

5 Saint-Gobain's first project was the glass for the famous Hall of Mirrors in Versailles in _____ .

3 🎧 **9.1** Listen to an interview with Oliver Gore, the author of a book called *For Over a Century*. Check your answers in **2**.

4 Work in pairs. Say what you remember about

1 Oliver Gore's books.

2 some of the oldest companies in the world.

3 James Bond.

4 the Louvre Pyramid and the windscreens of the Shinkansen train.

5 🎧 **9.1** Listen to the interview again. Check your answers in **4**.

Present Perfect Simple and Present Perfect Continuous

Read the examples and grammar rules.

Present Perfect Simple

- You've **written** a lot of books about the business world.
- Saint-Gobain **has developed** hundreds of products in its long history.
- Use the Present Perfect Simple for past activities and situations in a time up to the present.

You've written a lot of books about the business world.

Past	Now

- Some famous banks **have been** in the same family for generations.
- Some wine producers **have had** the same vineyards for hundreds of years.
- Use the Present Perfect Simple for a situation which began in the past and continues up to the present.

She's been a doctor for 10 years.

Past	Now

 Pocket Book p. 13

Present Perfect Continuous

- Saint-Gobain **has been making** glass since 1665.
- Barone Ricasoli **has been producing** wine for more than 850 years.
- How long **has** Beretta **been making** guns?

- To make the Present Perfect Continuous, use *has/have + been + -ing* form of the verb.
- Use the Present Perfect Continuous for an activity that began in the past and continues up to the present.

Saint-Gobain has been making glass since 1665.

Past	Now

Read the examples and complete the grammar rule.

- Exports **have grown** by 8% this financial year.
- The company's export market **has been growing** since the beginning of this year.

Write *the Present Perfect Simple or the Present Perfect Continuous.*

- Use _____ to focus on an activity which is not finished and _____ to focus on the result or completion of an activity.

 Pocket Book p. 14

since and *for*

Read the examples and complete the grammar rule.

- The Banca Monte dei Paschi di Siena has been in the banking business **since** 1472.
- The Beretta family has been making guns **for** nearly five hundred years.

Write *since* or *for*.

- Use _____ with a point of time and _____ with a period of time.

Past			Now

for a long time
for 2 years
for 2 weeks

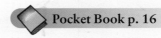 **Pocket Book p. 16**

Practice

1 Write *since* or *for* with these time expressions.

1 _____ nine o'clock
2 _____ a week
3 _____ yesterday
4 _____ last Saturday
5 _____ three hours
6 _____ centuries
7 _____ 20 January
8 _____ a long time
9 _____ 2001
10 _____ he left university

2 Underline the correct verb form.

1 Some companies *are/have been* family businesses for hundreds of years.
2 How long *have you had/have you been having* your company?
3 Some families *are making/have been making* the same product since their company was founded.
4 They *have produced/have been producing* 50,000 bottles of wine this year.
5 How long *is the company/has the company been* in business?

3 Work in pairs. Complete the questions about the interview with Oliver Gore. Look at Listening script 9.1 on p. 132 to help you.

1 What _____?

He's written a lot of books about the business world.

2 How long _____?

It's been the same family since the year 1000.

3 How long _____?

It's been producing wine for more than 850 years.

4 How long _____?

It's been making guns since 1526.

5 What _____ in its long history?

It's developed hundreds of products.

4 Complete these extracts from Oliver Gore's book, *For Over a Century*. Use the verbs in the boxes.

| has created | has been doing | builds | can order |
| has built | repairs | was founded | has included |

Kongo Gumi

The oldest company in the world is a Japanese company called Kongo Gumi that _____ ¹ in 578. Kongo Gumi _____ ² and _____ ³ temples and it _____ ⁴ this for more than 1,400 years. For its 21st-century customers it _____ ⁵ a website and _____ ⁶ on its home page photos of the different styles of temples it _____ ⁷ and which customers _____ ⁸ today.

AN EFFICIENT
5/-
FILM CAMERA.

THE BROWNIE.

Not a Toy. Takes splendid Photographs, 2¼ by 2¼ inches. Complete with Hand-book of Instructions. Price only **5/-**

Of all Photographic Dealers, or from—

KODAK, Limited,

43, Clerkenwell Road, E.C.;
60, Cheapside, E.C.;
115, Oxford Street, W.;
and 171-3, Regent Street, W.

grew	was	has been producing	has made	
wanted	cost	has been extending	has established	made

Kodak

Kodak _____ [9] cameras since 1888. Its founder, the American George Eastman, _____ [10] to make photography available to the greatest number of people at the lowest cost. His business _____ [11] rapidly in the early years and large-scale production _____ [12] this possible. In 1900 the first Brownie camera _____ [13] only $1 and there _____ [14] a huge expansion in the market. In the last 100 years Kodak _____ [15] its operations worldwide and _____ [16] manufacturing facilities in Canada, Mexico, Brazil, the UK, France, Germany, and Australia. This growth _____ [17] Kodak one the 25 largest companies in the United States.

5 Look at the verbs in the Present Perfect Simple and Continuous in the texts in **4**. Which verbs refer to

a a past activity in a time up to the present?

b an activity which began in the past and continues up to the present?

6 Work in pairs. Prepare questions for an interview with another student. You want to find out
  • where they live. (house/flat, town/suburbs/country)
  • how long they've been living there.
  • where they work. (company, organization)
  • what job they do.
  • how long they've had their job.
  • how many jobs they've had until now.
  • if they make business trips.
  • how many business trips they've made this year.
  • what sports/leisure interests they have.
  • how long they've been doing them.

7 Work with a different partner. Ask your partner questions. Answer your partner's questions.

8 Write three things about your partner on a piece of paper. Do not write his/her name. Give your teacher the piece of paper.

Example X *has been living in (Milan) for ten years.*
          X *has made two business trips this year.*
          X *has been playing tennis for five years.*

9 Your teacher will give you another student's piece of paper. Read the sentences to the class. Which of your colleagues do you think they describe?

Property developer wins
$20 million contract

Finance Minister
forecasts 2% growth
in economy

Rapid industrialization
changes the face of China

Government promises to
invest more in public services

Car makers cut prices as
competition grows

PRODUCTION STOPPED
AS STRIKE CONTINUES

Rise in employment
good news for government

Top industrialists unhappy
with latest government plan

Consumers buy more
goods on credit

Business headlines file. Word families and collocation

1 Work in pairs. Read the headlines. Answer the questions below. Use a dictionary if necessary.

1 Why is it a good time to buy a new car?

2 Are people spending more money than they have?

3 Is unemployment going up?

4 Is the economic forecast good or bad?

5 Why has production stopped?

6 Find words in the headlines which mean
  a put money into
  b says in advance what will happen
  c people who manage large industrial companies
  d people who buy goods
  e time when employees refuse to work
  f process of developing industries in an area
  g opposite of *loses*

 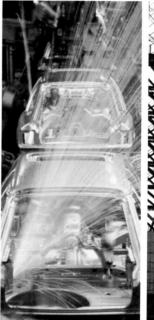 

2 Complete the table. Some of the missing words are in the headlines. If necessary, use a dictionary.

Verb	Noun (activity, thing)	Noun (person)
_____	development	_____
_____	_____	employer
_____	_____	investor
manage	_____	_____
compete	_____	competitor
_____	consumption	_____
_____	product/_____	_____
_____	_____/economics	economist
industrialize	industry/_____	_____

Pronunciation

1 🎧 **9.2** Listen to the examples. Notice the different stress patterns.

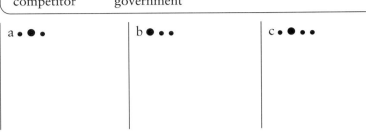

a employer   b industry   c development

2 Work in pairs. Put the words in the box in the correct column.

> management   develop   industrial   producer
> company   investment   economy   consumption
> competitor   government

a • ● •	b ● • •	c • ● • •

3 🎧 **9.3** Listen and check your answers.

4 🎧 **9.3** Listen again and repeat the words twice quietly to yourself.

5 Look at the words in the list. Mark the stress pattern a, b, or c.

consumer _____   manager _____

customer _____   production _____

economize _____   employment _____

developer _____   economist _____

6 Work in pairs. Practise saying the words in **5**.

❸ Match words from A and B to make collocations (words which we often use together). For some of the words, there is more than one possible combination.

Examples *consumer society*
            mass production

A	**B**
consumer	skills
management	society
free-market	development
developing	goods
developed	production
industrialized	market
industrial	economy
mass	countries

❹ Work in pairs. Write two business headlines for a newspaper. Use words from ❶, ❷, and ❸.

❺ Give your headlines to another pair of students. Read the headlines you receive. Decide what the articles will be about. Write the first sentence of each article.

❻ Read your headlines and first sentences to the class.

Changing China

1 Work in groups. Do you think these statements about China are true or false? Give your opinion. Write T (true) or F (false) under 'My opinion'.

	My opinion	What the article says
1 Today China has a free-market economy.	____	____
2 Its population is almost one billion.	____	____
3 In 2001, foreign companies invested the same amount of money in China and Africa.	____	____
4 Most Chinese people are in favour of modernization.	____	____
5 Average income has increased by almost 50% in the last decade.	____	____
6 The world's top ten car makers are thinking about investing in China.	____	____
7 China's rapid industrial development has brought pollution problems.	____	____

2 Read the article *The world's fastest-growing economy*. Write T (true) or F (false) under 'What the article says' in **1**.

The world's fastest-growing economy

In less than three decades there have been enormous economic and social changes in China. Until 1978 industrial production was under the control of the communist state. Today the state controls less than a quarter of industrial production and China has a free-market economy. In recent years its economy has been growing faster than any other major country and is now the sixth largest economy in the world.

More and more foreign companies have been investing in China, attracted by its market of 1.3 billion people and its very competitive low-cost labour force. In 2001 China received $47 billion in foreign investment, four times more than the whole of Africa, and in 2002 more than half of China's exports were from foreign firms.

China's major cities, too, have changed dramatically. Huge new office blocks, hotels, and shopping malls have appeared where before there were traditional Chinese houses and markets. In Beijing and other big cities, many areas of great cultural and historical interest have disappeared, but most Chinese are in favour of modernization and very happy with their 21st-century cities of glass and steel.

Consumer goods are everywhere, and millions of Chinese can now afford them because average income has more than doubled in the last decade. In cities many people now have not only a TV, washing machine, video, and mobile phone, but also a car and an apartment.

Since 2002, when there were only sixteen million cars in China, car sales have been rising rapidly and the world's top ten global car makers have set up joint ventures with Chinese car manufacturers.

But, as in every industrialized country, rapid industrial development has brought many problems, especially pollution. As industrialization continues and huge numbers of people enjoy western standards of living for the first time, the worry is that the impact on the environment may also be huge.

3 Read the article again. Find the words and phrases that mean

1 putting money into
2 total number of workers
3 changed very much
4 covered areas with many shops
5 have enough money to buy
6 business activities where two organizations work together
7 effect
8 the natural world

4 What do these numbers and phrases from the article refer to?

1 sixth largest
2 1.3 billion
3 $47 billion
4 more than doubled
5 sixteen million
6 top ten

5 Work in groups. Discuss the questions and give reasons for your answers.

1 Do you think China will become the largest economy in the world?
2 Have you visited, or would you like to visit, China for a holiday?
3 Would you like to live and work in China for a year or more?
4 What impact do you think China's industrialization will have on the environment?

Offers and requests

1 🎧 **9.4** Listen to a conversation between Duncan Ross and his secretary, Carol. Write down what Duncan wants Carol to do.

Book flight _____

Book hotel _____

Get information about _____

2 🎧 **9.5** Listen to another conversation between Duncan and Carol later the same day. Answer the questions.

1 How does Duncan want to travel back to London?

2 Why doesn't he need a hotel in Bordeaux?

3 🎧 **9.4, 9.5** Listen to the two conversations again and tick (✓) the phrases you hear.

Requesting

Can you ... ?

Could you ... ?

Do you mind ... (+ -*ing*)?

Would you mind ... (+ -*ing*)?

Would you ... ?

Do you think you could ... ?

Offering

Shall I ... ?

Do you want me to ... ?

If you like, I can ...

Would you like me to ... ?

Agreeing

Yes, of course.

Yes, certainly.

Not at all.

No, of course not.

Refusing

I'm sorry, but that's not possible.

I'm afraid not.

Accepting

Yes, please.

Thank you.

That's very kind of you.

Thank you. I'd appreciate that.

Declining

Thanks, but please don't bother.

Thanks, but that won't be necessary.

That's very kind of you, but ...

4 Work in pairs.

Student A Student B is visiting your company. Practise making, accepting, and declining offers in these situations. Add two more situations.

Student B You are a visitor to Student A's company. Practise making, accepting, and declining offers in these situations. Add two more situations.

Student A	**Student B**
Offer	
1 to carry Student B's suitcase.	Decline.
2 to get him/her a drink.	Accept.
3 to show Student B round your company.	Accept.
4 to explain the programme you've arranged.	Accept.
5 to accompany Student B to his/her hotel.	Decline.
6 to order a taxi to his/her hotel.	Decline.
7 _____	_____
8 _____	_____

Now change roles.

5 Work in pairs. Practise making and responding to requests. Add two more requests.

Student A	**Student B**
Ask Student B	
1 to lend you his/her newspaper.	Agree.
2 to look after a visitor tomorrow.	Refuse (you are out all day).
3 to give you next year's budget.	Agree.
4 _____	_____

Student B	**Student A**
Ask Student A	
5 to give you a lift to the station.	Agree.
6 to show you how some new software works.	Refuse (you don't understand it yourself).
7 to lend you a calculator.	Agree.
8 _____	_____

6 Work in pairs. Practise making offers and requests for these situations. Add more situations.

1 Offer to show a visitor round your city.
2 Offer to explain the menu in a restaurant to a foreign guest.
3 Ask a friend to lend you some money.
4 Ask a colleague for some advice.
5 Offer to book a hotel room for a visitor.
6 Ask a colleague to help you write a report.
7 Offer to take a visitor out to lunch.
8 Offer to help a colleague prepare a presentation.
9 Ask a friend to pick you up at the airport.

UNIT 10
Will our planet survive?

▼ **AGENDA**

▸ Future: *will* + infinitive

▸ 1st Conditional, *if* and *when*

▸ Prepositions of place file. Preposition diagrams

▸ Living longer, growing younger

▸ Asking for information

Language focus

1 Work in groups. Look at the headlines from different newspaper and magazine articles. Guess what the content of each article will be.

Global warming – real or imagined?

One planet is not enough

Wildlife habitats disappearing

Hope for forests?

US puts economy first

Water – a global crisis

2 The words in A are in the extracts in **3**. Match them with their meaning in B.

A		B	
1	the world's resources	a	damage very badly
2	destroy	b	100% necessary
3	essential	c	impossible to believe
4	destruction	d	continue to exist
5	global warming	e	the noun of *to destroy*
6	habitat	f	increase in the world's temperature
7	incredible	g	e.g. oil, forests, water
8	survive	h	natural home of a plant, bird, or animal

3 Read the extracts from the articles. Write the correct headline from **1** for each extract.

1 _____

... There are 6 billion people in the world today. The richest 1.5 billion use 75% of all the world's resources. To give the other 4.5 billion people who live in poverty a better life, we will need the resources of another four or five planets. But we have only one, and 1.5 billion of us have already destroyed a large part of it. ...

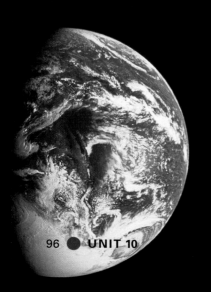

2 _____

... Forests are essential to life. They give us clean air and plants for medicines, and contain over half the world's animals, birds, and plants. Humans destroy an area of forest the size of Greece every year. If we don't stop this destruction, it will be too late. There are some signs of hope, but we will have to work very hard if we want to save the planet. ...

3 _____

... Scientists have predicted that global warming will destroy 80% of the 115 most important wildlife habitats. If we don't save these habitats, 20% of the world's birds, animals, and plants will disappear for ever. ...

4 _____

... Some people say we can't be sure global warming is really happening. They say they'll worry about it when we are sure. But it will be too late to do anything about it when we are sure. It won't be possible to save the planet if we don't take action now. ...

④   Underline five verbs which refer to the future in the extracts in **③**.

Future: *will* + infinitive; 1st Conditional, *if* and *when*

Read the examples. Answer the question and complete the grammar rules.

will + infinitive

- This percentage **will increase** by 43% in the next 20 years.
- Our planet **won't survive**.

- Use *will* + infinitive to predict future situations and actions.

How do we make questions and short answers with *will* + infinitive?

    Pocket Book p. 5

Note   *Will* becomes *'ll* in spoken English, except in short answers.
Will not becomes *won't* in spoken English, including short answers.

1st Conditional

- We'll **have** to act now **if** we **want** to save the planet.
- **If** we **don't stop** this destruction, it **will be** too late.
- It **won't be** possible to save the planet **if** we **don't take action** now.

- Use the 1st Conditional to express a future possibility, and its result.

Write *will* + *infinitive* or *the Present Simple*.

- In a 1st Conditional sentence, use
_____ after *if* and
_____ to express
the result.

Look at the extracts in **③**. Find other 1st Conditional sentences.

if and *when*

- It will be too late to do anything about it **when** we are sure.
- We'll have to work very hard **if** we want to save the planet.

Write *if* or *when*.
- Use _____ to express a possibility and _____ to express a certainty.

    Pocket Book p. 2

5 _____
... Today a billion people in the world don't have clean drinking water. If we don't improve our use of water, this number will rise to four billion by the year 2025. It seems incredible, but we have to live on less than 1% of the world's water because 97% of the water on our planet is seawater, 2% is ice, and we can use only part of the 1% underground. That is what we have to survive on. ...

6 _____
... The USA produces 25% of the gases that cause global warming and says this percentage will increase by 43% in the next 20 years. It says we can do little to change the situation. If the USA works with other countries to reduce global warming, we'll be able to limit the damage. If it doesn't, we won't, and our planet won't survive. ...

The world warms up

If we _____ ¹ (do) nothing to stop global warming, we _____ ² (see) big changes in the future. If world temperatures _____ ³ (continue) to rise, as scientists have predicted, there _____ ⁴ (be) less snow and some countries _____ ⁵ (lose) their skiing industry. We _____ ⁶ (have) hotter, drier summers and more wind and rain in winter.

Rising sea levels

Three hundred top American scientists have predicted that sea levels _____ ⁷ (rise) by between 50 and 100 centimetres over the next century. If their predictions _____ ⁸ (be) correct, half the US population who live in coastal areas _____ ⁹ (lose) their homes.

World's capitals at risk

Scientists believe that temperatures in Greenland _____ ¹⁰ (increase) more than in other parts of the world. If this _____ ¹¹ (happen), the ice will melt completely and sea levels _____ ¹² (rise) by about seven metres. They say this _____ ¹³ (put) most of the world's capitals under water.

Your summer holidays are bad for the planet

We all enjoy travelling and air travel is getting cheaper. That's good news for holidaymakers but bad news for the environment because aircraft emissions increase global warming. There has been a huge increase in air travel in recent years. If this increase _____ ¹⁴ (continue), the damage _____ ¹⁵ (get) worse.

Water wars

In the future, people _____ ¹⁶ (not fight) wars over oil, or religion, or politics, but over water. Nearly 40% of the world's population depends on rivers from which two or more countries get their water. Many of these countries want to develop their agriculture and industry. If they _____ ¹⁷ (not have) enough water, they _____ ¹⁸ (fight) wars to get it because without water they _____ ¹⁹ (not survive).

2 Work in pairs. Ask and answer questions. Give your opinion.

Examples   **Ask** *Do you think we'll stop the destruction of the forests?*
Answer *Yes, I'm sure we will./No, I'm sure we won't.*
Yes, I think so./No, I don't think so.
Maybe. I'm not sure.

1 stop/destruction/forests?
2 weather/get hotter and wetter?
3 many birds, animals, and plants/disappear?
4 the world's capital cities/be under water?
5 countries/lose ski industry?
6 people/fight wars over water?

Pronunciation

1 🎧 **10.1** Listen to the examples. Which of the underlined vowel sounds is long? Which is short?

/ɪ/   /iː/
a w<u>i</u>ll   b wh<u>ee</u>l

2 🎧 **10.2** Listen to the pronunciation of the underlined vowels. Which sound do you hear? Tick (✓) a or b.

	a (short)	b (long)
1 Are you going to l<u>ea</u>ve?	_____	_____
2 Where do you l<u>i</u>ve?	_____	_____
3 Do s<u>i</u>t down.	_____	_____
4 Do take a s<u>ea</u>t.	_____	_____
5 Would you like some ch<u>i</u>ps?	_____	_____
6 That restaurant is very ch<u>ea</u>p.	_____	_____
7 Shall I f<u>i</u>ll your glass?	_____	_____
8 Do you f<u>ee</u>l better?	_____	_____

3 🎧 **10.2** Listen again and repeat the sentences.

4 Are the underlined vowels short or long? Tick (✓) a or b.

	a (short)	b (long)
1 Is this your k<u>e</u>y?	_____	_____
2 We invited thirty p<u>eo</u>ple.	_____	_____
3 Did you have a good tr<u>i</u>p?	_____	_____
4 Is it time to <u>ea</u>t?	_____	_____
5 Did you sl<u>ee</u>p well?	_____	_____
6 He was very <u>i</u>ll.	_____	_____

5 🎧 **10.3** Listen and repeat the sentences twice quietly to yourself.

3 Complete the sentences. Use *if* or *when* at the beginning. Finish the sentences with your own ideas.

Example *When we meet again, I'll give you the information.*

1 _____ we meet again …
2 _____ I become rich …
3 _____ I get home tonight …
4 _____ I change my job …
5 _____ I go abroad …
6 _____ I have more time …

4 Say what you think will happen in your country, and why. Begin *I think/I don't think* …

Example *I don't think the economic situation will improve because the world economic situation isn't good.*

1 the economic situation/improve
2 the present government/win the next election
3 unemployment/increase
4 the cost of living/stay at the same level
5 taxes/increase
6 transport system/improve

5 Complete the sentences with your own ideas. Add two more examples of your own.

Examples *I'll do an English course in the UK if my company pays.*
If I get a promotion at work, I'll have a big party.

1 I'll do an English course in the UK if …

2 If I get a promotion at work, …

3 If my company makes a big profit, …

4 I'll move to another city if …

5 If my company wants me to learn another language, …

6 I'll look for another job if …

6 Read what Sir David Attenborough, Britain's best-known wildlife film maker, says about the future of our planet. Then discuss the questions in groups.

'The future of life on earth depends on our ability to take action. Many individuals are doing what they can but real success can only come if there's a change in our societies, in our economies, and in our policies. I've been lucky in my lifetime to see some of the greatest spectacles that the natural world has to offer. Surely we have a responsibility to leave for future generations a planet that is healthy and habitable by all species.'

Sir David Attenborough

1 What kind of changes do you think Sir David Attenborough is referring to?

2 Do you think both developed and developing countries need to make changes?

3 Do you think the planet will be 'healthy and habitable by all species' in future?

Prepositions of place file. Preposition diagrams

1 Look at the picture of an office. Write the correct number in the key.

Key

_____ bin
_____ chair
_____ clock
_____ coffee machine
_____ computer
_____ desk
_____ desk lamp
_____ filing cabinet
_____ keyboard
_____ lift
_____ mouse
_____ mouse mat
_____ paper
_____ pen
_____ personal organizer
_____ phone
_____ photocopier
_____ plant
_____ printer
_____ year planner

2 Describe the location of the objects in the office. Use the prepositions in the diagrams.

Examples *The year planner is above the desk.*
The mouse mat is on the right of the keyboard.

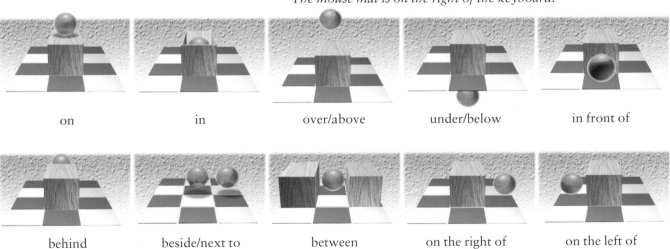

on   in   over/above   under/below   in front of

behind   beside/next to   between   on the right of   on the left of

3 Work in pairs.

1 Describe your office/work area to your partner. Draw the office/work area your partner describes. Do not show your partner the drawing until you have finished.

2 When you have finished, tell your partner if there are any mistakes in their drawing.

Example *The bin isn't on the right of the desk, it's on the left.*

Living longer, growing younger

1 Read the newspaper extracts. What do these numbers refer to?

1 49   2 80   3 $2,600   4 1.3   5 42%   6 4 out of 10

... 100 years ago, in developed countries, life expectancy for a woman was 49. Today it is 80 and scientists say it will be 101 by 2070. A female born today in France and Japan, the two countries in the world with the longest life expectancy, has a 50% chance of living to 100. ...

... The Japanese government is so worried about the falling birth rate that it is giving women $2,600 as soon as they have a baby. It is also providing 'baby hotels' where working women can leave their babies when they are away on business trips. Japanese women have an average of only 1.3 children. To maintain its present population level, Japan needs an average birth rate of 2.1 children per woman.

... In 2002 the World Bank forecast a fall in the working-age population of countries in the European Union, down from 230 million to 167 million by 2050. The biggest fall predicted is for Italy, down by 42%, followed by Spain and Germany. ...

... By 2030, four out of ten people will be over 65. That is double the number in the 1960s.

2 Discuss the questions.

1 Why are countries worried about a decrease in the birth rate and in the working-age population, and an increase in the number of older people?

2 Would you like to live to be 100?

3 🎧 **10.4** Listen to a discussion between three friends about the topics in the newspaper extracts in **1**. Answer the questions.

1 Does Alma want to live to be 100?

2 What does she say about life expectancy?

3 In Tonia's opinion, what will be a big problem for governments in the future?

4 According to Eddie, why will developed countries have the biggest problem?

5 Does Eddie think the retirement age will stay the same?

4 Discuss the question in groups.

Which of these options would you prefer as a solution to the problem of paying for pensions in the future?

1 work until the age of 70 or more

2 pay more in taxes and social security

3 save money for a private pension

5 The words and phrases in A are from the article, *The ageing future*. Match them with their meaning in B.

A	B
1 tripled	a to be afraid of
2 centenarian	b having advantages most people don't have
3 to fear	c increased by 300%
4 privileged	d person who is 100 years old or more

6 Read the article *The ageing future*. Answer the questions.

1 What has happened to the world's population since 1950?

2 Why do fewer people die from infectious diseases today than in the past?

3 According to the OECD what will happen in the next 25 years?

4 What did Helen Klein do when she was 72?

The ageing future

Since 1950, the world's population has almost tripled. All of us are living longer than any generation in human history.

In the year 2000 there were 100,000 people around the planet who were 100 years old or more. Yet, when they were born, before aeroplanes and antibiotics and atom bombs, before cars and computers, there were very few centenarians anywhere in the world. Now millions of people will live into their 70s, 80s, and 90s, and centenarians will no longer be rare.

Advances in medicine and public sanitation mean that infectious diseases no longer kill millions of children and adults as they did in the past. Healthier food and better health care have made stronger, fitter bodies. Average life expectancy has gone up by 25 years and more in many parts of the world.

At the same time the contraceptive pill has had a huge impact on world population levels since the 1970s. Women are having fewer babies and more people are living longer, so the balance between the number of young and old people in the population is changing dramatically. According to the OECD*, over the next 25 years the number of pensioners will rise by 70 million, while the working-age population will rise by only 5 million.

But this is good news rather than bad. To be old is not to be ill. Studies have shown that healthy food and regular physical exercise keep mind and body young, and that it's never too late to start getting fit or learning new things. At 72 the remarkable Helen Klein successfully completed the first Eco-Challenge, a 480-kilometre desert adventure race with swimming, canoeing, white-water rafting, running, horse-riding, and rock climbing.

Many older people are active, productive, and useful. Freer than they have ever been, they are not retired from life but actively part of it. There will be millions more like them in the future, as the most privileged generations that have ever lived find they, too, grow old.

OECD = Organization for Economic Co-operation and Development

7 Discuss the questions in groups. Give reasons for your opinions.

1 Do you agree with the author that the rising number of old people is 'good news rather than bad'?

2 Do you think life expectancy will go on increasing?

3 Is there 'a recipe' for living longer? For example, do you think factors like a healthy diet, sport and exercise, lack of stress, a healthy climate, and happiness help you live longer?

Asking for information

1 🎧 **10.5** Duncan Ross's secretary, Carol, phones British Airways reservations office to get information about flights. Listen to the conversation. Note down the times of flights.

> Flight times
> Sun p.m.   Edinburgh   Paris
> _____   _____
> _____   _____
> _____   _____
> Fri   Bordeaux   London
> _____   _____

2 🎧 **10.5** Listen to the conversation again and tick (✔) the phrases you hear.

Asking for information
I'd like | some information about …
         | to know …
Do you know …?
Can you tell me …?
Could you tell me …?

Apologizing
I'm afraid I don't have any
   information about …
I'm sorry, I can't tell you …

Showing understanding
I see.
Right, I've got that.
So …

Asking for repetition
Could you repeat that, please?
Could you say that again?

Checking
Let me check.
I'll look that up.

3 🎧 **10.6** Carol phones French Railways in London. Listen to the conversation and note down the information.

> Train times   Paris _____
>   Bordeaux _____
>   Wed. arrive by 1 p.m.
>   Which station _____

4 🎧 **10.6** Listen to the conversation again and complete the questions.

1 Can you tell me when _____ ?

2 Could you tell me when _____ ?

3 Do you know which station _____ ?

5 Compare the questions from the two conversations. Which are more polite, the direct or indirect questions? What is the difference in the form of the verb?

Direct questions
What time **does** the first flight **arrive**?
When **do** the later flights **arrive**?
Do I **need** to make a reservation?

Indirect questions
Do you know if Air France **flies** from Bordeaux to London?
Can you tell me when you **want** to travel?
Could you tell me when it **leaves** Paris?
Do you know which station it **leaves** from?

6 Work in pairs. Some of these questions are not correct. Write the correct question.

1 Could you tell me what the fare is?

2 I'd like to know how long does the journey take.

3 Do you know if there's a dining car on the train?

4 Can you tell me which airport does the flight leave from?

5 Do you know how much is the fare?

6 I'd like to know where can I buy a ticket.

7 Work in pairs. Ask for and give information. Practise asking indirect questions. Begin your questions with the phrases in **2**.

British Airways Flight Information
From London Gatwick to Madrid

	Depart	Arrive	Flight number	Economy class fare*
Daily	0900	1230	BA 2464	£178
	1125	1450	BA 2468	£53
	1435	1810	BA 2466	£33
	1930	2300	BA 2470	£33

* airport taxes not included

Italian State Railways

	ES	ES	ES	ES	IC
Bologna	0824	0848	0905	0916	0932
Rome	1105	1130	1155	1205	1313

Direct service – no changes

Trains
ES = Eurostar   IC = Intercity

Fares	1st class	2nd class
ES	€ 42.56	€ 29.74
IC	€ 34.40	€ 25.73

Situation 1

Student A
Phone British Airways. Ask for information about flights from London Gatwick to Madrid.

You want to know
- how many flights/a day
- when flights depart/arrive
- how much/Economy class fare
- if fare includes airport taxes

Student B
You work for British Airways. Use this information to answer an enquiry.

Situation 2

Student A
You work for Italian State Railways in London. Use this information to answer an enquiry.

Student B
Phone Italian State Railways. Ask for information about trains from Bologna to Rome.

You want to know
- how many trains/between 8 a.m. and 10 a.m.
- when trains depart/arrive
- how much/1st and 2nd class fares
- if you have to change trains

UNIT 11
Getting around in cities

▼ AGENDA

▶ 2nd Conditional

▶ City description file. Topic groups and collocations

▶ The best cities to live in

▶ Social responses

Language focus

1 Work in groups. What different methods of transport do people in your country use to get around in cities? Make a list.

2 Read the newspaper extracts about transport in cities. Answer the questions.

1 What did Trondheim and Singapore do in order to reduce traffic congestion?

2 How does use of public transport in Zürich compare with other cities?

3 Which countries have the highest percentage of cyclists in cities?

4 Why did Curitiba choose a bus system, not an underground or light-rail system?

5 What new scheme has been introduced in Edinburgh?

In 1991 Trondheim in Norway became the first city in the world to reduce traffic congestion by charging motorists to drive in the city centre. Other cities in Scandinavia did the same and used the money to improve public transport. Singapore also charges motorists, and its efficient public transport system makes private cars unnecessary for most city journeys.

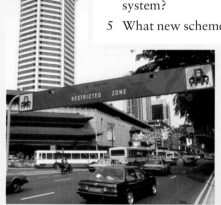

In Zürich 40% of journeys are by public transport compared with 10 to 15% in most European cities and only 3% in the USA. A lot of people in Zürich own a car, but private car traffic is half the level of other European cities of similar size. This was achieved by introducing a high-quality fast light-rail system integrated with buses and trains.

In the Netherlands and Denmark more people use bicycles in cities than in other countries in Europe. There are cycle paths everywhere in city centres and a lot of roads have special cycle lanes. In Copenhagen 25% of city journeys are made by bike. In the Dutch cities of Groningen and Utrecht the figure is 50%.

Curitiba in Brazil has a population of 2.5 million. It has more cars per person than any other Brazilian city except Brasilia, but it has few traffic jams. It is not a rich city, so it chose a bus system rather than an underground or light-rail system because it was a lot cheaper. Its fast, efficient bus system transports 75% of city commuters. They can change easily from one route to another, using a single ticket for all journeys.

Seven thousand employees who work at the Edinburgh Business Park in Scotland's capital city have been invited to join a car-sharing scheme. It is the first time a computer has been used to match employees' journeys to work, and is part of a plan to reduce traffic congestion in a city where eight out of ten cars carry just one person. The scheme was introduced after 40% of the staff said they would join it.

3 🎧 **11.1** Listen to part of a TV panel discussion programme called *Ask the panel*.

Match the speakers with their suggestions for reducing traffic congestion in cities.

John _____ Susanna _____ David _____ Kate _____ Nick _____

a Make people park outside the city centre and then take a bus.

b Charge motorists for driving in city centres.

c Get companies to organize car-sharing schemes for their staff.

d Provide a really good inexpensive public transport system.

e Encourage people to use bikes.

2nd Conditional

Read the examples and complete the grammar rule.

- **If I were** responsible for transport, **I'd ban** private cars from city centres.
- **If** cycling **was** safer, more people **would travel** that way.
- **We'd have** less congestion **if** more people **used** bikes for short journeys.
- **If** they **organized** car-sharing schemes, people from different companies **could join in**.

- Use the 2nd Conditional to talk about an unreal or imaginary present or future possibility, and its result.

Write *Past Simple* or *would*.

- In a 2nd Conditional sentence, use the _____ after *if* and _____ or *could* + infinitive to express the result.

We often use '*d* for *would*.

We can use *were* instead of *was* with *I/he/she/it*, but in the expression *If I were you, I'd …* we can only use *were*.

Look at Listening script 11.1 on p. 133–4. Find other 2nd Conditional sentences.

What is the difference in meaning between these two sentences?
If I buy a bike, I'll cycle to work.
If I bought a bike, I'd cycle to work.

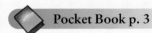 **Pocket Book p. 3**

Pronunciation

1 🎧 **11.2** Listen to the examples. Notice the contractions.

    a If they don't reply soon, we'll send another letter.

    b I wouldn't accept the offer if I were you.

2 🎧 **11.3** Listen to the sentences. Write the missing verbs. Some are contractions.

    1 If she _____ late, she _____ the plane.

    2 I _____ to work if I _____ a car.

    3 If you _____ tomorrow, I _____ you at the airport.

    4 We _____ fewer problems if we _____ the system.

    5 We _____ a solution if we _____ something quickly.

    6 If they _____ here before six o'clock, I _____ them.

    7 They _____ the company if there _____ a problem.

    8 She _____ if she _____ the money.

3 🎧 **11.3** Listen again and check.

4 Which sentences in **2** are 1st Conditional? Which are 2nd Conditional?

5 Work in pairs. Practise the sentences in **2**, paying particular attention to the pronunciation of the contractions.

Practice

1 Complete the sentences. Use the Past Simple or 2nd Conditional form (*would/could*) of the verbs in brackets.

1 If I _____ (live) near my office, I _____ (walk) to work.

2 She _____ (not drive) to work if there _____ (be) a good bus service.

3 If public transport _____ (not be) overcrowded, more people _____ (use) it.

4 He _____ (cycle) to work if it _____ (be) safer.

5 If our roads _____ (be) less crowded, journeys _____ (be) quicker.

6 Fewer people _____ (drive) in city centres if we _____ (introduce) charges.

2 If you were responsible for transport in your town/city, which of the following would you do? Which wouldn't you do? Explain why/why not.

Begin *If I were responsible for transport I would/wouldn't ... because ...*

1 make public transport free

2 provide cycle lanes in the centre

3 build more roads

4 charge motorists for driving in the centre

5 encourage car-sharing schemes

What other things would you do, and why?

3 Work in pairs. We often use the 2nd Conditional to give advice, e.g. *If I were you, I would/wouldn't ...* . What advice would you give to someone who wants to

1 work in Germany but speaks only a little German?

2 get fitter but never does any sport?

3 study for a new career but thinks she's too old at 30?

4 pass the exam at the end of the English course but often misses lessons?

5 buy an expensive new car but never saves any money?

4 Work in pairs. Your employer has offered you three months off work, with salary and all expenses paid, in order to get to know another country and its culture. Decide

- which country you would go to.
- what five things you would do to get to know that country's culture.

5 Work with a different partner. Tell your partner where you would go and what you would do. Ask questions to find out more.

City description file. Topic groups and collocations

1 Read the description of Brussels. Find the answers to the questions.

1 Why is Brussels called 'the capital of the EU'?

2 What are its most important industries?

3 What is Grand Place?

4 What can you find in Butchers' Street?

5 What cultural attractions does Brussels offer?

Brussels

Brussels is Belgium's capital city and its administrative, financial, and cultural centre. It has two official languages, French and Dutch, and a population of almost a million inhabitants. It is also the 'capital of the EU*', as the European Parliament is there. The headquarters of NATO* are in Brussels and many multinational companies have their European head offices in the city.

Manufacturing and service industries are important to its economy. The main manufacturing industries are metal, electrical, pharmaceutical, and chemical, and the main service industries banking, financial services, and tourism.

Brussels has a modern and efficient metro, bus, and tram network. It has Eurostar train connections to Paris and London, and an international airport. The historic centre is Grand Place, one of Europe's most beautiful city squares. In December a traditional Christmas Market is held there. North of Grand Place are elegant 19th-century shopping arcades and Butchers' Street, a lively area called 'the stomach of Brussels' because it is full of restaurants. Brussels also has many attractive cafés and bars. It is one of the best places in Europe to eat and drink, and is known as 'the beer capital of the world'.

It has an impressive cathedral and offers all the cultural attractions of a European city – museums, theatre, music, dance, opera, and international films.
There are sports and leisure facilities in the city centre, and golf courses and woods outside where you can enjoy walking, cycling, and jogging, and boating or ice-skating on the lake, depending on the season.

EU = European Union
NATO = North Atlantic Treaty Organization

2 Match words in A and B to make collocations from the description of Brussels.

Example *financial centre*

A		B	
capital	financial ✓	centre ✓	attractions
official	shopping	arcades	companies
multinational	cultural	city	industries
manufacturing		languages	

3 Work in pairs. Organize words and phrases from the description of Brussels in the following topic groups. Add other useful words to the groups.

- geography/economy
- transport
- eating/drinking
- culture
- sports/leisure

4 In the box below find

1 four pairs of opposite adjectives.

2 five adjectives which have an opposite adjective beginning with the prefix *un-* or *in-*.

attractive	beautiful	efficient	important	lively	best	
impressive	traditional	modern	official	worst	dull	ugly

5 Make notes to talk about your home town or city. Choose two of the topic areas in **3** (e.g. *geography/economy* and *transport*). Use suitable vocabulary from the lists you wrote in **3**, and from **2** and **4** above.

6 Work in groups. In turn, tell your colleagues about your home town or city. Answer any questions from your colleagues.

The best cities to live in

1 Work in groups. Give your opinion of your own city, or one you know well. Rate it E (excellent), G (good), A (average), or P (poor) in each of the categories below. Give reasons for your opinion.

1 public transport _____
2 traffic congestion _____
3 pollution _____
4 crime _____
5 schools and education _____

6 health care _____
7 choice of restaurants _____
8 cultural facilities (e.g. theatres, cinemas, music, museums) _____
9 sports and leisure facilities _____

2 If your city had the money to make improvements in two of the categories in **1**, which two would you choose?

3 🎧 **11.4** Listen to an extract from another radio programme in the series *Working Week*, about the best cities to live in. Tick (✓) to show which cities have the

- overall best quality of life
- best restaurants, cultural, and leisure facilities

Some answers are given as examples.

The best cities to live in

City	Overall best quality of life	Best restaurants, cultural, and leisure facilities	City	Overall best quality of life	Best restaurants, cultural, and leisure facilities
Budapest			Prague		
Buenos Aires			Sydney		
Copenhagen			Tokyo		
Geneva			Vancouver	✓	
London			Vienna		
Los Angeles			Warsaw		
Montevideo			Washington DC		
New York		✓	Yokohama		
Paris			Zürich		

4 🎧 **11.4** Listen to the extract again. Answer the questions.

1 How many cities does the survey cover?
2 Why are Paris and London lower in the list this year than a year ago?
3 How many US cities are in the top 50 in the list? Why don't they come higher?

5 Work in groups. Discuss your ideas.

Your organization wants you to live and work in one of these cities for a year. Which city would you choose and why?

Sydney   Vancouver

Social responses

❶ How would you respond politely to the following?

1 Sorry I'm late. 3 Have a good weekend.

2 Thanks for all your help. 4 Do you mind if I smoke?

❷ **11.5** Listen to some social comments at a party. Tick (✓) the most appropriate response.

1 a Didn't you? 5 a Yes, you can.

  b It's Simon. Simon Grant.   b Thank you. That would be very nice.

2 a Not at the moment, thanks. 6 a Oh, I'm sorry to hear that.

  b I've had one.   b Don't mention it.

3 a Yes, that's right. 7 a It doesn't matter.

  b Yes, I'm from Spain.   b Not at all.

4 a Yes, you are. 8 a Thanks, the same to you.

  b Don't worry.   b Yes, I hope so.

❸ **11.6** Listen to the complete conversations. This time you will hear the most appropriate response. Check your answers to **❷**.

❹ Work in pairs. Look at this picture of guests at a cocktail party. Think of suitable responses to their comments and questions.

❺ Match the replies with the comments and questions in the picture in **❹**.

a Really! f Don't mention it.

b Please do. g Well, I'd rather you didn't.

c Yes, that's right. h Yes, here you are.

d It doesn't matter. i Never mind. Better luck next time.

e Thanks. I'll have a whisky. j No, I've been here before.

❻ You are at Duncan Ross's party at Glencross Castle. Walk around and make small talk with your class colleagues. Practise offering drinks, thanking, apologizing, asking permission, and making appropriate responses.

❼ **11.7** Listen to the social comments. Tick (✓) the response if it is appropriate.

1 Yes, of course. 5 It doesn't matter.

2 Thanks. You, too. 6 I'm sorry to hear that.

3 Yes, here you are. 7 Yes.

4 Don't worry. 8 Congratulations.

❽ **11.8** Listen to the social comments in **❼** again. This time you will hear an appropriate response. Check your answers.

UNIT 12
The story of cork

▼ AGENDA

▷ Passives: Present Simple, Past Simple, Present Perfect, Future

▷ Descriptions file. Word building

▷ Strange but true

▷ Thanking for hospitality. Saying goodbye

Language focus

1 Do the quiz. Guess the answers if you don't know.

What do you know about cork?

1 Where does cork come from?

2 What is the most important product made from cork?

3 Which country is the world's biggest producer of cork?

4 Why does NASA use cork in rocket engines?

2 Read the article *Cork – from past to present*. Check your answers to the questions in **1**.

Cork – from past to present

Cork comes from only one tree in the world, the cork oak tree, *Quercus suber*. Cork oak forests are found in Mediterranean and Asian countries but only cork from Mediterranean trees has the quality which is needed to make commercial products, including the most important product – wine stoppers. Over 50% of the world's cork is produced in Portugal and 80% of all cork products are made there. This makes cork Portugal's second most important export after port wine. In fact cork is so important to the Portuguese economy that cork trees, forests, and farmers are all protected by the law.

Cork has been used since ancient times. Cork stoppers have been found in Egyptian, Greek, and Roman amphorae where wine and olive oil were stored. The ancient Romans wore sandals made of cork and used it to make roofs for houses, and it is still used in this way in north Africa today. Since the 18th century, when champagne was invented by the French monk, Dom Pérignon, cork stoppers have been used for all champagne and sparkling wine. Today it also has a hi-tech use – it is put in the engines of NASA's rockets because it is an excellent insulation material against heat.

The cork is not removed from the oak until it is 25 years old. After that it will be removed every 9 years for the next 150 to 200 years, depending on the tree. Only the best quality cork is used to make wine stoppers, and this is not produced until the tree is over 40 years old. When the cork has been removed, a number is painted on the tree to show the year this was done. Under ideal conditions, cork oaks can live for 300 to 400 years.

3 In the article *Cork – from past to present*, underline one example of a verb in the passive form in each of these tenses: Present Simple, Past Simple, Present Perfect, Future.

The Passive

Read the examples. Complete the grammar rules and answer the questions.

Present Simple

- Cork oak forests **are found** in Mediterranean and Asian countries.
- The cork **is not removed** from the oak until it is 25 years old.

Past Simple

- Champagne **was invented** by the French monk, Dom Pérignon.
- Wine and olive oil **were stored** in Egyptian, Greek, and Roman amphorae.

Present Perfect

- Cork **has been used** since ancient times.
- Cork stoppers **have been found** in Egyptian, Greek, and Roman amphorae.

Future

- The cork **will be removed** every 9 years for the next 150 to 200 years.

Write *passive* or *active*.

- Use the _____ form when the person or thing that did the action is important.
- Use the _____ form when the person or thing that did the action isn't important, or when we don't know who or what did the action.

Find other examples of verbs in the passive in the article.

When do we use *by* after a verb in the passive?

How do we make questions in the passive?

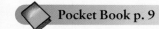 Pocket Book p. 9

Practice **1** Complete this description of the process of making cork wine stoppers. Use the Present Simple passive form of the verbs in brackets.

From tree to wine stopper

Cork trees _____ ¹ (plant) when they are a year old. Most planting _____ ² (do) by hand. When the tree is 25 years old the cork _____ ³ (remove) for the first time. After that it _____ ⁴ (cut) every 9 years for another 150 to 200 years, depending on the tree. The cork _____ ⁵ (leave) in the forest to dry for about a year. Then it _____ ⁶ (boil). This process cleans the cork and makes it stronger and more flexible.

After boiling, the cork _____ ⁷ (cut) into strips and the wine stoppers _____ ⁸ (make) from the strips. Then the wine stoppers _____ ⁹ (wash), dried, and checked for quality. At this stage most of the stoppers _____ ¹⁰ (transport) to their destination, but some _____ ¹¹ (mark) with the name of the wine producer before they leave the factory.

2 Cross out the incorrect verb form.

Plastic wine stoppers – a threat to wildlife?

In about 7% of the market, plastic wine stoppers *have replaced/~~have been replaced~~* traditional cork stoppers, especially in the USA, Australia, Chile, South Africa, and New Zealand. Their use in all these countries is on the increase.

Plastic wine stoppers *introduced/were introduced*¹ because it *believed/was believed*² cork was the cause of problems with wine quality. But studies *have shown/have been shown*³ there are other causes and the cork industry *has spent/has been spent*⁴ a lot of money on improving the product.

Wildlife experts are worried about the growing use of plastic stoppers because the cork forests are an important habitat for wildlife. In some areas cork forests *have destroyed/have been destroyed*⁵ and holiday villages and roads *have built/have been built*⁶ in their place.

Wildlife organizations *have started/have been started*⁷ campaigns to inform people about the problem and *have asked/have been asked*⁸ supermarkets to show what type of stopper a bottle has. If the use of plastic stoppers *continues/is continued*⁹ to increase, there is a real danger that cork forests and important wildlife habitats *will lose/will be lost*¹⁰ for ever.

3 Work in pairs. Make questions in the passive form for these answers from the article *Cork – from past to present*.

Examples *Where were oil and wine stored?*
What percentage of cork products are made in Portugal?
How long have cork stoppers been used for champagne and sparkling wine?

1 Where _____ ?
They're found in Mediterranean and Asian countries.

2 What percentage _____ ?
Over 50% is.

3 Why _____ ?
Because cork is so important for the Portuguese economy.

4 How long _____ ?
It's been used since ancient times.

5 Where _____ ?
They've been found in Egyptian, Greek, and Roman amphorae.

6 When _____ ?
It was invented in the 18th century.

7 Why _____ ?
Because it's an excellent insulation material against heat.

8 When _____ ?
It is removed after the tree is 25 years old.

Pronunciation

1 🎧 **12.1** Listen to the examples. Notice how the final consonant sound is linked to a following vowel sound.

    a Were any products exported in April?

    b How are the engines assembled?

    c Two hundred engines have been imported.

2 Join the words you think are linked.

    1 Cork is produced in Portugal.

    2 Many cork products are exported abroad.

    3 Champagne was invented in the 18th century.

    4 Experts are worried about increasing sales of plastic stoppers.

    5 A lot of money has been spent on improving quality.

    6 Cork is used for insulation in rocket engines.

3 🎧 **12.2** Listen and check your answers.

4 🎧 **12.2** Listen again and repeat.

---

4 Work in pairs, Student A with another Student A, Student B with another Student B. Look at p. 115.

Student A

1 Read Datafile A.

2 Write the questions you need to ask to complete your datafile. Begin with the words in brackets and use the passive form in all your questions.

Examples *How many products are made out of rubber?*
How long ago was rubber used by the Mayan people of Central America?

Datafile A

Facts and figures

a Rubber is one of the world's most important industrial materials. _____ products are made out of rubber. (How many … ?)

b Natural rubber is made from a white liquid, called latex, which comes from a tree. After the latex is collected it is processed for industrial use. Synthetic rubber is made from _____ . (What … ?)

c 90% of natural rubber is supplied by Malaysia, Thailand, and Indonesia.

d More than 60% of natural rubber is used for _____ . (What …?)

e Car tyres are made from synthetic and natural rubber, but aircraft tyres are made entirely from natural rubber because it is a lot stronger.

The history of rubber

f Rubber was used _____ ago by the Mayan people of Central America. (How long ago … ?)

g Rubber has been known to Europeans since the end of the 15th century when Christopher Columbus brought it back from South America.

h The word 'rubber' was first used in 1770 by an English chemist called Joseph Priestley, who discovered it could rub out pencil marks.

i Raincoats have been called 'mackintoshes' since _____ , when a Scottish chemist called Charles Mackintosh first used rubber to make them waterproof. (How long …?)

j In _____ a process called vulcanization was discovered by an American called Charles Goodyear. (When …?) In this process, rubber is heated with chemicals to make it stronger and more flexible. This discovery made it possible to manufacture tyres from rubber, and was the beginning of the Goodyear tyre company.

Student B

1 Read Datafile B.

2 Write the questions you need to ask to complete your datafile. Begin with the words in brackets and use the passive form in all your questions.

Examples *What happens after the latex is collected?*
How long has rubber been known to Europeans?

Datafile B

Facts and figures

a Rubber is one of the world's most important industrial materials. More than 50,000 products are made out of rubber.

b Natural rubber is made from a white liquid, called latex, which comes from a tree. After the latex is collected _____ . (What happens after …?) Synthetic rubber is made from petroleum.

c _____ of natural rubber is supplied by Malaysia, Thailand, and Indonesia. (What percentage …?)

d More than 60% of natural rubber is used for tyre and automotive products.

e Car tyres are made from synthetic and natural rubber, but aircraft tyres are made entirely from natural rubber because _____ . (Why …?)

The history of rubber

f Rubber was used 2,500 years ago by the Mayan people of Central America.

g Rubber has been known to Europeans _____ , when Christopher Columbus brought it back from South America. (How long …?)

h The word 'rubber' was first used in _____ by an English chemist called Joseph Priestley, who discovered it could rub out pencil marks. (When …?)

i Raincoats have been called 'mackintoshes' since 1823 when a Scottish chemist called Charles Mackintosh first used rubber to make them waterproof.

j In 1839 a process called vulcanization was discovered by an American called Charles Goodyear. In this process, rubber is heated with chemicals _____ . (Why …?) This discovery made it possible to manufacture tyres from rubber, and was the beginning of the Goodyear tyre company.

5 Work with a different partner, Student A with Student B. Ask your questions and complete your datafile. Answer your partner's questions.

Descriptions file. Word building

1 The suffixes *-y*, *-al*, or *-able* make the nouns in the box into adjectives. Complete the table with the adjectives. Check the spelling in a dictionary if necessary.

hunger✓	economy✓	knowledge✓	health	industry	fashion
noise	profit	politics	cloud	centre	comfort
value	anger	commerce			

-y	*-al*	*-able*
hungry	economical	knowledgeable
_____	_____	_____
_____	_____	_____
_____	_____	_____
_____		

2 Work in pairs. Choose two adjectives from each group in the table in **1** and use them in sentences of your own.

3 We can make some nouns into adjectives by adding the suffixes *-ful* (= full of) or *-less* (= without). Six of the adjectives in the table below have an opposite adjective ending in *-less*. Which are they? Write them next to the adjectives.

-ful	*-less*
beautiful	_____
careful	_____
harmful	_____
hopeful	_____
painful	_____
powerful	_____
successful	_____
useful	_____
wonderful	_____

4 Complete the sentences with a suitable adjective ending in *-ful* or *-less* from the table in **3**.

1 The accident was caused by _____ driving.

2 You won't feel any pain. In fact the treatment is completely _____ .

3 Smoking is _____ to your health.

4 Thank you for all the work you've done. You've been really _____ .

5 This machine doesn't work at all. It's totally _____ .

6 We can't be sure of success, but we're very _____ we'll succeed.

Strange but true

① Which of the following do you do, and how often?
- watch the news on TV
- listen to the news on radio
- read newspapers
- read current affairs magazines

② Have you heard any unusual or amusing stories in the news recently? If so, what were they about?

③ 🎧 **12.3** The cartoons illustrate two true news reports. Listen to the reports and answer the questions.

Report 1
What new policy has the company introduced?

Report 2
Why does the new company have more staff than it needs?

④ 🎧 **12.3** Listen to the two reports again. Then say what you remember about the following.

Report 1	Report 2
1 profits	1 47
2 a hug	2 €15,000
3 music	3 in a year's time
4 birthday	4 five
5 relaxed and friendly	5 two more

⑤ Work in pairs. Use the words and phrases in **④** to present the two news reports again.

⑥ Discuss the questions and give reasons for your opinions.

Report 1
1 What do you think of the policy of being nice to its staff introduced by the company?
2 What do you think makes a company 'a great place to work'?

Report 2
1 If you were one of the university graduates, would you agree to stay with the company and accept €15,000 to travel round the world for a year?
2 Why do you think only five of the 47 graduates have accepted the offer?

7 Work in Group A or Group B. Read the words and phrases from your news report and try to guess its content. The words are in the same order as in the reports.

Group A – Report A

goats – fires – San Francisco –
400 goats – dry grass – catches fire –
company – rents out – business has doubled – enough goats

Group B – Report B

Australia – Saudi Arabia – 120 camels –
trade – to grow – about 5,000 a year –
from the Canary Islands in 1840 – Saudi Arabian client

8 Work in pairs, one student from Group A and the other student from Group B. Tell your partner what you think your news report is about.

9 🎧 **12.4** Listen to the news reports for Groups A and B. Were you right about any of the content?

10 Look at Listening scripts 12.3 and 12.4 on p. 135. Underline all the examples of passive verb forms in the news reports. Why is the passive used in these examples?

11 Discuss the following questions about the two news reports you heard in **9**. Give reasons for your opinions.

Report A

In San Francisco the authorities used herbicides and controlled fires to reduce the risk of fires before they discovered goats could do the job better. Why do you think people in rich, developed countries often use expensive or harmful methods to solve a problem when a simple, inexpensive, and more natural solution exists?

Report B

Did the information in this report surprise or amuse you? Why? Why not?

Thanking for hospitality. Saying goodbye

❶ 🎧 **12.5** Duncan is saying goodbye to some of the guests who stayed at Glencross Castle after the *Wine & Dine* anniversary celebration. Listen to the three conversations and answer the questions.

Dialogue 1
1 What have Pierre and Anne-Marie invited Duncan to do?
2 Has Duncan accepted?

Dialogue 2
1 What does Monique promise Duncan?
2 When is their next meeting?

Dialogue 3
1 What does Duncan think James should write?
2 Why do you think James asks Duncan about his meeting with Monique?
3 Why do you think James says 'That's the problem'?

❷ 🎧 **12.5** Listen to the three conversations again and tick (✓) the phrases you hear.

Thanking for hospitality
Thank you for inviting us.
Thank you very much for your hospitality.
Thank you for everything.
Thanks a lot.

Positive comment
We've had a wonderful time.
I really appreciated it.
It was really enjoyable.
Everything was great.

Responding to thanks
I'm glad you | could come.
| enjoyed it.
| liked it.
| found it interesting.

Saying goodbye
I really must be going.
We really must leave now.
I must be off.
I look forward to ... (*seeing you again*).
I'm looking forward to ... (*our next meeting*).
See you | on the ...
| next week.
| soon.
Have a good | trip back.
| flight.

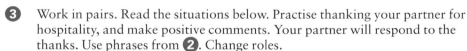

❸ Work in pairs. Read the situations below. Practise thanking your partner for hospitality, and make positive comments. Your partner will respond to the thanks. Use phrases from **❷**. Change roles.

1 A colleague has invited you to a restaurant to celebrate your promotion. You have just finished the meal.
2 A supplier has taken you to the theatre to see a play.
3 Some foreign friends have taken you on a sightseeing tour of their city.

❹ Read the situations on the left. Match them with an appropriate response on the right.

1 You're at a party. It's late and you want to leave.

a I really must be going, John. I've got another appointment now.

2 Your business meeting has just finished. You have a train to catch.

b Thanks for the lift, Sue. I must be off or I'll miss my plane.

3 You've had lunch with a visitor. You have to meet another person in fifteen minutes.

c Well, I really must leave now. I've got to get to the station.

4 A friend who drove you to the airport is talking to you. You're afraid you'll miss your flight.

d I must be going. I've got an early start tomorrow.

❺ Now walk round and say goodbye to your colleagues. Give your reason for needing to leave now.

REVIEW UNIT C

This unit reviews all the main language points from Units 9–12. Complete the exercises. Check your learning with the self-check box at the end.

1 **Present Perfect Simple and Continuous, *since* and *for***

Write sentences about these situations and activities with *since* and *for*.

Examples She has a flat in the city centre. She bought it two years ago.
She's had a flat in the city centre for two years.

The company makes computers. It started in 1980.
The company has been making computers since 1980.

1 Marc has his own company. He started it in 1999.

2 Franca works as an accountant. She qualified in 2001.

3 Claude and Anna are married. They got married six months ago.

4 Leon is learning Japanese. He began last year.

5 Mike lives in Dublin. He moved there three years ago.

6 The company manufactures electrical goods. It started five years ago.

2 **Present Perfect Simple and Continuous, *since* and *for***

Five of the sentences below have a grammatical mistake. Find the mistakes, then write the correct sentences.

1 She's been a doctor since 1998.

2 I study English for a long time.

3 How long has he had his job?

4 The company is doing very well since last October.

5 How many years are you teaching English?

6 I've known that family for ages.

7 How long have they been members of the club?

8 They've been living in Paris since a long time.

9 How long have they been married?

10 How long are you working for your company?

3 **1st and 2nd Conditional**

Match the two halves of these sentences.

1 If I had more leisure time,   a I wouldn't do that.
2 If I finish work early today,   b I'll look for another job.
3 If I got more exercise,   c I'd spend it with my family.
4 If I don't get a promotion,   d I'd be a lot healthier.
5 If I had longer holidays,   e I'll go to the sports centre.
6 If the salary and conditions were good, f we could find a solution.
7 If I were you,   g I'd travel to faraway places.
8 If we understood the problem,   h I'd accept a job in another country.

4 1st and 2nd Conditional

Write sentences about these future situations. If you think they are possible, write the sentence in the 1st Conditional. If you think they are unlikely, use the 2nd Conditional.

Example *If I get a big salary increase, I'll buy a new car.* (possible)
If I got a big salary increase, I'd buy a new car. (unlikely)

1 You get a big salary increase.

2 You take up a new sport.

3 Your company asks you to work in China for a year.

4 Your company moves to another city.

5 You decide to start your own business.

6 You lose your passport while on a business trip abroad.

7 Your company asks you to improve your English very quickly.

8 You win a safari holiday in Africa.

5 Passives

Complete the information about coffee. Write the correct passive form of the verb in brackets. Use the Present Simple, Past Simple, or Present Perfect.

Coffee facts

Did you know ...?

- Coffee is the most popular drink in the world.
  400 billion cups of coffee _____ [1] (consume) each year.
  It's the world's second most important commodity after oil.
- About 8,000 coffee beans _____ [2] (use) to make a kilo of coffee.
- The world's first coffee house _____ [3] (open) in Constantinople in 1475.
- Coffee _____ [4] (import) into Europe since 1600, when it arrived in the port of Venice for the first time.
- The first commercial espresso machine _____ [5] (manufacture) in Italy in 1905.
- Instant coffee _____ [6] (drink) since 1938 when it _____ [7] (invent) by Nescafé.
- The USA is the world's largest importer of coffee. About 30% of total production _____ [8] (export) to the USA.
- Scandinavia has the highest per capita consumption of coffee. On average seven kilos of coffee _____ [9] (buy) every year by Europeans, but in Finland, Denmark, and Sweden the figure is twelve kilos or more.

6 **Offers and requests**

Work in pairs. Make offers and requests and respond to them. Add two more each.

Example **Student A** *Can you help me with my luggage, please?*

Student B *Yes, certainly.*

Student A

1 Ask a colleague to lend you a dictionary.

2 Offer to help a colleague write a letter in English.

3 Offer to phone for a taxi for a visitor.

4 Ask _____

5 Offer _____

Student B

1 Ask a friend to give you a lift to the station.

2 Ask a colleague to explain a new system.

3 Offer to show a visitor round your company.

4 Offer _____

5 Ask _____

7 **Asking for information**

Change these direct questions to indirect questions.

Example Where's the KLM check-in desk?
Could you tell me where the KLM check-in desk is?

1 What's the plane fare from Barcelona to Paris?

Could you tell me _____?

2 How long does the flight take?

Do you know _____?

3 Which airport in Paris does the plane arrive at?

Can you tell me _____?

4 When do I need to check in?

Could you tell me _____?

5 Can I buy duty-free goods on the plane?

Do you know _____?

8 **Social responses**

Match the comments and questions in A to the responses in B.

A

1 Could I use your dictionary?
2 I didn't get the job I wanted.
3 Have a nice weekend.
4 I'm sorry I'm so late.
5 Do you mind if I smoke?
6 Thanks for all your helpful advice.
7 I've just become a father of twins!
8 Can I get you another drink?

B

a Don't mention it.
b Congratulations!
c Yes, of course.
d Not at the moment, thanks.
e I'm sorry to hear that.
f Thanks. The same to you.
g It doesn't matter.
h Well, I'd rather you didn't.

9 **Thanking for hospitality**

Work in pairs. What would you say in these situations?

1 Your boss has invited you to dinner at his home. You have just finished the meal.

2 A business associate has taken you to a local wine festival.

3 On a business trip, your host has taken you to a restaurant which has local specialities on the menu.

4 Some colleagues at work have given a party to celebrate your promotion.

⑩ **Saying goodbye**

Work in pairs. Read the four situations. Explain why you must leave and say goodbye.

Student A

Situation 1
You're talking to a friend on the platform. Your train is coming into the station.

Situation 2
You've just finished a meeting with your boss. You want to leave now to meet a visitor at the airport.

Student B

Situation 3
You've spent a long time helping a colleague. You have an important meeting with a client.

Situation 4
You've had dinner in a restaurant with a customer. It's late and you have to take an early morning flight the next day.

⑪ **Vocabulary**

Work in Group A or Group B. Write a vocabulary test to give to the other group. Choose ten of the words below. Write a sentence or phrase to help the other group guess each word.

Example Word *to win*
    Clue *the opposite of 'to lose'*

huge	century	worst	traffic jam	ugly
to win ✓	goat	life expectancy	headquarters	destruction
growth	to forecast	staff	noisy	population
overcrowded	consumer	decade	free-market economy	to afford

⑫ **Vocabulary test**

Give your vocabulary test to the other group. Do the other group's test. Return your answers for checking.

Look at the self-check box below. Tick the areas you need to review again.

SELF-CHECK BOX	Yes	No	Pocket Book
• Present Perfect Simple and Continuous, *since* and *for*			13, 14, 16
• 1st and 2nd Conditional			2, 3
• The Passive			9
• Offers and requests			20
• Asking for information			17
• Social responses			21
• Thanking for hospitality			21
• Saying goodbye			21
• Vocabulary			

Listening scripts

Unit 1

1.1

R=Roberto, J=James, M=Monique

Dialogue 1

J Roberto! Good to see you again. How are things?

R Oh, hello, James. Fine, thanks – very busy – lots of work, lots of travelling as always. Can I introduce a good friend of mine, Monique Bresson? Monique, this is James Turner.

M How do you do?

J How do you do?

Dialogue 2

J Are you an importer?

M No, a translator. I'm here with the Vinexpo translation service. I'm with a group of Italian wine producers who don't speak French.

R Monique is a genius, James. She speaks five languages fluently.

J Really? Which ones?

M Spanish, Italian, and Hungarian, and of course French and English. What do you do?

J I'm a wine consultant, like Roberto. We both write about wine. I'm a journalist with *Wine & Dine* magazine.

Dialogue 3

J Actually, I have a job for someone who speaks English and Italian. Are you free later to discuss it?

M I'm not sure at the moment. I'm afraid I already have several appointments today. Perhaps this evening? How about 7.00 in the main bar?

J Fine.

1.2

M=Monique, J=James

J Ah, Monique.

M Sorry I'm late.

J That's OK. A glass of champagne?

M Thank you. So, what does a wine journalist do?

J Well, I go to the wine regions and I interview people in the business to get information for my articles. I travel to Italy two or three times a year.

M Do you enjoy your job?

J Oh, yes, I really love my work, especially the travelling. I meet so many interesting people.

M I enjoy travelling, too …

J Yes, I see from your business card that your translation agency has offices in Paris, London, and Rome.

M Yes, that's right. I live in London, of course, but I often travel in Europe and I come to Paris regularly, usually for work. Sometimes I come to visit my parents. They live near Dijon. So, why do you need a translation agency?

J Well, to help with interviews for my book about Italian wines.

M Oh, really? How interesting. We have a lot to discuss!

J Yes, we do. Do you have time for dinner? The restaurant here is excellent.

M Thank you very much.

1.3

a Do you speak Italian?

b Which languages do you speak?

1.4

1 Do you travel a lot?

2 How often do you come here?

3 Do you speak French?

4 How often do you go to Italy?

5 Do you work here every year?

6 Who do you meet here?

7 Where does he live?

8 Does James speak Italian?

9 What does Roberto do?

10 Which languages does Monique speak?

1.5

The world's ten most important languages are: first, Mandarin Chinese, which 726 million people speak as a first language; second, English, with 377 million speakers; third, Spanish, with 266 million; fourth, Hindi, with 182 million; fifth, Arabic, with 181 million; then sixth, Portuguese, which has 165 million; seventh, Bengali, with 162 million; eighth, Russian, with 158 million; then ninth, Japanese, which has 124 million; and tenth, German, with 121 million.

1.6

I=Interviewer, L=Language expert

I Do we know how many people in the world speak English as a second or foreign language?

L Well, we don't know the exact number, of course, but we know the approximate number, and that's more than 1.1 billion.

I And today I imagine it's the main language used on the Internet?

L Yes, that's certainly the case at the moment. Over three quarters of the information on the Internet is in English and 80% of the people who use the Internet communicate in English, although we expect that percentage to decrease as the number of people using the Internet increases.

I How many people in the European Union speak English?

L Well, including the population of the UK and Ireland, who speak it as a first language, at present about half the population of the EU – the European Union – speaks English, so it's quite a high number, but as more countries join, this number will go down. But 69% of the people in the EU who don't speak English as a first language think it's the most important language to learn.

I And are there any figures for the number of people in the world who are learning English at present?

L Again, it's not possible to know the exact number but the estimated number is over two billion.

1.7

Dialogue 1

T=Tony, M=Monique

T Excuse me, are you Ms Bresson?

M Yes, that's right.

T May I introduce myself? I'm Tony White. How do you do?

M How do you do, Mr White?

Dialogue 2

J=Jeanne, R=Roberto

J   Roberto! Nice to see you again. How are you?

R   Hello, Jeanne. Fine, thanks. How are you? How's the family?

J   Oh, very well, thank you, Roberto.

Dialogue 3

R=Roberto, L=Luigi, J=James

R   James, I'd like to introduce you to Luigi Bastini. He represents some growers in the Chianti area of Italy here at Vinexpo. Luigi, this is a journalist friend of mine, James Turner.

L   Pleased to meet you, Mr Turner.

J   How do you do? Please call me James.

L   Then you must call me Luigi.

1.8

M=Monique, J=James

J   Monique, I must go now. It was very nice meeting you, and I look forward to seeing you in London next month.

M   I really enjoyed meeting you, too, James. Have a good trip back.

J   Thank you, and the same to you. Bye.

M   Bye. See you soon.

Unit 2

2.1

Extract 1

I=Interviewer, JM=José Manuel

I   José Manuel, you're from Portugal but you live and work in Spain?

JM   Yes, that's right. I'm the Operations Director in Unilever's Food Division, and I live and work in Barcelona.

I   Do you need to speak good English, working for a big international company like Unilever?

JM   Yes, English is the company language so I use it every day for emails and phone calls, and all international meetings are in English.

I   How often do you go to international meetings?

JM   I go to our head office in the Netherlands twice a year, and I sometimes have meetings in other countries in Europe too. But most of my meetings are in Spain, with Spanish people, so I don't have to speak English then!

Extract 2

I=Interviewer, G=Geneviève

I   Geneviève, you work for a TV production company in Paris called Téléimages. Do you need English in your job?

G   Yes, every day. We have a lot of foreign visitors in our office and we usually communicate in English, and I make lots of phone calls in English because I contact people in different countries to arrange meetings and so on. And I use English for emails, too.

I   Do you have any problems speaking English on the phone?

G   Sometimes, with some nationalities. I find Japanese and Americans more difficult to understand. But I think my English is improving because it's getting easier!

Extract 3

I=Interviewer, K=Kensuke

I   Kensuke, as Sales Manager, Professional Products, for Electrolux in Tokyo, do you travel a lot for work?

K   Yes, I travel a lot in Japan, for meetings with managers and salesmen, and to visit our most important retailers to negotiate sales. And I go to Sweden, two or three times a year.

I   To your company's head office?

K   Yes. I usually stay there for about a week.

I   And you have to speak English then?

K   Yes. I also speak English in Japan, in meetings with the President of Electrolux Japan, because he's Swedish.

I   And he doesn't speak Japanese?

K   No, and our company language is English!

2.2

Extract 1

I=Interviewer, JM=José Manuel

I   José Manuel, are any things changing in Unilever, Spain at the moment? Are there any new developments?

JM   Yes, in fact there's a very big change. We're changing our distribution system, from the present system of three distribution centres to just one big centre. So right now I'm having a lot of meetings with consultants, to find the best system to use in the new centre. It's a lot of work, and it's very important I make the right decision!

Extract 2

I=Interviewer, G=Geneviève

I   Geneviève, are any changes taking place in your company, or your job?

G   Well, Téléimages is expanding very quickly, so that means I'm making new contacts and working with more people in my job. And in France right now the number of TV channels is increasing. My company wants to buy a TV channel so we're working hard in order to be successful. We're hoping to get the news soon that Téléimages has got its own TV channel.

Extract 3

I=Interviewer, K=Kensuke

I   Kensuke, there are problems in the economy at present. Are companies like Electrolux having problems, too?

K   Yes, most companies are having problems. In my division, Electrolux Professional Products, sales are decreasing, but the Consumer Products Division isn't having this problem, in fact sales are going up a little there. But I expect an improvement in my division in two to three years …

2.3

1   a   Do you work in Paris?   b   Yes, I do.

2   a   Does she live in Madrid?   b   Yes, she does.

2.4

1   Where do they live?

2   Does she speak English?

3   Yes, she does.

4   What time do we arrive?

5   Do you often travel abroad?

6   Yes, I do.

2.5

First, I'd like to welcome you all to Electrolux, and give you a brief introduction to the company before we begin our tour. As you know, Electrolux is a Swedish company with its head office here in Stockholm. Now I expect when you hear the name 'Electrolux' you probably think of a refrigerator – or a fridge as we usually call it – or maybe a vacuum cleaner, and in fact these were the company's first two products.

Electrolux started as a company in 1921 when it produced the world's first vacuum cleaner. Four years later, in 1925, it produced its first refrigerator, and these are still two of its best-known products. But today the company is very different from what it was in 1921. What you perhaps don't know is that it now owns many well-known consumer brands, including AEG, Zanussi, Frigidaire, Flymo, and Husqvarna and Partner, and this makes it the world's largest producer of powered appliances for kitchen, cleaning, and outdoor use.

Today it employs 81,971 people and sells its products in more than 150 countries. Its worldwide turnover in 2002 was 14,552 million euros.

It has two global divisions, called Consumer Durables and Professional Products. Seventy-five per cent of the company's sales comes from the Consumer Durables Division. This division includes the appliances we have in our homes, for example cookers, vacuum cleaners, and washing machines. Professional Products includes much larger appliances, for example food service equipment for hotels and restaurants, and outdoor products for the garden.

Right, that's all I'll say about the company for the moment. I hope that gives you a general idea to start with. I'll be happy to answer any questions, then we'll begin our tour …

2.6

R=Receptionist, J=James

R Good morning. Bresson Translation Services.

J Oh, hello. Could I speak to Monique Bresson, please?

R Who's calling, please?

J This is James Turner from *Wine & Dine* magazine.

R Hold the line, please, Mr Turner. … I'm sorry, she's in a meeting. Can I take a message?

J Yes. Could you ask her to call me? My number is 020 7331 8582.

R 7331 8582. Thank you. I'll give her your message.

J Thank you. Goodbye.

2.7

R=Receptionist, J=James, M=Monique

R Bresson Translation Services.

J Can I speak to Monique Bresson, please?

R Who's calling, please?

J It's James Turner.

R Hold the line, Mr Turner. Monique?

M Speaking.

R I have James Turner for you …

2.8

R=Receptionist, J=James

R Good afternoon. Bresson Translation Services.

J Good afternoon. This is James Turner speaking. Is Ms Bresson there, please?

R I'm afraid she's in Paris this afternoon. Can I give her a message?

J Er … yes. Could you tell her that the meeting with Mr Michelmore is on Wednesday at 11.00?

R Could you spell that, please?

J Yes. It's M-I-C-H-E-L-M-O-R-E. And could you ask her to call him? His number is 020 7623 4459.

R Yes, Mr Turner. I'll give her your message.

J Thank you.

Unit 3

3.1

I=Interviewer, T=Tim Smit

I Tim, in 1998 Eden was just a hole in the ground, but today it's a great success story and one of the UK's top visitor attractions. Where did the idea of the Eden Project come from?

T One evening I was in a pub with a friend, an architect from Cornwall called Jonathan Ball. We had a discussion about Cornwall and its problems. We wanted to bring more visitors to the area and create more jobs. At that time there was a lot in the newspapers and on TV about the Amazonian rainforest, and we thought why not build the biggest greenhouse in the world and put a rainforest inside it!

I And three years later you and Jonathan Ball founded the Eden Project?

T Amazingly, yes. And the idea became a reality.

I What was your biggest challenge in creating Eden?

T Oh, there were lots. Money, for example.

I How much did the project cost?

T £86 million.

I And where did you get the money from?

T Half of it, £43 million, came from the Millennium Commission – that was the organization that gave money to special projects to celebrate the year 2000. The problem was that we needed to find the same amount, another £43 million, ourselves, before they gave us the money.

I Did you find it?

T Yes, we did. But it wasn't easy. And the weather certainly didn't help us. When work began in 1998 it rained every day for 100 days. The workers didn't make any progress for three months. That gave us a lot of problems. We thought it was the end of our great idea.

I A million people visited Eden in the first year. Did you expect so many visitors?

T No, we didn't. It was the best thing that happened.

I The Eden Project was a huge challenge. How did you do it?

T We did it because we had a wonderful team of people. We all had the same vision. We believed in the idea of Eden and worked incredibly hard to make it a success.

I Do you have plans for the future?

T Oh, certainly – exciting plans, but that's the topic of another interview.

3.2

a lived
b helped
c visited

3.3

arrived	rained	watched
started	increased	received
worked	expected	needed
wanted		

3.4

Yesterday, a 57-year-old mother of three became the first woman to fly solo around the world in a small one-engine aeroplane. Polly Vacher, a music teacher, arrived back at Birmingham Airport 124 days after she left the same airport on the 12th of January. On the 46,670-kilometre journey she flew over deserts and oceans and survived tropical thunderstorms, engine problems, and a frightening experience over the Pacific when her plane ran out of fuel. Her flight was a personal challenge, but it also raised £150,000 for a charity which gives disabled people the chance to learn how to fly.

3.5

R=Receptionist, J=James

R Good afternoon, can I help you?

J Good afternoon. My name's James Turner. I have an appointment with Wayne Brown.

R Oh, yes, Mr Turner. Mr Brown is expecting you. Please take a seat and I'll tell him you're here. … Mr Brown, I have Mr Turner in reception for you. ... OK. Mr Turner, Mr Brown will be with you in a moment.

3.6

W=Wayne, J=James

W Hello, James! Welcome to California! It's good to meet you.

J It's good to be here at last.

W Did you have any problems finding us?

J No. Jack Michelmore gave me directions in London last week. I got a taxi here.

W Good. How was your flight?

J There was a short delay in London, but the flight was fine. Fortunately, I slept on the plane, so I'm not very tired.

W Glad to hear it. You've got a busy programme ahead. Let's discuss it over lunch. I booked a table for 1.30. Do you like Mexican food?

3.7
W=Wayne, J=James

W Where did your career in the wine business begin?

J Right here, actually. I came to San Francisco when I was a student. That was when I discovered Californian wines.

W When was that?

J Nearly fifteen years ago.

W Did you work in California?

J No. I returned to Europe, and I got a job with a wine merchant. Later, I wrote an article for a wine magazine. That's how it all began! How did you get into the wine business?

W Well, actually, I'm a lawyer. But I grew up in Napa Valley, and my uncle owns a winery there.

J Really? How big is it?

W Its production is quite small, but the wines are excellent. Anyway, when I finished university my uncle asked me to work for him. I look after his business affairs.

Unit 4

4.1
J=Jan, M=Mark

J Hello.

M Hi, Jan, it's Mark. I'm phoning to give you the final details for the seminar in Prague next weekend and to tell you which sessions we're doing.

J Right.

M You're not doing anything on Saturday morning. I'm giving the first presentation, from 9.00 to 10.45. Then after the coffee break Vana's talking about cultural differences from 11.00 to 12.45. We're having lunch from 1.00 to 2.00 and your first session is after lunch. You're giving a presentation on intercultural communication. I hope that's OK?

J Yes, that's fine. How much time do I have?

M From 2.00 to 3.30. As you can see from the programme, we're having three sessions in the afternoon.

J OK. Is Vana doing the workshop on working with multicultural teams?

M Yes. Then I'm giving the talk about body language.

J What times are those sessions?

M Vana's workshop is from 4.00 to 5.30 and my session is from 5.30 to 6.30.

J Right. What are we doing in the evening?

M We're meeting in the hotel bar for drinks at 7.00 and then going to a restaurant for dinner.

J Good. So that's everything for Saturday?

M Yes, I think that's everything.

4.2
M=Mark, J=Jan

M OK, let's move on to Sunday now. I didn't send you any information because we're not going to have a fixed programme on Sunday. The activities are going to be more informal and practical, and give everyone the chance to find out about our training materials and ask us lots of questions.

J Are we going to demonstrate any of our materials?

M Yes. We're going to show our training videos and our online courses, and give people the chance to learn how they can use them in their companies. They can choose what they want to watch, and how long to spend on each one, and ask us questions about them.

J How much time are we going to spend on the videos and online courses?

M I think we need about three hours, so say from 9.00 until about 12.15, which will give us time for a coffee break in the middle. Then that leaves fifteen minutes to bring everything to a conclusion and finish at 12.30. After that we can talk to people individually about their company's needs and discuss what training we can do for them …

4.3
a Who are you writing to?
b Are you writing to Mark?

4.4
1 Is he going to Japan?
2 He's going to change his job.
3 Which country is he travelling to?
4 Are they coming to see us?
5 Which companies is he writing to?
6 Where are you going to stay?
7 Which airport are you flying to?

4.5
R=Receptionist, S=Secretary

R Good morning. Meridiana Hotel. How can I help you?

S Oh, hello. I'm looking for a suitable hotel for a group of managers and I wanted to check what facilities your hotel offers. Do you have a restaurant and a bar?

R Yes. We have a restaurant and a cocktail bar on the top floor with lovely views over the city, and there's another bar and a lounge on the ground floor.

S Oh, good. What about parking?

R The hotel has its own car park. We also have a fitness room and a sauna, and a business centre which provides fax, Internet, and photocopying services.

S Right. Are there connections for PCs in the guest rooms?

R Yes, all guest rooms have computer and fax points, and of course multi-line phones and satellite TV.

S OK. And air-conditioning?

R Yes, all rooms are air-conditioned.

S And are there tea- and coffee-making facilities in the rooms?

R No, but all rooms have a minibar, and we offer 24-hour room service.

S Right. Well, I think you have everything we need. Oh, oh, just a couple more things – do the guest rooms have hairdryers and safes?

R They have hairdryers, but not safes. Guests can leave money and valuables in the hotel safe at reception.

S Well, thanks very much for the information. I need to check on the dates with the managers and I'll get back to you to make the booking …

4.6
R=Receptionist, J=James

R *Hotel Leon d'Oro. Buongiorno.*

J *Buongiorno.* Do you speak English?

R Yes. How can I help you?

J My name is James Turner. Last week I booked a room from the 3rd to the 6th of April … um, you confirmed the reservation by email.

R Oh, yes, Mr Turner. I remember.

J I'd like to book a single room, for a colleague, for the 4th of April.

R Let me see. Oh, I'm very sorry, Mr Turner, but we're fully booked on the 4th of April, because of Vinitaly.

J Oh, what a pity.

R You could try the Hotel Europa.

J Yes, I'll do that. Thank you for your help. Goodbye.

R We look forward to seeing you on the 3rd of April, Mr Turner. Goodbye.

4.7

J=James, R=Receptionist

J   Good evening. My name is Turner. I have a reservation.

R   Yes, a single room for four nights?

J   Yes, that's right.

R   Could you fill in this form, please, and sign here? Thank you. Here's your key. Your room is on the first floor. The porter will take your luggage.

J   Thank you. Oh, could I have an early morning call, at 6.30?

R   Yes, certainly. Do you need anything else?

J   No, that's all, thank you.

4.8

J=James, R=Receptionist

J   Could I have my bill, please? Can I pay by credit card?

R   Yes, that's fine.

J   Good.

R   I hope you enjoyed your stay here.

J   Oh, yes, very much. And I'm sure I'll be back here for Vinitaly next April.

R   We'll be delighted to see you again, Mr Turner. Goodbye, and have a good flight back.

J   Thank you. Goodbye.

Unit 5

5.1

a coffee

b champagne

c exercise

5.2

1 vegetable

2 problem

3 alcohol

4 research

5 sandwich

6 advice

5.3

1 butter

2 holiday

3 colleague

4 weekend

5 headache

6 energy

5.4

Speaker 1

For me one of the great pleasures of travelling to another country or to another part of your own country is eating different food – discovering local dishes and specialities that are completely new to you. That's why I think Slow Food is important. I don't want to find the same food everywhere I go, but that's what fast food is doing to us. I want to stop that.

Speaker 2

Some people say Slow Food is only for people who have lots of money to buy the best food and wine, and have lots of time to sit, eat, drink, and talk. But Slow Food can be simple and inexpensive. What's important is that it's fresh, that it tastes good, and that it's healthy and good for you. And of course that you don't eat it fast!

Speaker 3

There's a saying, 'families that eat together stay together'. I think it's true. But in a lot of families that doesn't happen any more. A meal is something you buy, ready to eat, from the supermarket. All you do is put it in the microwave for two minutes and eat it in five minutes in front of the TV. Or if you're not at home, you can eat your food walking along the street. I don't think that's the way to live. Things were much better in the past.

Speaker 4

A lot of our towns and cities have squares in the centre, and they're great places to sit and eat, have a drink, and meet friends. But in many towns the main square isn't for people at all – it's just a big car park. That's why I think it's good that Slow Cities promise to keep town squares for people and not use them as car parks. And of course that they improve lots of other things so the quality of life really is better for the people who live there.

5.5

W=Waiter, M=Monique, J=James

W   Good evening.

M   Good evening. I booked a table for two. The name is Bresson.

W   Oh, yes, madam. Your table is over here.

J   This is a wonderful surprise, Monique. How did you know it was my birthday?

M   Oh, that's a secret. Anyway, I would like to discuss the trip to Hungary with you, but let's order first.

J   Mm, it's a difficult choice. What do you recommend?

M   Well, the meat is usually excellent here. Let's see ... I recommend the beef or the lamb cutlets.

W   Are you ready to order?

M   James?

J   Yes, I'll have the duck and red cabbage as a starter, and then beef in red wine with onions.

M   And I'd like cold cucumber soup with prawns, and lamb cutlets with roast potatoes and courgettes.

W   Certainly, madam. And what would you like to drink?

M   You choose.

J   OK. A bottle of Beaujolais, please.

5.6

M=Monique, J=James

M   This wine is very good, isn't it? Do have some more.

J   Mm. Yes, it's very good. And the beef is excellent.

M   Good, I'm pleased you like it. Now, how about a dessert?

J   I'm sure they're all wonderful, Monique. Thank you, but I couldn't eat any more.

M   Are you sure? Would you like some coffee, then?

J   Yes. That would be very nice.

M   Now, about the trip to Hungary ...

5.7

M=Monique, J=James

J   Thank you for a lovely evening, Monique.

M   I'm glad you enjoyed it, James.

J   Now ... when's *your* birthday?

Unit 6

6.1

I=Interviewer, C=Travel industry consultant

I   I'd like to ask you about no-frills airlines. More people are flying with them and fewer people are flying with the traditional airlines, which are of course usually a lot more expensive. How can airlines like Ryanair and easyJet offer such cheap fares?

C   They can do it by having much lower costs than the traditional airlines and saving money in different ways. First, they sell directly to the customer, either online – that's on the Internet – or by phone. Their biggest number of sales is online and because that's the least expensive way of selling, they save money. Second, they don't use tickets. Passengers just get a reference number, then a letter which they show when they check in.

I So it's a much easier way of booking a flight?
C Exactly. And this means they can employ fewer people because there's much less paperwork. A third way they save money is by not serving meals on the flight.
I What about flight attendants? Do they have as many flight attendants as on traditional airlines?
C No they don't, so again that's another way of cutting costs.
I But passengers can buy drinks and sandwiches on the plane?
C Yes, so they make a little money from that. Another way they cut costs is by having just one type of aircraft, which is a lot cheaper than having different types of aircraft, and they use them in a more efficient way. Their turnaround time – that's the time between when the aircraft lands at an airport and takes off again – is only thirty minutes, so that's another way they save money.
I Do they use the big airports, like Heathrow, those nearest to the city centres?
C No, when they fly to a big city it's normally not to the main airport nearest to the city centre but the one that's farthest away.
I So you get the cheapest fare but you have the longest journey to the city centre?
C Yes, that's certainly one disadvantage, but then smaller airports are usually not as busy as the big ones, and less crowded, so getting your luggage is often quicker.

6.2
a a lot cheaper
b quicker than
c the most popular
d as busy as

6.3
1 easier than
2 a higher fare
3 the same as
4 much quicker than
5 not as cheap as

6.4
Speaker 1
What methods of travel do I use, and why? Well, when I make business trips I always travel by plane because it's faster. For holidays I go either by plane or car. I prefer going by car because you're more independent, but for longer distances flying is of course quicker. To get to work every day I travel by train and then underground. I never go anywhere by bus. I use my car to go out in the evenings, and at weekends in the summer I get my bike out and go cycling.

Speaker 2
I travel by plane only for holidays – I don't travel in my job. And for shorter distances, when I'm not going far on holiday, I prefer to use my motorbike. For me it's the most enjoyable way to travel. To get to work I go by train or motorbike. Going by train is more expensive, of course. I could go by bus but it's the slowest way because of all the traffic, so I don't use buses. I don't have a car but I've got a bike and I use it to go to my local sports club and to go cycling with friends.

6.5
1 Your attention, please. Will Mr Carlos Siga, travelling on a connecting flight to Dubai, please go to the British Airways information desk.
2 May I have your attention, please. Will Mr and Mrs Harcon, the last remaining passengers travelling to Madrid on Flight IB3615, please go immediately to Gate 14 where the aircraft is waiting to depart.
3 We are now ready to board. Would passengers in seat rows 15 to 23 board first. Please have your boarding cards and passports ready.

4 This is a security announcement. Passengers are reminded that they must keep their bags with them at all times. Any unattended luggage may be taken away and destroyed.

6.6
I=Interviewer, E=Tourist guide (Erica)
I Erica, both the Musée d'Orsay and Tate Modern are very different from other famous modern art museums because they weren't originally designed as museums. What do people think of them?
E Well, some people like them and others don't. Most people find the exterior of the Musée d'Orsay a lot more attractive because it was a hotel. Tate Modern is an industrial building and some people think the exterior is very ugly. They think a modern art museum should be beautiful like the Guggenheim Museum in Bilbao, for example. Other people think Tate Modern is a perfect place to show modern art because you need a lot of space, and Tate Modern has an enormous amount of space.
I Yes, when you go in you're in this enormous hall. There aren't many museums with an entrance hall of that size.
E No, in fact that hall is 200 metres long – as big as a square in the middle of a city. When the building was a power station that huge area was the turbine hall and the architects decided to keep it as a huge space. The Musée d'Orsay's got an enormous hall as well, almost as long as the Tate's, which was the area where the trains and platforms were when it was a station. Now it's ideal as an exhibition space for an art museum.
I It's interesting that the museums are similar in other ways, too – their locations, for example …
E Yes, it's true. They're both on the banks of rivers and the advantage for visitors is that you get wonderful views from them. From the Musée d'Orsay you can see the River Seine in front and the Louvre and the Tuileries Gardens opposite. From Tate Modern you've got a great view of the River Thames and St Paul's Cathedral opposite. And now there's a new bridge for pedestrians so you can get to St Paul's Cathedral on foot, by walking straight across the river.
I … Or to Tate Modern if you come from the other side. Well, thank you very much, Erica, for describing these two museums – it's been really interesting …

6.7
R=Receptionist, M=Monique, D=Duncan
R Monique, I have a Mr Duncan Ross on the line.
M Oh, yes, put him through. … Hello, Mr Ross.
D Hello.
M Thank you for your letter. I'd be very interested to meet you and discuss the new project …
D That's very good news. Oh, please call me Duncan, by the way. When would be convenient for you?
M Let me see … I'm rather busy this week. Is next week possible for you? I'm free on Friday … or Tuesday, if you prefer?
D Yes, Tuesday suits me fine. Shall we say lunch on Tuesday, then?
M Yes, that's fine. What time would suit you?
D How about 1.30 at the Riverside Restaurant?
M Oh, that'll be very nice.
D Good. Well, I look forward to meeting you again.
M It'll be very nice to see you again, too. Goodbye.

6.8
M=Monique, D=Duncan
D Hello.
M Hello. Is that Duncan Ross?
D Yes, speaking.

M Oh, hello, Duncan. It's Monique Bresson here. I'm very sorry, I'm afraid I can't manage our meeting on Tuesday – I have to go to Rome. Could we arrange another time?

D Oh, what a pity. But yes, of course. When are you free?

M Is Thursday the 17th possible for you?

D No, I'm afraid I've got another appointment then. What about Friday the 18th?

M Yes, I can make it on the 18th.

D Excellent. So, the same time and place? One thirty, at the Riverside?

M Yes. Thank you, Duncan. And I do apologize.

D It's no problem at all. Have a good trip to Rome. See you on Friday …

Unit 7

7.1

I=Interviewer, H= Harriet Lamb

I Harriet, can you tell us first, when did the idea of Fairtrade start?

H Well, in the UK, it started in 1992, but the first country to have Fairtrade was the Netherlands – that was in 1988. Today 90% of Dutch supermarkets sell Fairtrade coffee. Since 1988 Fairtrade has expanded into many other countries.

I How many countries?

H At present it's in seventeen countries, mostly in western Europe but also the USA, Canada, Australia, New Zealand, and Japan. And Fairtrade has just started in eastern Europe, with Hungary as the first country.

I What was the reason for starting Fairtrade?

H The reason was to help some of the poorest people in the world get a fair price for their crops. In recent years the price of coffee, cocoa, and bananas has fallen but the cost of growing them has risen. This has been a disaster for people in the Third World. But with Fairtrade, the producers get a price that covers the cost of production, plus an extra 'social premium' which they can use to improve their living and working conditions.

I What kind of improvements have they made?

H Oh, they've done so many things. They've built wells to give them clean water, they've built schools so their children can have an education, and health centres so they can get basic health care.

I So Fairtrade has made a big difference to their lives?

H Oh, yes. It's made a very big difference. It's really changed their lives.

I And what about the sales of Fairtrade products? Have they increased?

H Yes, they have, especially in the last five years. For example, in the UK sales went up by 50% in 2001. But we need a much bigger market. At present producers can only sell a very small percentage of what they grow to Fairtrade because the market is still very small.

I How much more does a Fairtrade product cost?

H Usually about 10 to 20% more than the average price. But sales are increasing and this shows more and more people are willing to pay a bit extra to help people escape poverty.

I So you're optimistic about the future of Fairtrade?

H Yes, there's still a lot to do but I'm optimistic.

I Thank you, Harriet, and I hope …

7.2

1 a Carla hasn't left.　　b I think she has.
2 a Have sales increased?　b No, they haven't.

7.3

1 The company has expanded.
2 Has it made a lot of changes?
3 No, it hasn't.
4 Their prices have increased.
5 I'm sure they haven't.
6 I think they have.

7.4

1 Has she made any progress?
2 I'm sure she has.
3 I hope they haven't forgotten the meeting.
4 Do you think they have?
5 Have they finished the work?
6 They haven't started it yet!

7.5

We sold 100 units in January and sales remained stable until March when there was an increase of 10% and sales went up to 110. They continued to rise steadily in the next two months and reached a peak of 145 units in June. In July and August they fell slightly, to 140, and there was a further decrease in September, to 130. Sales levelled off at this figure in October and November, and in December we saw an improvement to 135.

7.6

P=Presenter, M=Markus

P Good evening and welcome to tonight's *Working Week*. As usual, we begin with one of the week's most interesting business stories. Markus, what are you going to tell us about tonight?

M Well, this week we've had the latest survey on the best companies to work for in the UK – so that's our topic today.

P Right. Does the survey tell you what makes a company one of the best?

M Well, it shows that the best companies to work for have quite a lot of things in common. And of course these include things like good pay and holidays, and opportunities for career development. Then there are the company benefits like private health care, company pension, bonuses – that sort of thing. In many companies only the top people get these benefits, but in the best companies everyone gets them, not just the people at the top. There are also other benefits like free meals at lunchtime, and quite a lot of companies have fitness centres and make sure their employees spend some time in them every day!

P Sounds like a very good idea. What about working hours – flexitime, for example?

M The survey shows that the best companies in the UK give staff more freedom about when they work so they have flexible working hours, and if an employee wants to change from full-time to part-time work then that's not a problem.

P So the best companies are more 'family-friendly'?

M Yes, in many cases they are, and today it's important for a company to be family-friendly, especially companies who employ more women.

P What about a crèche for staff with babies or young children?

M Only two of the 50 best companies in the survey have a crèche at the company, but quite a lot offer staff subsidized places at a local crèche.

P Where staff pay less than the normal cost?

M That's right. The survey also looks at company culture and it's interesting to see that some of the best companies have a very open and democratic company culture. They treat everyone in the same way. There are no private offices, no executive dining-rooms – everyone eats in the same place, and when anyone in the company flies, they go economy class. And in these companies it's easy for anyone to meet and talk to the company's chief executive.

P Do you think this is the model for all companies in the future?

M Maybe. This kind of very open culture is common in American companies, but I think a company's culture depends on its nationality and on the country it's in.

P Well, thank you, Markus, for that look at the best companies to work for. And if you'd like to tell us your views on what makes a company one of the best you can phone us on 020 4368 7665 or email us via our website which is www.radio6.com/workingweek. And now it's time for our round-up of this week's news …

7.7

J=James, D=Duncan

J Sorry I'm late, Duncan. The traffic was terrible …

D Oh, don't apologize. I'm glad you could find time for a meeting.

J OK, so you want to discuss how we celebrate the tenth anniversary of *Wine & Dine*, right?

D Yes. First, what do you think about having the celebration at my castle in Scotland, instead of at a London hotel?

J Well, in my opinion, Scotland is too far for people to travel.

D I agree – it's a long way. But I thought of chartering a plane from London. Then we could include travel to Scotland in the invitation. What's your opinion of that idea?

J I think it sounds really great!

D Good. Second, how do you feel about celebrating the publication of your new book on Italian wines at the same time?

J That's a wonderful idea, Duncan! I certainly agree with that.

D I thought you would! Now, we need to decide on the programme. What do you think about this idea …

7.8

D=Duncan, J=James

D … OK, James. Then I suggest you give a talk on Italian wines.

J How about having a wine-tasting too?

D Yes, let's do that. Right, that's a very full programme on the first day. Do you have any suggestions for the second day?

J Why don't we make the second day more relaxing? Give people an opportunity to socialize, to get to know each other better. Why not start the day with a champagne breakfast?

D Yes, and we could follow that with a treasure hunt in the garden, with a bottle of something very special as the treasure?

J Hmm, I'm not sure about that. What if it rains?

D Don't worry, James. We have wonderful summers in Scotland. And then people can choose – there's tennis, swimming, golf.

J In fact everything for a great weekend!

D That's right. And we finish with a big party in the evening. Well, James, I think we've agreed on everything. All we need now is to check the guest list, and make sure we haven't forgotten anyone …

Unit 8

8.1

In Russia

1 It's important not to give an even number of flowers as a present because Russians only give an even numbers of flowers when people die.

2 Smoking in Red Square, Moscow, is forbidden and you can get a large fine which you have to pay immediately.

3 Russians think it's very bad manners to put your coat on the back of your chair in a restaurant or a theatre.

4 When it snows, Russians always take off their outdoor shoes when they go indoors. They offer visitors shoes to wear indoors, but you give a very good impression if you take your own indoor shoes with you.

In Japan

1 The Japanese consider talking loudly or showing anger a very rude way to behave. In their culture it's important to be calm and to control emotions.

2 If you pour your own drink, they may think you are an alcoholic.

3 Westerners normally stand closer to each other than Japanese people do. Japanese people feel uncomfortable if a foreigner stands close to them.

4 A Japanese communal bath is not for washing but for relaxing, so you should wash before getting into a bath in Japan.

8.2

You might have a few problems, but you won't have many.

8.3

1 You should always be punctual, but you don't have to be formal.

2 You don't have to wear a suit, but you must wear a tie.

3 You have to get permission first, but the managers don't.

4 The Japanese may think you rude, but the Italians won't.

5 It's important to be serious at work, but not when you're at a party.

8.4

The countries that Richard Lewis gives as examples of the three different cultural groups are the USA and northern Europe for the Linear-active group, southern Europe and Latin America for the Multi-active group, and south-east Asia and Finland for the Reactive group. Of course it's important to remember when someone describes different nationalities in this way they're not saying every person who lives in a particular country is the same. They're giving a general picture, to help people who are going to another country understand why things are different.

8.5

Now, looking at the differences between the groups, you can understand there are often problems when they do business together because they have a different idea of what is 'normal'. Let me give you a few examples. People in Linear-active and Reactive cultures think punctuality is normal. So they think a southern European who arrives ten minutes late is rude. But in Multi-active cultures it's normal to be unpunctual.

Another example. An American asks a Japanese a question. The Japanese doesn't reply so the American asks another question. The Japanese is surprised. In a Reactive culture like Japan's, long pauses in a conversation are normal. In the other two cultures long pauses are uncomfortable, so someone speaks to end the silence. To work together without problems people need to understand their differences. If they don't, they may get a bad impression of the other culture.

Another difference is eye contact. For example, a southern European talking to a Japanese doesn't understand why the Japanese doesn't look at him but at the window behind him. The Japanese is uncomfortable because the southern European looks at him directly. The reason? In Multi-active cultures there's a lot of eye contact. In Linear-active cultures less, and in Reactive cultures very little eye contact at all.

The last example I'll give you is people's different sense of personal space – that's how close you stand to the person you're talking to. In Linear-active and Reactive cultures people stand further away from each other. In Multi-active cultures they stand much closer. So, for example, when a Brazilian and a Finn are in conversation together, the Brazilian moves closer but the Finn moves further away. Each is trying to find the personal space that is normal for them. And when they communicate, people in Multi-active cultures use a lot of gestures. In Linear-active cultures they use some, but in Reactive cultures almost no gestures at all.

8.6

D=Duncan, M=Monique

D Hello. Duncan Ross.

M Hello, Duncan. It's Monique Bresson. My secretary said you called.

D Yes. Thank you for calling back. I wanted to make sure you've received the invitation.

M Yes, I have. Thank you. I'd be delighted to accept.

D Good. Er … Monique, some friends of mine are going to stay at Glencross for a few days after the celebration, and I'd like to invite you to stay, too. Would you join us for four or five days?

M Oh, I'd love to, Duncan, but I'm afraid I can't. I've already arranged to go to Brussels on the 18th …

D Well, would you like to stay until the 17th? I'm sure you need a break from your busy schedule. You work too much, Monique!

M You're right. Thank you, Duncan, I'd love to stay until the 17th.

8.7

J=James, D=Duncan

J Hello.

D Hello, James, it's Duncan. How's everything? I hope you're ready for the big event at Glencross!

J Not yet, but there's still time.

D James, some friends are going to stay at Glencross for a few days after the celebration. How about joining us?

J Thanks a lot, Duncan, but I'm going to be very busy during that week.

D Ah, that's a pity. Monique Bresson is going to stay and I know you enjoy her company.

J Is she really? Then let me think about it, Duncan. Perhaps I can manage to change a few appointments …

Unit 9

9.1

I=Interviewer, O=Oliver Gore

I Oliver, you've written a lot of books about the business world including several best-sellers. Your latest book, called *For Over a Century*, will be in the bookshops next week. Can you tell us what it's about?

O Yes, it's about companies that have been doing business for more than 100 years, and in some cases much longer than that.

I Does that make them the oldest companies in the world?

O Some of them certainly are. Some of the oldest companies in the world are family businesses and you find that the same family has been running the business since it started. For example, some wine producers in countries like France, Italy, and Spain have had the same vineyards for hundreds of years. The oldest wine business in France, the Château de Goulaine, has been in the same family since the year 1000, and Barone Ricasoli in Italy has been producing wine for more than 850 years. Some famous banks, too, have been in the same family for generations, although this isn't true of the world's oldest bank.

I Which bank is that?

O An Italian bank called Banca dei Paschi di Siena that's been in the banking business since 1472, when it was founded in Siena. But it is true of another Italian company, Beretta, which makes guns for police forces such as the Italian Carabinieri and the French Gendarmerie – and for James Bond and other Hollywood stars, of course!

I How long has Beretta been making guns?

O It was founded in 1526 so the Beretta family has been making guns for nearly 500 years.

I That's quite something!

O Sure is. Another company with a long history, but not a family business, is the French company, Saint-Gobain, which is today the world's biggest manufacturer of glass and building materials. Its first project was the glass for the famous Hall of Mirrors in Versailles in 1665, at a time when mirrors were more valuable than paintings by great artists. It's been making glass since then and has developed hundreds of products in its long history, including more recently the glass for the Louvre Pyramid in Paris and an incredibly strong glass for the windscreens of one of the fastest trains in the world, the Japanese Shinkansen.

I Well, thank you, Oliver. Unfortunately we don't have time to hear about more of the companies in your book, but we'll look forward to reading about them and hope this book will be another best-seller for you …

9.2

a employer
b industry
c development

9.3

Stress pattern a
develop, producer, investment, consumption
Stress pattern b
management, company, government
Stress pattern c
industrial, economy, competitor

9.4

D=Duncan, C=Carol, Duncan's secretary

D Oh, Carol, can you come into my office? It's about my trip to France.

C Yes, of course. So, you have meetings in Paris on Monday and Tuesday.

D Yes. I'll be in Scotland at Glencross the week before, so could you book me a flight from Edinburgh to Paris, on Sunday afternoon or evening if possible?

C Right. Shall I book a hotel in Paris?

D Yes, please, for three nights. Then on Wednesday I want to travel to Bordeaux, either by plane or by train.

C Would you like me to get some information on both?

D Thank you, I'd appreciate that. I need to be in Bordeaux by about 1 p.m. I think the TGV is probably best. Would you mind checking arrival times of the TGV and flights?

C No, of course not.

D Right, thanks very much, Carol. That's all for the moment. I'm not sure about the trip back yet, but we can arrange that later.

9.5

D=Duncan, C=Carol

D Carol, I'd like to give you the other details about my trip to France.

C Yes, fine.

D Right. I need to be back in London on the Friday evening. Do you think you could check the times of direct flights from Bordeaux?

C Yes, certainly. What about accommodation? Do you want me to book you a hotel in Bordeaux?

D Thanks, but that won't be necessary. I'm going to stay with some friends. They've got a little château and some vineyards, and they produce some very good wine.

C Mm, it sounds a lot more enjoyable than a hotel.

D Yes, I think it will be.

Unit 10

10.1

a will
b wheel

10.2

1 Are you going to leave?
2 Where do you live?
3 Do sit down.
4 Do take a seat.
5 Would you like some chips?
6 That restaurant is very cheap.
7 Shall I fill your glass?
8 Do you feel better?

10.3

1 Is this your key?
2 We invited thirty people.
3 Did you have a good trip?
4 Is it time to eat?
5 Did you sleep well?
6 He was very ill.

10.4

E=Eddie, A=Alma, T=Tonia

E According to this newspaper report we've got a 50% chance of living to be 100. It seems incredible, doesn't it? I'm not sure I want to live to be 100. Do you, Alma?

A Well, if I'm healthy and enjoying life, why not? People are living much longer today. And it's what you'd expect because we've got better health care, and we know more about what we should do to stay healthy. I'm sure that 50 years from now there'll be a lot more people living to be 100 because life expectancy is increasing with each generation. What do you think, Tonia?

T I agree, and yes, it's a good thing that so many older people are healthier and more active today – but unfortunately we won't all be wonderfully healthy and active at 90. Most of us will need more help and medical care as we get older, and the cost of providing this will increase as more of us live longer. I think that'll be a big problem for governments in future. I don't know what you think, Eddie?

E Yes, it'll certainly be a problem. And as well as the cost of medical care, there's the cost of paying pensions. I think the biggest problem will be in developed countries. I read an article the other day which said that in 50 years' time, for the first time in history, there'll be more old people than children in the developed countries of the world.
That means the working population will be smaller so there'll be fewer people to pay the pensions of all the retired people. Today there are four workers for every pensioner – by 2050 there'll only be two.

A So we'll all have to work longer?

E Yes, I'm sure we will. Most likely until we're 70 or more. And I don't think there'll be a fixed retirement age. If you want to work until 75, the government won't stop you.

T Mm, I can't say I like that idea.

E Nor do I, but if you think about it the retirement age has stayed the same for 50 years, but our life expectancy hasn't. It's gone up quite a lot – so you can see why governments want to change it.

T Yes. I can also see that we'll need to live longer and be healthier and more active because we'll still have to get up and go to work in our seventies!

10.5

R=Reservations clerk, British Airways, C=Carol

R British Airways reservations. How can I help you?

C I'd like some information about flights from Edinburgh to Paris, on a Sunday afternoon, please.

R Certainly. Let me check. … OK. There's one flight at 14.45, and two later flights at 16.00 and 18.00 hours. They all involve a transfer at Heathrow.

C What time does the first flight arrive?

R At 18.45.

C Could you repeat that, please?

R It arrives at 18.45.

C And when do the later flights arrive?

R The 16.00 gets in at 20.50, and the 18.00 at 23.05.

C Right, I've got that. Could you tell me the times of flights from Bordeaux to London, travelling on a Friday?

R One moment, please. … Right, there's just one British Airways flight daily, leaving at 14.40 and arriving at Gatwick at 15.10.

C Do you know if Air France flies from Bordeaux to London?

R I'm afraid I don't have any information about Air France flights. I can give you their telephone number.

C No, don't worry, I think the 14.40 flight will be fine. Thank you for your help. I'll get back to you later to book the flights.

10.6

R=Reservations clerk, French Railways, C=Carol

R Good afternoon, French Railways.

C Good afternoon. I'd like to know the times of trains from Paris to Bordeaux.

R Um … Can you tell me when you want to travel?

C Yes, on a Wednesday, arriving in Bordeaux by about 1 p.m.

R There is a TGV which arrives in Bordeaux at exactly 1 p.m.

C Oh, good. Could you tell me when it leaves Paris?

R Yes, it leaves at 10 a.m.

C So the journey takes three hours?

R Yes, that's right.

C And do you know which station it leaves from?

R Yes, from Paris Montparnasse.

C Thank you. Oh, just one more question. Do I need to make a reservation?

R Yes, it's advisable.

C OK. I'll check with my boss, then phone you back. Thank you for your help.

R You're welcome.

Unit 11

11.1

C=Chairman, A=Member of audience, J=John, S=Susanna, D=David, K=Kate, N=Nick

C Welcome to tonight's discussion programme, *Ask the panel*. As usual our panel is here to answer questions from the audience. So let's have our first question, please.

A If members of the panel were responsible for transport in towns and cities, what would they do to reduce the problem of traffic congestion and pollution?

C John, would you like to begin?

J Well, I think the problem is so bad in big cities that the only solution is to follow the example of places like Singapore and introduce a system of charges. I'm sure that if we charged motorists for driving in city centres, we'd reduce traffic congestion. It would be very unpopular, of course, and it certainly wouldn't solve the problem completely, but

I think it would make a big difference. Then we could use the money to improve our public transport system, as Singapore and other cities have done.

C Susanna?

S I think the only way to reduce traffic congestion in our cities is to have a good public transport system. People use their cars because they just don't have a choice – our public transport is expensive, inefficient, and overcrowded, and takes longer than using your car. If we had a really good public transport system, people would use it. Just look at the cities that do have good systems – they're the ones that don't have all the traffic jams!

C David, what do you think?

D I agree with Susanna about public transport. But there are other ways we can reduce the number of cars in cities. For example, encouraging people to use bicycles. Most journeys in town centres are very short, just a few kilometres. We'd have less congestion if more people used bikes for short journeys. You'd need special cycle lanes, though, to make cycling safer, but if cycling was safer, more people would travel that way, I'm sure.

C Are you in favour of bikes, Kate?

K Well, bikes aren't much good when it rains. If I were responsible for transport, I'd ban private cars from city centres and have lots of free car parks outside the centre. If we did that, and had a good bus service from the car parks to the centre, we'd have less traffic in cities and we'd all get around faster.

C Nick?

N You'd be surprised how many of the people who live in the same area travel the same route to work every day, but they all travel in their own car. Most of the cars on our roads have only one person in them. If more people travelled in the same car, there'd be a lot less traffic. Companies could do a lot to help, too. If they organized car-sharing schemes, people from different companies could join in. That way everyone would save money, and maybe they'd make new friends, too.

C Right, so quite a few ideas from our panel there. Can we have our next question, please? . . .

11.2

a If they don't reply soon, we'll send another letter.
b I wouldn't accept the offer if I were you.

11.3

1 If she's late, she'll miss the plane.
2 I'd drive to work if I had a car.
3 If you come tomorrow, I'll meet you at the airport.
4 We'd have fewer problems if we changed the system.
5 We won't find a solution if we don't do something quickly.
6 If they don't get here before six o'clock, I won't see them.
7 They wouldn't leave the company if there wasn't a problem.
8 She wouldn't work if she didn't need the money.

11.4

P=Presenter, M=Markus

P Good evening and welcome to *Working Week*. In an earlier programme in this series, Markus reported on the best companies to work for. In this programme, he's going to tell us about the results of the latest survey on the best cities to live in. Markus, which cities are the winners in this survey?

M Well, first I should explain that the survey looks at a lot of different categories to decide which cities offer the best quality of life. These include areas like public transport, traffic problems, pollution, and crime. It also includes the political and economic situation, schools and education, and health care. And the things we enjoy – restaurants,

cultural facilities like theatres, cinemas, and music, and sports and leisure facilities.

P How many cities does the survey cover?

M Altogether, 215 cities, in all five continents.

P Quite a lot. So, based on all those factors, which cities come top of the list?

M For overall best quality of life there are two cities at the top – Vancouver and Zürich, followed by Vienna. Then three other cities are very close to Vienna – they're Copenhagen, Geneva, and Sydney.

P So of the top six cities in the list, four are in Europe?

M Right.

P What about cities like Paris and London?

M Paris and London are both lower down the list. Paris comes thirty-third and London fortieth. In the same survey a year ago they were both higher. I think the main reason they've gone down is because crime has increased in both cities. If a city does well in most categories but badly in one or two areas, that puts it further down the list. The USA, for example, has twelve cities in the top fifty. They do well in many areas – political and economic situation, health care, sport and leisure facilities, and so on, but they have more crime so they come lower down.

P Which other cities do well in the 'best quality of life' category?

M Well, in Central Europe, Prague, Budapest, and Warsaw are at the top for best quality of life – they were also at the top last year. In Latin America, Buenos Aires and Montevideo are the winners, and in Asia, Tokyo comes first, followed by Yokohama.

P Which cities offer the best choice of restaurants and cultural and leisure facilities?

M Not surprisingly this is where Paris and London do well – in fact they come right at the top here, together with Sydney and three cities in the USA – New York, Los Angeles, and Washington DC.

P Right, well, thank you for that Markus. And let's hope not all our listeners are going to get on the next plane to Vancouver or Zürich! Now it's time to move on to our round-up of this week's business stories from around the world . . .

11.5

1 I'm sorry. I didn't catch your name.
2 How about a drink?
3 You're from Spain, aren't you?
4 Sorry I'm late.
5 Can I get you something to eat?
6 We've got a lot of problems at the moment.
7 Thanks very much for your help.
8 Have a good weekend.

11.6

1 I'm sorry. I didn't catch your name.
  It's Simon. Simon Grant.
2 How about a drink?
  Not at the moment, thanks.
3 You're from Spain, aren't you?
  Yes, that's right.
4 Sorry I'm late.
  Don't worry.
5 Can I get you something to eat?
  Thank you. That would be very nice.
6 We've got a lot of problems at the moment.
  Oh, I'm sorry to hear that.
7 Thanks very much for your help.
  Not at all.
8 Have a good weekend.
  Thanks. The same to you.

11.7

1 May I use your phone?
2 Have a good holiday.
3 Could I ask you something?
4 I'm sorry, I've got the wrong number.
5 Thanks for the lovely flowers.
6 Someone stole my car last night.
7 Do you mind if I join you?
8 I'm getting married tomorrow.

11.8

1 May I use your phone?
   Yes, of course.
2 Have a good holiday.
   Thanks. You, too.
3 Could I ask you something?
   Yes, go ahead.
4 I'm sorry, I've got the wrong number.
   Don't worry.
5 Thanks for the lovely flowers.
   Don't mention it.
6 Someone stole my car last night.
   I'm sorry to hear that.
7 Do you mind if I join you?
   Not at all.
8 I'm getting married tomorrow.
   Congratulations.

Unit 12

12.1

a Were any products exported in April?
b How are the engines assembled?
c Two hundred engines have been imported.

12.2

1 Cork is produced in Portugal.
2 Many cork products are exported abroad.
3 Champagne was invented in the 18th century.
4 Experts are worried about increasing sales of plastic stoppers.
5 A lot of money has been spent on improving quality.
6 Cork is used for insulation in rocket engines.

12.3

Report 1

A British company reports that its profits have increased by 200% since it introduced a new policy of being nice to its staff. When they arrive at work every morning, staff get a hug from the boss. Music is played in the office and no one works on their birthday. Every two weeks there are social activities where everyone gets together. The new policy has been welcomed by the staff. They think a hug from the boss is an excellent way to start the day and say everyone is more relaxed and friendly, and their company has become a great place to work.

Report 2

Forty-seven university graduates who were given jobs by two UK companies have now been offered €15,000 to spend a year travelling round the world before they start work. The graduates were offered jobs before the two companies agreed to join together and become one company. The new company now finds it has more staff than it needs, but it wants to keep the graduates because it believes it will need more people in a year's time. So far, the offer has been accepted by five of the forty-seven graduates and the company hopes it will be accepted by two more.

12.4

Report A

For the first time, goats have been used to help reduce the risk of fires in San Francisco, California. Four hundred goats have been put in areas where machines can't be used and where the dry grass easily catches fire in hot weather. The company that rents out the goats says they offer a better solution than other methods. Business has doubled in the last five years, and the company is having problems finding enough goats for all its customers.

Report B

Australia has started selling camels to Saudi Arabia. So far 120 camels have been sold and the trade is expected to grow to about 5,000 a year. Camels were first introduced into Australia from the Canary Islands in 1840 and this number has grown to about 400,000 today. The camels have been bought by a Saudi Arabian client.

12.5

P=Pierre, D=Duncan, A=Anne-Marie, M=Monique, J=James
Dialogue 1

P Duncan, we really must leave now or we'll miss our plane back to Bordeaux. Thank you for inviting us, we've had a wonderful time.
D I'm glad you enjoyed it. And thank you for inviting me to stay with you. I'm really looking forward to it.
A And so are we. Goodbye, Duncan. See you next week in Bordeaux.
D Goodbye, Anne-Marie, Pierre. Have a good flight.

Dialogue 2

M Duncan, thank you very much for your hospitality. I really appreciated it.
D Well, I'm very pleased you agreed to stay a few more days. You must come and stay whenever you like.
M Thank you, I promise I will. So, goodbye, Duncan. See you in London on the 22nd.
D Yes, I'll ring you next week to fix the time. Goodbye, Monique.

Dialogue 3

D Well, James, thanks for all your help organizing the *Wine & Dine* celebration, and congratulations – everybody was very impressed by your book. I think you should write another one!
J Yes, I'll think about it. Er, Duncan, you're meeting Monique in London on the 22nd?
D Yes, to discuss the French edition of *Wine & Dine*. Monique has agreed to do all the translation work.
J Oh, good. I thought ... well ...
D Don't worry, James, it's strictly business. Although I must say Monique's a very attractive and interesting person!
J Yes, I know, that's the problem. Well, I must be off. I'm driving Monique to the airport. Thanks a lot, Duncan. Everything was great.
D Bye, James, and don't forget to think about that second book, not just your social life! Bye, James. Bye, Monique.

Answer key

Unit 1
Language focus p.6

2 (Possible answers)
Roberto is a wine consultant. He works in Florence.
His telephone number is 055 53 75 866.
Bresson Translation Services has offices in London, Paris, and Rome.
James is a wine journalist.
He works in London.
His office is in Honeywell Street.

3
1 No, he doesn't.
2 How do you do? How do you do?
3 She is with the Vinexpo translation service, to translate for a group of Italian wine producers.
4 What do you do?
5 Because he has a job for her.
6 At 7 o'clock that evening.

4
1 interviews people
2 two or three times a year
3 London

- Use the Present Simple to talk about long-term situations and routine activities.
- To make the question, use *do* + *I/you/we/they* + infinitive.
- The positive form always ends in *-s*.
- To make the negative, use *does* + *not* (*doesn't*) + infinitive.
- To make the question, use *does* + *he/she/it* + infinitive.

Practice p.7

1
1 writes
2 doesn't import
3 meet
4 doesn't live
5 don't speak
6 travels

2
1 Who?
2 (blank)
3 Which?
4 When?
5 Where?
6 How often?

3
1 Where do they live?
2 How often does he go there?
3 Where do they meet?
4 When does she visit them?
5 Who do they meet at Vinexpo?
6 What does he write about?

Pronunciation p.8
2 1 a 2 b 3 a 4 b 5 a 6 b 7 b 8 a 9 b 10 b

4
1 Does Monique speak Italian? Yes, she does.
2 Where does she work? In London, Paris, and Rome.
3 Do James and Roberto write about wine? Yes, they do.
4 Does James work for *Wine & Dine*? Yes, he does.
5 Does Roberto know Monique? Yes, he does.
6 Does James live in Italy? No, he doesn't.
7 Does he love his work? Yes, he does.
8 Does James go to France and Italy? Yes. Two or three times a year.
9 Where do Monique's parents live? Near Dijon.
10 Does she travel to Paris? Yes, she does.

5

Group A (Possible questions)	Group B (Possible questions)
Which magazine is the letter from?	Why is Monique at Vinexpo?
What does James do?	Which stand is she on?
Does he often travel in Europe?	Does she live in Paris?
Who does he interview?	Does she know a lot about the wine business? Why?
What are his hobbies/interests?	Where do her parents live?
Which sports does he play?	Where is her father from?
Does he enjoy cooking?	What are her hobbies/interests?

- We write words like *always/usually/never* after the verb *to be* but before other verbs.

Wordpower p.10
Organizing vocabulary

1 1 (Possible answers)
Work   office, salary, meeting
Jobs   manager, doctor, sales person
Family   children, uncle, grandmother

2 (Possible answers)
to make   a mistake, an appointment, a decision
to have   a holiday, an English lesson, a party

3 **at**   10 a.m., midday
in   2001, the afternoon
on   Tuesday morning, 5 July

2 (Possible answers)

travel	activities
car	swimming
train	skiing
plane	walking

3 send an email, meet a visitor, make a business trip, do a job, attend a meeting

4 cheap – expensive, cold – hot, difficult – easy, tall – short, sad – happy, hard-working – lazy

---

Skills focus p.12
2 3 Spanish 5 Arabic 8 Russian 9 Japanese 10 German
3 1 726 m 2 377m 4 182m 6 165m 7 162m
4 a eighty per cent
b sixty-nine per cent
c two billion
d one point one billion
e (a) half
f three-quarters
5 1 1.1bn 2 ³/₄ 3 80% 4 ½ 5 69% 6 2bn
7 **Food and drink**   hamburger, chicken, beer, juice
Communication   radio, television, fax, email

Focus on functions p.13
1
1 Usually, people in Britain only shake hands when they meet for the first time, or when they meet again after a long time.
2 I'm sorry, I didn't hear your name.
Could you repeat that/say that again, please?
3 *Good morning/Good afternoon/Good evening* are greetings.
We say *Good night* to say goodbye/end a conversation at night.

2
1 Excuse me, are you ...?
May I introduce myself?
I'm ...
How do you do?
3 Let me introduce you to ...
I'd like to introduce you to ...
Pleased to meet you.
2 How are you?

3
1 Excuse me, are you ...? May I introduce myself? I'm ... How do you do?
2 Nice to see you again. How are you? How's the family?
3 I'd like to introduce you to ... Pleased to meet you.

4 Pleased to meet you. Pleased to meet you, too.
How do you do? How do you do?
Please call me James. Then you must call me Luigi.
How's life? Not too bad, but very busy.
Hello, are you Roberto? Yes, that's right.

5 I must go now.
It was very nice meeting you.
I look forward to seeing you.
I really enjoyed meeting you, too.
Have a good trip back.
Thank you, and the same to you.

Unit 2
Language focus p.14
1 **Extract 1**   Operations Director, Barcelona
Extract 2   Paris
Extract 3   Sales Manager, Tokyo

2 José Manuel emails, phone calls, international meetings
Geneviève talking to foreign visitors, phone calls, emails
Kensuke visits to company head office in Sweden, meetings in Japan

4 Extract 1
1 It's changing it, from three centres to one big centre.
2 To find the best system to use in the new centre.

Extract 2
1 It's expanding very quickly.
2 That it has got its own TV channel.

Extract 3
1 Sales are decreasing.
2 Sales are going up.

5 All the questions in **4** refer to current activities.

- Use the Present Simple to talk about regular activities.
- Use the Present Continuous to talk about current activities.
- To make the Present Continuous, use *am/is/are* + *ing* form of the verb.

Pronunciation p.15
2 2 a 3 b 4 a 5 a 6 b
4 We pronounce it as the strong form.

Practice p.16

1 Student A
a How many children does José Manuel Faria have?
b What language does he speak at home?
c What work does his wife do?
d Where does he spend most of his work time?
e How often does he travel to Bilbao?
f Why does he go to Bilbao?
g Does he like living in Barcelona?
h What does he enjoy doing in his free time?

Student B
a Where does Kensuke Matsumura work?
b Does he live in Tokyo?
c How long does his journey to work take?
d How many hours a day does he work?
e How much time does he spend on phone calls and emails?
f What does he do to relax?
g What does he do once a month?
h How many weeks' holiday a year does he have?

3 1 starts 4 produces 7 doesn't have 10 am recording
2 finishes 5 sells 8 is working 11 is
3 works 6 work 9 is writing 12 don't forget

Wordpower p.18

1 do some work, a job, an exam
make a phone call, a decision, a business trip
have a meeting, a holiday, a discussion
work full-time, part-time, flexitime

2 2 unemployed, out of work 6 on maternity leave, on paternity leave
3 self-employed
4 retired, a pensioner 7 on strike
5 on sick leave

Skills focus p.20

1 1 cooker 4 lawnmower 6 freezer
2 vacuum cleaner 5 washing machine 7 dishwasher
3 refrigerator

2 Nationality Swedish
Head office Stockholm
Started 1921
World's first vacuum cleaner 1921
First fridge 1925
Employs 81,971 people
Sells its products in more than 150 countries
Worldwide turnover €14,552 million
Consumer Durables 75% of sales

Focus on functions p.22

1 Message for Monique Bresson
Caller's name James Turner
Company *Wine & Dine* magazine
Number 020 7331 8582
Please call ✓

2 Could I speak to Monique Bresson, please?
Who's calling, please?
Hold the line, please.
I'm sorry, she's in a meeting.
Can I take a message?
Could you ask her to call me?

4 1 speak 2 calling, please 3 It's 4 the line

5 1 b 2 b 3 a 4 b

6 /eɪ/ (as in *say*): a, h, j, k
/iː/ (as in *she*): e, b, c, d, g, p, t, v
/e/ (as in *ten*): f, l, m, n, s, x, z
/aɪ/ (as in *fly*): i, y
/əʊ/ (as in *go*): o
/ɑː/ (as in *bar*): r
/uː/ (as in *who*): u, q, w

Unit 3
Language focus p.24

2 1 three 3 £43 million 5 100
2 £86 million 4 1998 6 a million

3 (Possible answers)
1 They wanted to bring more visitors to the area and create more jobs.
2 From newspapers and TV.
3 No, they didn't. It was the best thing that happened.
4 The fact that they had a wonderful team of people, who worked incredibly hard to make it a success.

4 All the verbs refer to finished actions or situations in the past.

- To make the Past Simple of regular verbs, add *-ed* to the end of the verb.
- To make the negative, use *did not* or *didn't* + infinitive.
- To make the question, use *did* + subject + infinitive.
- To make short answers use *did* (positive) and *didn't* (negative).

Practice p.25

1 become/became, begin/began, come/came, cost/cost, do/did, find/found, get/got, give/gave, have/had, make/made, think/thought

---

Pronunciation p.25
2 started /ɪd/, worked /t/, wanted /ɪd/, rained /d/, increased /t/, expected /ɪd/, watched /t/, received /d/, needed /ɪd/
4 We pronounce the *-ed* ending as /ɪd/.

---

2 1 worked 4 went 7 studied 10 didn't earn 13 had
2 lived 5 hated 8 got 11 began 14 moved
3 didn't live 6 became 9 loved 12 started 15 brought

Wordpower p.28

2 play football, tennis, volleyball
do yoga, exercises, weight training
go sailing, skiing, windsurfing

5 go to a restaurant, a concert, the theatre, the cinema, a nightclub
watch TV, a video
play music, a computer game, chess, a musical instrument, cards
listen to the radio, a concert, music
read books, magazines, newspapers

Skills focus p.29

2 1 c 2 d 3 e 4 b 5 f 6 a

❸ Debra Veal
age 27
travelled in a rowing boat
left Tenerife on 7 October 2001
arrived in Barbados on 26 January 2002
length of journey 4,768km
number of days 113
problems – hurricanes, sharks, loneliness

❹ (Possible answers)
1 the time the Veals trained for the race
2 the time after which Andy began to have panic attacks
3 Andy's experience as a rower
4 the time Debra started rowing every morning
5 when Debra woke in the night to check for supertankers
6 a wave
7 the telephone bill

❼ Polly Vacher
age 57
travelled in a one-engine aeroplane
left Birmingham Airport on 12 January 2002
arrived at Birmingham Airport on 17 May 2002
length of journey 46,670km
number of days 124
problems – tropical thunderstorms, engine problems, ran out of fuel

❽ (Possible answers)
Similarities
Both their journeys took over 100 days.
They both had frightening experiences on their journeys.
Both journeys were great personal challenges.
Differences
Polly is 30 years older than Debra.
Polly's journey was 11 days longer.
Polly's journey raised money for charity.

Focus on functions p.31
❶ 1 Wayne Brown   2 to take a seat
❸ Did you have any problems finding us?
How was your flight?
❹ 1 He came to San Francisco as a student, and discovered Californian wines.
2 He got a job with a wine merchant, then wrote an article for a wine magazine.
❺ 1, 3, 4, and 5 are important to make a good conversation.
❻ James and Wayne do all these things, so their conversation is a good model.

Unit 4
Language focus p.32
❶ 1 Cross-cultural training.
2 Videos, online self-access courses, country briefings, and *Cross-culture Journal*.
3 Mark Grady, Jan Kirsten, and Vana Bell.
❸ 1 Vana   3 Jan   5 Vana   7 Mark
2 2.00 – 3.30   4 4.00 – 5.30   6 5.30 – 6.30
❹ (Possible answers)
1 No, they aren't.
2 Their training videos and online courses.
3 Talk to people about their company's needs and discuss what training they can do for them.

- Use the Present Continuous for fixed future arrangements.
- Use *going to* + infinitive for future plans, intentions, and decisions.

Practice p.33
❶ 2 is spending/'s spending   5 are having
3 is going/'s going   6 is arriving/'s arriving
4 is flying/'s flying   7 are coming
❷ 2 is he interviewing   4 is he preparing   6 is he eating
3 is he having   5 is he getting   7 is he playing

Wordpower p.36
❶ 1 A *double room* has a double bed, a *twin room* has two single beds.
2 You sit or lie in a *bath* but stand under a *shower*.
3 A *suitcase* is one item of luggage and is a count noun. *Luggage* usually refers to several bags/suitcases and is a mass noun.
4 *Half-board* is bed, breakfast, and evening meal, *full-board is* bed, breakfast, lunch, and dinner.
5 A *keycard* is like a credit card, you put it into a slot to open the door.
6 A *bill* shows the amount you have to pay. A *receipt* shows you have paid.
7 *lift* = British English, *elevator* = American English
❷ 1 car park   5 fitness room   8 safe
2 restaurant   6 hairdryer   9 conference facilities
3 lounge   7 air-conditioning   10 swimming pool
4 cocktail bar
❸ **Hotel facilities** restaurant, cocktail bar, lounge, sauna, fitness room, car park, business centre
Guest rooms satellite TV, multi-line phone, computer and fax point, air-conditioning, minibar, 24-hour room service, hairdryer
❺ (Possible answers)
1 in a guest room   4 and 5 hanging on the door of a guest room
2 over a door   6 and 7 by a phone in a guest room
3 by a fire alarm

Skills focus p.37
❷ 1   British English   American English
a 11 April 2003   November 4 2003
b 12 August 2002   December 8 2002
c 3 May 2004   March 5 2004
2 b is correct
3 a for a single woman or girl
b for a single or married woman
c for a married woman
4 a information   c For the attention of   e enclosures
b numbers   d as soon as possible
5 a iii   b iv   c i   d ii
❸ 1 C   2 D   3 B   4 A
❹ 1 Following, Thanks for   6 Unfortunately
2 This letter is, This email is   7 Sorry
3 Could you please, Would you please   8 Let me know, Hoping, See you
4 I attach
❺ E
1 Thank you for   2 I enclose   3 Please contact me again
F
1 Thank you for   3 I am pleased
2 I apologize for   4 I look forward to
G
1 Thanks for   2 sorry   3 Could you please

Focus on functions p.40
❶ 1 To book another room for a colleague for 4 April.
2 The hotel is fully booked for 4 April.
❷ 1 single room   3 what a pity
2 I'm very sorry   4 Thank you for your help
❸ I have a reservation.
Could you fill in this form, please, and sign here?
Here's your key.
The porter will take your luggage.
Could I have an early morning call, at 6.30?
Do you need anything else?
❹ 1 False   2 True
❺ 1 Could I have   3 that's fine   5 very much
2 Can I pay   4 you enjoyed

Review unit A

❷ meet foreign visitors at work
make business trips
speak English on the phone
attend international meetings
write emails in English
work flexitime
go to work by car

❸ 1 They often travel on business.
2 At present our business is doing very well.
3 He has meetings with customers every week.
4 They are always early for work.
5 How often do you visit them?
6 She's talking to some clients right now.
7 When do you usually finish work?
8 I have five weeks' holiday every year.
9 He's studying for an exam at the moment.
10 Do you always travel to work by car?

❹ 1 became 3 brought 5 found 7 gave 9 said
2 began 4 cost 6 flew 8 grew 10 thought

❺ 1 comes 3 works 5 spent 7 is staying 9 wrote
2 lives 4 decided 6 moved 8 is renting 10 is working

❻ 1 Where did you go? 5 How many meetings did you attend?
2 How long were you there?
3 Where did you stay? 6 When did you get back?
4 Who did you meet?

❿ (Possible answers)
1 Could I speak to 5 isn't here
2 's calling 6 take a message
3 This is 7 Could you ask him
4 the line 8 I'll give him your message

Unit 5

Language focus p.46

❷ 1 (Possible answers)
a Make sure you get some regular breaks.
b Take some long, slow breaths; do lots of physical exercise; get some relaxation.
c A lot of alcohol and coffee is bad for you; a little wine, and fruit and vegetables are good; a diet without cheese or butter is healthier.
d Try and get seven or eight hours' sleep each night.
e Find time to relax.

Mass and count nouns
Mass alcohol, coffee, butter, research, energy
Count office, sandwich, parks, vegetables, holiday

- Count nouns have a singular and plural form. We can count them.
- Mass nouns do not have a plural form. We cannot count them.

some/any, a lot of/lots of, much/many, a little/a few

	any	a lot of/ lots of	much	many	a little	a few
count nouns	✓	✓		✓		✓
mass nouns	✓	✓	✓		✓	
positive sentences		✓		✓	✓	✓
negative sentences	✓		✓		✓	
questions	✓	✓	✓	✓		

Practice p.49

❶ 1 A any B a little, some 3 A some B a little
2 A any B a few 4 A some B a few, some

❷ traffic M, money M, information M, business trip C, meeting C, article C, news M, advice M

❸ 1 B much, many
2 A much B a lot of/lots of
3 A many, much
4 A many B much
5 A much B a lot of/lots of

Pronunciation p.50
2 2 a 3 c 4 b 5 a 6 b
4 1 a 2 c 3 a 4 b 5 a 6 c

Wordpower p.51

❶ **Meat** lamb, pork, chicken
Fish/Seafood prawns, salmon, Dover sole
Vegetables cucumber, red cabbage, onions, potatoes, courgettes, aubergines
Fruit lemon, pears, strawberries, grapes, peaches, cherries

❹ 1 grilled 2 roast 3 boiled 4 fried

Skills focus p.52

❶ (Possible answers)
1 It began in 1986. An Italian food writer started the movement in protest at the opening of McDonald's in the Piazza di Spagna in Rome.
2 No, only cities with a maximum of 50,000 inhabitants.
3 The world's largest food and wine event, and the world's largest cheese festival.
4 Guides on Italian food, wine, and culture.

❹ a 2 b 4 c 1 d 3

Focus on functions p.54

❶ Duck and red cabbage, beef with red wine and onions, cold cucumber soup with prawns, lamb cutlets with roast potatoes, a bottle of Beaujolais.

❷ Monique (because she offers James more wine, dessert, coffee).

❸ (Possible answer)
Perhaps James wants to ask Monique out for dinner to celebrate her birthday.

❹ **Recommending** **Ordering**
What do you recommend? I'll have …
The … is usually excellent here. I'd like …
I recommend … **Declining**
Offering Thank you, but I couldn't eat any more.
Do have some more …
How about …? **Accepting**
Would you like…? Yes. That would be very nice.
Thanking and responding
Thank you for a lovely evening.
I'm glad you enjoyed it.

❺ (Possible answers)
1 do you recommend 8 how about
2 tuna and red pepper salad 9 I couldn't eat any more
3 what about beef in red wine 10 Are you
4 that would be nice 11 What about
5 what would you like 12 Yes, I'd like that
6 A bottle of Beaujolais 13 for a lovely evening
7 that would be very nice 14 I'm glad you enjoyed it, Steve

Unit 6

Language focus p.56

❷ (Possible answers)
1 Their biggest number of sales is online.
2 They don't use tickets.
3 They don't have as many flight attendants as traditional airlines.
4 They have just one type of aircraft.
5 Their turnaround time is only thirty minutes.
6 When they fly to a big city they normally fly to the airport that is farthest away.

❺ biggest, cheaper, cheapest, fewer, longest, lower, nearest, quicker, smaller, easier, crowded, efficient, expensive, furthest, less, more

One-syllable adjectives
- To make the superlative, add *-est* to the end of the adjective.

Two-syllable adjectives ending in *-y*
- To make the comparative, change the *-y* to *-i* and add *-er*.
- To make the superlative, change the *-y* to *-i* and add *-est*.

Other adjectives with two or more syllables
- To make the superlative, put *most* or *least* before the adjective.

Practice p.57

❶
2	lower	8	cheapest	14	longer
3	highest	9	earliest	15	easier
4	worst	10	latest	16	higher
5	most important	11	better	17	more complicated
6	more expensive	12	worse	18	highest
7	more crowded	13	more	19	most flexible

Pronunciation p.58

3 1 easier than   3 the same as   5 not as cheap as

2 a higher fare   4 much quicker than

---

❹
Travel by	Speaker 1	Speaker 2
train	to get to work	to get to work
underground	to get to to work	
car	holidays, going out in evening	
bus		
motorbike		holidays, to get to work
bike	weekends in summer	to go to local sports club, cycling with friends

❺ faster, more independent, longer, quicker, shorter, most enjoyable, more expensive, slowest

---

Wordpower p.59

❶ arrivals screen, landing card, customs, aisle seat, label, trolley, briefcase/hand luggage, overhead locker

❷ **Documents**   passport, ticket, landing card
Terminal   check-in desk, arrivals screen, information desk, passport control, duty-free shop, security check, customs
On board   window seat, safety instructions, flight attendant, seat-belt, aisle seat, overhead locker
Luggage   suitcase, trolley, label, briefcase, hand-luggage

❸ 1 C   2 C   3 P   4 C   5 P   6 P   7 C   8 P   9 P
❹ 1 c   2 d   3 a   4 b

Skills focus p.60

❸ (Possible answers)
1 unattractive
2 very large area
3 very large room which contains a turbine
4 area to show pictures, objects, etc. to the public
5 resemble each other

❹ (Possible answers)
1 Some people like them and others don't.
2 Both museums have got an enormous amount of space.
3 They're both on the banks of rivers.

Focus on functions p.62

❶ (Possible answer)
Duncan is writing to invite Monique to lunch to discuss business with her.

❷ lunch with Duncan Ross, Tuesday, 1.30 p.m. at the Riverside Restaurant

❸
Making an appointment	Saying 'yes'
When would be convenient for you?	Yes, Tuesday suits me fine.
Is next week possible for you?	Yes, that's fine.
Shall we say …?	I look forward to meeting
What time would suit you?	you …
How about …?	

❹ 1 She can't come to the meeting on Tuesday.
2 No, he has another appointment then.
3 Friday 18th

❺
Making an appointment	Saying 'yes'
When are you free?	Yes, I can make it on …
Is … possible for you?	See you on …
What about …?	Saying 'no'
Changing an appointment	No, I'm afraid I've got
I'm very sorry …	another appointment …
I'm afraid I can't manage our meeting on …	
Could we arrange another time?	

---

❻ (Possible answers)
1	Chris	6	What about
2	Andrew	7	that suits me fine
3	When would be convenient	8	Shall we say
4	How about	9	Yes, that's fine
5	I'm afraid I'm busy		

❽ (Possible answers)
1	Jan	7	are you free
2	speaking	8	Monday convenient
3	Armand	9	I'm afraid I've got another appointment then
4	I have to cancel our meeting on Saturday	10	Tuesday
5	arrange another time	11	that's fine
6	that's fine	12	See you on Tuesday at 9 a.m.

Unit 7

Language focus p.64

❷ 1 guarantees
2 deal
3 Third World, developing countries
4 benefit
5 developed countries

❸ (Possible answers)
1 A better deal.
2 Millions of farmers in 36 countries in the Third World.
3 The rich developed countries.

❹ 1 c   2 a   3 e   4 d   5 b

❻
1	1992	4	Canada	7	living	10	2001
2	1988	5	Japan	8	working	11	10
3	17	6	Hungary	9	50	12	20

1	a the Past Simple	b the Present Perfect Simple
2	a the Past Simple	b the Present Perfect Simple

Practice p.65

❷ 1 a   2 b   3 b   4 b   5 a
❸
1	has fallen	5	earned	8	has made
2	has increased	6	fell	9	has been
3	have not received	7	went down	10	have grown
4	have decreased				

Pronunciation p.66

1 They are stressed.
2 1 company, expanded   3 No, hasn't   5 sure, haven't
2 made, changes   4 prices, increased   6 think, have
3 They are stressed when they are at the end of a sentence.
They are not stressed in other positions in the sentence.
4 1 made, progress   4 think, have
2 sure, has   5 finished, work
3 hope, forgotten, meeting   6 started, yet

---

❹ **Student A**
a What has Fairtrade given people in the Third World?
b What have producers improved?
c What have they stopped using?
d How have communities used the social premium?
e What have Edgar and Blanca built?
f What have their children received?
g What has Edgar done all his life?
Student B
a Who did Edgar and Blanca work for?
b Did they earn a lot of money?
c What did they buy?
d What did they decide to grow?
e What did Edgar join?
f When did the price of coffee fall?
g Why was Edgar lucky?

Wordpower p.69

❶ 1 b   2 d   3 a   4 c
❷
Verb (infinitive)	Past Simple	Noun
go up	went up	–
improve	improved	an improvement
increase	increased	an increase
rise	rose	a rise
decrease	decreased	a decrease
fall	fell	a fall
go down	went down	–

③ 1 steadily   2 dramatically   3 slightly   4 sharply
④ 1 by   2 at   3 in   4 from, to   5 by   6 of, in

Skills focus p.70
❶ 2 c   3 b   4 i   5 f
❸ (Possible answers)
1 Everyone gets them, not just the people at the top.
2 No, it isn't a problem.
3 Two out of the 50 companies in the survey.
4 You don't find private offices and executive dining rooms.

Focus on functions p.72
❶ 1 The tenth anniversary of *Wine & Dine* magazine.
2 Because Scotland is too far for people to travel.
3 The publication of James's book on Italian wines.
4 He thinks it's a wonderful idea.

❷
Asking for opinions	Giving opinions
What do you think about ...?	In my opinion ...
What's your opinion of ...?	I think ...
How do you feel about ...?	**Agreeing**
	I agree.
	I certainly agree with that.

❸ 1 T   2 F   3 F   4 T
❹
Making suggestions	Accepting suggestions
I suggest ...	Yes, let's do that.
How about ...?	**Asking for suggestions**
Why don't we ...?	Do you have any suggestions for ...?
Why not ...?	**Rejecting suggestions**
We could ...	I'm not sure about that.

❺ I suggest we go skiing next weekend./go to a restaurant in the evening.
How about buying tickets for the music festival?/going away for a few days?
What about going away for a few days?/buying tickets for the music festival?
Why don't we invite some friends for dinner?/spend next Sunday in the country?
Why not spend next Sunday in the country?/invite some friends for dinner?
We could go to a restaurant in the evening./go skiing next weekend.

Unit 8
Language focus p.74
❷ 1 b   2 g   3 f   4 a   5 c   6 d   7 e
❸ Extract 1   Germany
Extract 2   Japan
Extract 3   Italy
❺ it's important to, should/shouldn't
(*have to* is used to describe necessity/obligation rather than advice.)

---

should/shouldn't
● Use *shouldn't* to say *it's a bad idea.*

have to/ don't have to
● Use *have to* to say *it's necessary or obligatory.*
● Use *don't have to* to say *it's not necessary or obligatory.*

may/might
● Use *may* to say *it's about 50% possible.*

Other examples of modals from book extracts in **❸**.

Extract 1	Extract 3
... you should focus on facts ...	People may be late ...
You should also prepare well ...	... their way of working may seem ...
... you shouldn't use first names ...	... they don't feel they have to ...
Extract 2	... you should dress well ...
... you should do the same	
... it may mean 'I understand' ...	
... it might be because ...	

Practice p.76
❶ 1 have to   3 may/might   5 shouldn't
2 don't have to   4 should

Wordpower p.78
❶
Adjective	Opposite adjective	Noun
efficient	inefficient	efficiency
honest	dishonest	honesty
polite	impolite	politeness
punctual	unpunctual	punctuality
reliable	unreliable	reliability

❸ 1 sociable   5 ambitious   8 creative
2 patient   6 organized   9 outgoing
3 hard-working   7 adaptable   10 sensitive
4 easy-going

❹
Adjective	Opposite adjective	Noun
ambitious	unambitious	ambition
organized	disorganized	organization
patient	impatient	patience
sensitive	insensitive	sensitivity

Skills focus p.80
❸
long pauses in conversation	R		L,M	no long pauses in conversation
a lot of eye contact	M	L	R	very little eye contact
stand close together	M		L, R	stand further away
use gestures a lot	M	L	R	use gestures very little

Focus on functions p.81
❶ 1 He invites Monique to stay at Glencross after the celebration.
2 She agrees to stay until the 17th.
❷ 1 Because he's going to be very busy.
2 Duncan tells him that Monique is going to stay.
❸
Inviting	Declining
I'd like to invite you to ...	I'd love to, but (*I'm afraid I can't*).
Would you join us ...?	Thanks a lot, but ...
Would you like to ...?	
How about ...?	
Accepting	
Thank you. I'd be delighted to accept.	
Thank you. I'd love to.	

Review unit B
❶ 3 Could you give me some information, please?
5 The news isn't very good.
7 Did she give you good advice? (any/some good advice – also correct)
8 How much money did you spend?
10 I didn't buy any coffee.
❸ 1 bigger, biggest   7 worse, worst
2 easier, easiest   8 farther/further, farthest/furthest
3 nearer, nearest   9 earlier, earliest
4 better, best   10 more crowded, most crowded
5 more efficient, most efficient   11 more flexible, most flexible
6 more, most   12 less, least
❹ 1 increased   5 have they visited   8 started
2 has improved   6 has grown   9 have gone up
3 did you finish   7 did you spend   10 have had
4 went
❺ **Student A**
1 Have you seen any good films this month?
2 Have you written any emails in English this week?
3 Have you had a holiday in the last six months?
4 Have you bought anything expensive recently?
Student B
1 Have you visited any interesting places recently?
2 Have you eaten any foreign food in the last two weeks?
3 Have you spoken English at work this week?
4 Have you done any sport in the last five days?

Unit 9

Language focus p.86

❸ 1 d 1000   2 c 850   3 a 1472   4 e 500   5 b 1665

❺ (Possible answers)
1 They are about the business world. Several are best-sellers.
2 They are family businesses.
3 He uses Beretta guns.
4 Saint-Gobain makes the glass for them.

Present Perfect Continuous
● Use the Present Perfect Continuous to focus on an activity which is not finished and the Present Perfect Simple to focus on the result or completion of an activity.

since and *for*
● Use *since* with a point of time and *for* with a period of time.

Practice p.87

❶ 1 since   3 since   5 for   7 since   9 since
    2 for   4 since   6 for   8 for   10 since

❷ 1 have been   4 have produced
    2 have you had   5 has the company been
    3 have been making

❸ (Possible answers)
1 What has Oliver Gore written?
2 How long has the oldest wine business in France been in the same family?
3 How long has Barone Ricasole been producing wine?
4 How long has Beretta been making guns?
5 What has Saint-Gobain done in its long history?

❹ 1 was founded   7 has built   13 cost
    2 builds   8 can order   14 was
    3 repairs   9 has been producing   15 has been
    4 has been doing   10 wanted   extending
    5 has created   11 grew   16 has established
    6 has included   12 made   17 has made

❺ Kongo Gumi
    a has created, has included, has built
    b has been doing
    Kodak
    a has established, has made
    b has been producing, has been extending

Wordpower p.90

❶ (Possible answers)
1 Because car makers are reducing prices.
2 Yes, because they're buying goods on credit.
3 No, there's a rise in employment.
4 It's good – the forecast is a 2% growth.
5 Because of a strike.
6 a invest   c industrialists   e strike   g wins
   b forecasts   d consumers   f industrialization

❷
Verb	Noun (activity, thing)	Noun (person)
develop	development	developer
employ	employment	employer
invest	investment	investor
manage	management	manager
compete	competition	competitor
consume	consumption	consumer
produce	product/production	producer
economize	economy/economics	economist
industrialize	industry/industrialization	industrialist

Pronunciation p.91
3 a develop, producer, investment, consumption
    b management, company, government
    c industrial, economy, competitor
5 consumer a   manager b
    customer b   production a
    economize c   employment a
    developer c   economist c

---

❸ consumer society/goods   developed countries
management skills/development   industrialized economy
free-market economy   industrial production
developing countries   mass production/market

Skills focus p.92

❷ What the article says
    1 T 2 F 3 F 4 T 5 F 6 F 7 T

❸ 1 investing in   5 afford
    2 labour force   6 joint ventures
    3 changed dramatically   7 impact
    4 shopping malls   8 the environment

❹ (Possible answers)
1 China's economy
2 China's market
3 the foreign investment China received in 2001
4 average income in China
5 the number of cars in China in 2002
6 global car makers that have set up joint ventures with Chinese car firms

Focus on functions p.94

❶ Book flight: Edinburgh – Paris on Sunday afternoon/evening
    Book hotel: Paris – three nights
    Get information about: plane and train to Bordeaux on Wednesday

❷ 1 By direct flight from Bordeaux.
    2 Because he's going to stay with some friends.

❸
Requesting	Agreeing
Can you ...?	Yes, of course.
Could you ...?	Yes, certainly.
Would you mind ... (+ -*ing*)?	No, of course not.
Do you think you could ...?	**Accepting**
Offering	Yes, please.
Shall I ...?	Thank you. I'd appreciate that.
Do you want me to ...?	**Declining**
Would you like me to ...?	Thanks, but that won't be necessary.

Unit 10

Language focus p.96

❷ 1 g 2 a 3 b 4 e 5 f 6 h 7 c 8 d

❸ 1 One planet is not enough   5 Water – a global crisis
    2 Hope for forests?   6 US puts economy first
    3 Wildlife habitats disappearing
    4 Global warming – real or imagined?

1st Conditional
● In a 1st Conditional sentence, use the Present Simple after *if* and *will* + infinitive to express the result.

if and *when*
● Use *if* to express a possibility and *when* to express a certainty.

Practice p.98

❶ 1 do   6 will have   11 happens   16 will not fight
    2 will see   7 will rise   12 will rise   17 do not have
    3 continue   8 are   13 will put   18 will fight
    4 will be   9 will lose   14 continues   19 will not survive
    5 will lose   10 will increase   15 will get

Pronunciation p.99
2 1 b 2 a 3 a 4 b 5 a 6 b 7 a 8 b
4 1 b 2 b 3 a 4 b 5 b 6 a

Wordpower p.101

❶ bin 20, chair 19, clock 2, coffee machine 4, computer 7, desk 11, desk lamp 10, filing cabinet 6, keyboard 12, lift 5, mouse 13, mouse mat 14, paper 8, pen 16, personal organizer 15, phone 17, photocopier 18, plant 3, printer 9, year planner 1

Skills focus p.102

❶ (Possible answers)
1 The life expectancy for a woman 100 years ago.
2 The life expectancy for a woman today.
3 The gift from the Japanese government to women as soon as they have a baby.
4 The average number of children that Japanese women have.
5 The fall in the working-age population in Italy by 2050.
6 The number of people over 65 by 2030.

❸ (Possible answers)
1 Yes, if she's healthy and enjoying life.
2 It's increasing with every generation.
3 Providing help and medical care for older people.
4 Because there will be a lot of retired people and a smaller working population.
5 No, he doesn't.

❺ 1 c   2 d   3 a   4 b

❻ (Possible answers)
1 It has almost tripled.
2 Because of advances in medicine and public sanitation.
3 The number of pensioners will rise by 70 million, while the working-age population will rise by only 5 million.
4 She completed the first Eco-Challenge.

Focus on functions p.104

❶
	Edinburgh	Paris
Sun	14.45	18.45
	16.00	20.50
	18.00	23.05
	Bordeaux	London Gatwick
Fri	14.40	15.10

❷ **Asking for information**
I'd like some information about ...
Do you know ...?
Could you tell me ...?
Showing understanding
Right, I've got that.
Checking
Let me check.

Apologizing
I'm afraid I don't have any information about ...
Asking for repetition
Could you repeat that, please?

❸ **Paris**
10 a.m.
Paris Montparnasse

Bordeaux
1 p.m.

❹ 1 Can you tell me when you want to travel?
2 Could you tell me when it leaves Paris?
3 Do you know which station it leaves from?

❺ An indirect question is more polite.
In an indirect question, there is no inversion of the subject and verb and no auxiliary verb form, e.g. *do, does, did.*

❻ 2 I'd like to know how long the journey takes.
4 Can you tell me which airport the flight leaves from?
5 Do you know how much the fare is?
6 I'd like to know where I can buy a ticket.

Unit 11

Language focus p.106

❷ (Possible answers)
1 They charged motorists to drive in the city centre.
2 It's a lot higher – 40% of journeys are by public transport.
3 The Netherlands and Denmark.
4 Because it was a lot cheaper.
5 A car-sharing scheme.

❸ John b   Susanna d   David e   Kate a   Nick c

> ● In a 2nd Conditional sentence, use the Past Simple after *if* and *would* or *could* + infinitive to express the result.

> **Pronunciation p.107**
> 2 1 If she's late, she'll miss the plane.
> 2 I'd drive to work if I had a car.
> 3 If you come tomorrow, I'll meet you at the airport.
> 4 We'd have fewer problems if we changed the system.
> 5 We won't find a solution if we don't do something quickly.
> 6 If they don't get here before 6 o'clock, I won't see them.
> 7 They wouldn't leave the company if there wasn't a problem.
> 8 She wouldn't work if she didn't need the money.
> 4 1, 3, 5, 6 = 1st Conditional   2, 4, 7, 8 = 2nd Conditional

Practice p.108

❶ 1 lived, would/'d walk
2 wouldn't drive, was/were
3 wasn't/was not, weren't/were not, would use
4 would/'d cycle, was/were
5 were, would be
6 would drive, introduced

Wordpower p.109

❶ (Possible answers)
1 Because the European Parliament is there.
2 In manufacturing, metal, electrical, pharmaceutical, and chemical; in services, banking, financial services, and tourism.
3 The historic centre of Brussels and one of Europe's most beautiful squares.
4 A lot of restaurants.
5 Museums, theatre, music, dance, opera, and international films.

❷ capital city, official languages, multinational companies, manufacturing industries, shopping arcades, cultural attractions

❸ (Possible answers)
geography/economy capital city, administrative/financial/commercial centre, population, inhabitants, headquarters, multinational companies, head offices, manufacturing/service industries, metal/electrical/pharmaceutical/chemical industries, banking, financial services, tourism, shopping arcades
transport metro/bus/tram network, Eurostar train connections, international airport
eating/drinking restaurants, cafés, bars, 'beer capital' of the world
culture cultural/historic centre, traditional Christmas market, cathedral, cultural attractions, museums, theatre, music, dance, opera, international films
sports/leisure sports/leisure facilities, golf courses, walking, cycling, jogging, boating, ice-skating

❹ 1 beautiful – ugly, best – worst, lively – dull, modern – traditional
2 attractive – unattractive, efficient – inefficient, important – unimportant, impressive – unimpressive, official – unofficial

Skills focus p.110

❸ **Overall best quality of life** Budapest, Buenos Aires, Copenhagen, Geneva, Montevideo, Prague, Sydney, Tokyo, Vienna, Warsaw, Yokohama, Zürich
Best restaurants, cultural, and leisure facilities London, Los Angeles, Paris, Sydney, Washington DC

❹ 1 215
2 Because crime has increased in both cities.
3 Twelve. Because they have more crime.

Focus on functions p.111

❶ (Possible answers)
1 It doesn't matter./Don't worry.
2 Don't mention it./Not at all.
3 Thanks, and the same to you.
4 Please do./ Well, I'd rather you didn't.

❸ 1 b   2 a   3 a   4 b   5 b   6 a   7 b   8 a

❺ 1 e   2 d   3 f   4 c   5 g   6 a   7 i   8 b   9 h   10 j

❽ 1, 2, 4, 6, 8 are appropriate.

Unit 12

Language focus p.112

❷ (Possible answers)
1   From the cork oak tree, *Quercus suber*.
2   Wine stoppers.
3   Portugal.
4   Because it's an excellent insulation material against heat.

> - Use the active form when the person or thing that did the action is important.
> - Use the passive form when the person or thing that did the action isn't important, or when we don't know who or what did the action.

Practice p.113

❶
1 are planted	5 is left	9 are washed
2 is done	6 is boiled	10 are transported
3 is removed	7 is cut	11 are marked
4 is cut	8 are made	

❷
1 were introduced	5 have been destroyed	8 have asked
2 was believed	6 have been built	9 continues
3 have shown	7 have started	10 will be lost
4 has spent		

❸ (Possible answers)
1   Where are cork oak forests found?
2   What percentage of the world's cork is produced in Portugal?
3   Why are cork trees, forests, and farmers all protected by the law in Portugal?
4   How long has cork been used?
5   Where have cork stoppers been found?
6   When was champagne invented?
7   Why is cork put in the engines of NASA's rockets?
8   When is cork removed from the oak tree?

> ### Pronunciation p.114
> **3**
> 1   Cork is produced in Portugal.
> 2   Many cork products are exported abroad.
> 3   Champagne was invented in the eighteenth century.
> 4   Experts are worried about increasing sales of plastic stoppers.
> 5   A lot of money has been spent on improving quality.
> 6   Cork is used for insulation in rocket engines.

❹ Datafile A
a   How many products are made out of rubber?
b   What is synthetic rubber made from?
d   What is more than 60% of natural rubber used for?
f   How long ago was rubber used by the Mayan people of Central America?
i   How long have raincoats been called 'mackintoshes'?
j   When was the process of vulcanization discovered?

Datafile B
b   What happens after the latex is collected?
c   What percentage of natural rubber is supplied by Malaysia, Thailand, and Indonesia?
e   Why are aircraft tyres made entirely from natural rubber?
g   How long has rubber been known to Europeans?
h   When was the word 'rubber' first used?
j   Why is rubber heated with chemicals in the vulcanization process?

Wordpower p.116

❶ -y   healthy, noisy, cloudy, angry
        -al   industrial, political, central, commercial
        -able   fashionable, profitable, comfortable, valuable
❸ careless, harmless, hopeless, painless, powerless, useless
❹ 1 careless 2 painless 3 harmful 4 wonderful 5 useless
      6 hopeful

Skills focus p.117

❸ (Possible answers)
Report 1	A policy of being nice to its staff.
Report 2	Because the new company was formed from two companies. They recruited more staff than one company needs.

❹ (Possible answers)
Report 1
1   The company's profits have increased by 200% since it introduced its new policy.
2   Staff get a hug from the boss every morning when they arrive at work.
3   Music is played in the office.
4   No one works on their birthday.
5   Staff say everyone has become more relaxed and friendly.
Report 2
1   Forty-seven graduates were given jobs by two UK companies.
2   The two companies have offered the graduates €15,000 to travel round the world for a year.
3   The company believes it will need more people in a year's time.
4   Five of the forty-seven graduates have accepted the offer.
5   The company hopes the offer will be accepted by two more graduates.

❿
Report 1	is played, has been welcomed
Report 2	were given, have been offered, were offered, has been accepted, will be accepted
Report A	have been used, have been put, can't be used
Report B	have been sold, is expected, were (first) introduced, have been bought

Because we are interested in what was done, not in who or what did the action.

Focus on functions p.119

❶ Dialogue 1
1   To stay with them in Bordeaux.
2   Yes, he has.
Dialogue 2
1   To stay at Glencross Castle again.
2   In London on the 22nd.
Dialogue 3 (Possible answers)
1   Another book.
2   Because he is worried that their meeting might not be 'strictly business' (i.e. social or romantic).
3   Because other men find Monique attractive.

❷
Thanking for hospitality	Responding to thanks
Thank you for inviting us.	I'm glad you enjoyed it.
Thank you very much for your hospitality.	**Saying goodbye**
Thanks a lot.	We really must leave now.
Positive comment	I must be off.
We've had a wonderful time.	I'm looking forward to ...
I really appreciated it.	See you ... on the ...
Everything was great.	See you next week.
	Have a good flight.

❹ 1 d   2 c   3 a   4 b

Review unit C

❶
1   Marc has had his own company since 1999.
2   Franca has worked/been working as an accountant since 2001.
3   Claude and Anna have been married for six months.
4   Leon has been learning Japanese since last year.
5   Mike has lived/has been living in Dublin for three years.
6   The company has manufactured/has been manufacturing electrical goods for five years.

❷
2   I've been studying English for a long time.
4   The company has been doing very well since last October.
5   How many years have you been teaching English?
8   They've been living in Paris for a long time.
10 How long have you been working for your company?

❸ 2 e   3 d   4 b   5 g   6 h   7 a   8 f

❺
1 are consumed	4 has been imported	7 was invented
2 are used	5 was manufactured	8 is exported
3 was opened	6 has been drunk	9 are bought

❼
1   Could you tell me what the plane fare from Barcelona to Paris is?
2   Do you know how long the flight takes?
3   Can you tell me which airport in Paris the flight arrives at?
4   Could you tell me when I need to check in?
5   Do you know if I can buy duty-free goods on the plane?

❽ 2 e   3 f   4 g   5 h   6 a   7 b   8 d

Front and back cover:
Variety of vegetables
Slide/Okapia/Reinhard

Pages 2/3:
Beans
Slide/Okapia/Reinhard

Pages 7 and 11:
Pumpkins

This edition published in 2002 by
CHARTWELL BOOKS, INC.
A division of Book Sales, Inc
114 Northfield Avenue
Edison, New Jersey 08837

© Molière 2002, Paris
ISBN: 2-84790-021-7
Printed and bound in Italy
by Grafiche Zanini - Bologna

Photo credits:

Slide/Okapia: 1, 2/3, 11, 23, 25, 26/27, 31, 33, 35, 37, 39, 41, 42/43, 47, 49, 53, 55, 56/57, 61, 62/63, 64/65, 67, 68 /69, 71, 74/75, 81, 82/83, 85, 87, 89, 94/95, 99, 100/101, 102,103, 105, 109, 113, 115, 119, 129.
Slide: 45, 93, 117, 120.
Slide/Azambre: 29.
Slide/Binder: 96, 106/107.
Slide/Petri: 8.
Slide/Pontamier: 51.
Slide/Rosenthal: 78/79, 111.
Slide/Evans: 133.
Slide/Lemoine: 59, 73, 76/77, 91
Private collection, D.R.: 4, 7, 13, 15, 16, 17, 18, 19, 121, 122/123, 124/125, 126/127, 128, 133.

Text: E. Lemoine
Collaboration: F. B.S. B.

VEGETABLES
Then and Now

Elizabeth Lemoine

Foreword
Françoise Izrael

EDITIONS
MOLIÈRE

VEGETABLES

Then and Now

Elizabeth Lemoine

Foreword
Françoise Izrael

FOREWORD

Who would have said, at the end of the 40s, that in the 21st century, swedes and Jerusalem artichokes would be vegetables of choice? Or that gourds, pumpkins, chicories, colocynths, winter squash, turnips, and summer squash, which colored with their old-fashioned charm the kitchen gardens of our grandmothers, and were the basic ingredients of those soups we hated when we were younger, would become part of the most sophisticated cuisines and health practices? Or that we would be proud of growing tomatoes, peppers, fennel, cucumbers and radishes on our balconies and in our gardens?

Vegetables are lively plants which are not only subject to the cycles of nature, the sun, the moon, rain and frost, but also to people's whims. Formerly, when they did not accompany meat or fish, they were looked upon with a certain pity, as if they were orphans.

Today, vegetables have acquired their own autonomy, and, even when they are not part of a vegetarian diet, may be a meal by themselves. We keep finding in them new nourishing qualities and unsuspected medicinal properties and, at the same time, we rediscover to our great joy long forgotten vegetables the unusual flavors of which give free rein to our creativity. Let us hope that memory and imagination do combine to ensure that vegetables, the healthiest of foods for our bodies, are more and more present in our daily life.

Françoise IZRAEL

CONTENTS

A BRIEF HISTORY OF VEGETABLES

Who would have thought that at the beginning of the 21ˢᵗ century **beets** and **Jerusalem artichokes**, symbols of the deprivation that followed World War II, would become the preferred speciality served on silver plates in gastronomic temples? Or, that **aubergines** would be sold at prices comparable to those of caviar? These vegetables, which were once deemed the "meals of the poor" or as light and easily digestible dishes suitable only for those in convalescence, are popular today not only as the objects of detailed research, but as integral elements of vegetarian dishes present in the menus of some of the greatest restaurants.

The Romans, 2,000 years ago, were already familiar with the numerous properties of various vegetables, but they were not the first. In the words of *Pliny the Elder: "It would be impossible to enumerate the qualities of cabbage. Chrysippus already dedicated to it an entire volume divided into chapters each one dealing with a specific body part. Diocles also has written about it; even Pythagoras and Cato have praised this plant. A closer look at Cato's writings reveals the kind of medicine the Roman people have used for nearly 600 years. The early Greek authors distinguished three species: crinkled cabbage, which they named Selinas because its leaves resemble those of celery. This cabbage is good for the stomach and relaxes the abdomen. Smooth cabbage with large leaves which grow on a true stem [...] with no important medical properties. Cabbage, actually known as Crambe, with small, simple, very serrated leaves. It is very bitter, but very effective. Cato prefers the crinkled cabbage the most followed by the smooth cabbage with its large leaves and magnificent stem. He believes it is useful to treat headaches, flashing light sensations in the eye, blurred vision, stomach and diaphragm problems. It should be applied raw, mixed with vinegar, honey, coriander, rue, or mint [...]. To treat gout and joint illnesses it is mixed with rue, coriander, some salt and barley flour and applied in a compress. Use the decoction water, which is a marvellous aid for nerves and joints, in a compress. To heal old and fresh wounds, and to heal cartilage inflammations that cannot be cured by any other means, he recommends using the hot water in a compress and applying crushed cabbage twice a day."* The Roman naturalist observes the habits of his Roman predecessors with a certain condescension. Was he aware of the habits of the peoples of the Old Testament which, in fact, are surprisingly current today? *"(They) brought beds, and basins, and earthen vessels, and wheat, and barley, and flour, and parched corn, and beans, and lentils, and parched pulse, and honey, and butter, and sheep, and cheese of kine, for David, and for the people that were with him."* (Samuel II, 17 27:29). Despite the fact that none of the foods named have become obsolete, eating habits have evolved and vegetables have gone through waves of acceptance and rejection alike.

Lentils, which are mentioned very early in the book of Samuel, are an excellent example of the evolution and perpetuity of a vegetable. Before we begin, it is worth pointing out that we use the term "vegetable" in a very general sense, meaning: a food which is used as a side dish to compliment savory as well as sweet-and-savory dishes. **Lentils**, which are valued today because of their high iron content, are one of the oldest vegetables in the world. They can be traced as far back as the Neolithic Period. They have also been found in the Pharaohs' graves. The Romans allowed lentils to germinate before cooking them to intensify their sweetness and to prepare sweet and savory dishes. Later **lentils** were to experience a period of rejection. In the 19ᵗʰ century, for example, they were considered as meager refectory food.

The **pea** is also a very ancient vegetable with an interesting genetic history. During construction work on the Place du Carrousel in Paris, remains of **peas** dating from the Bronze Age were found. In the same way,

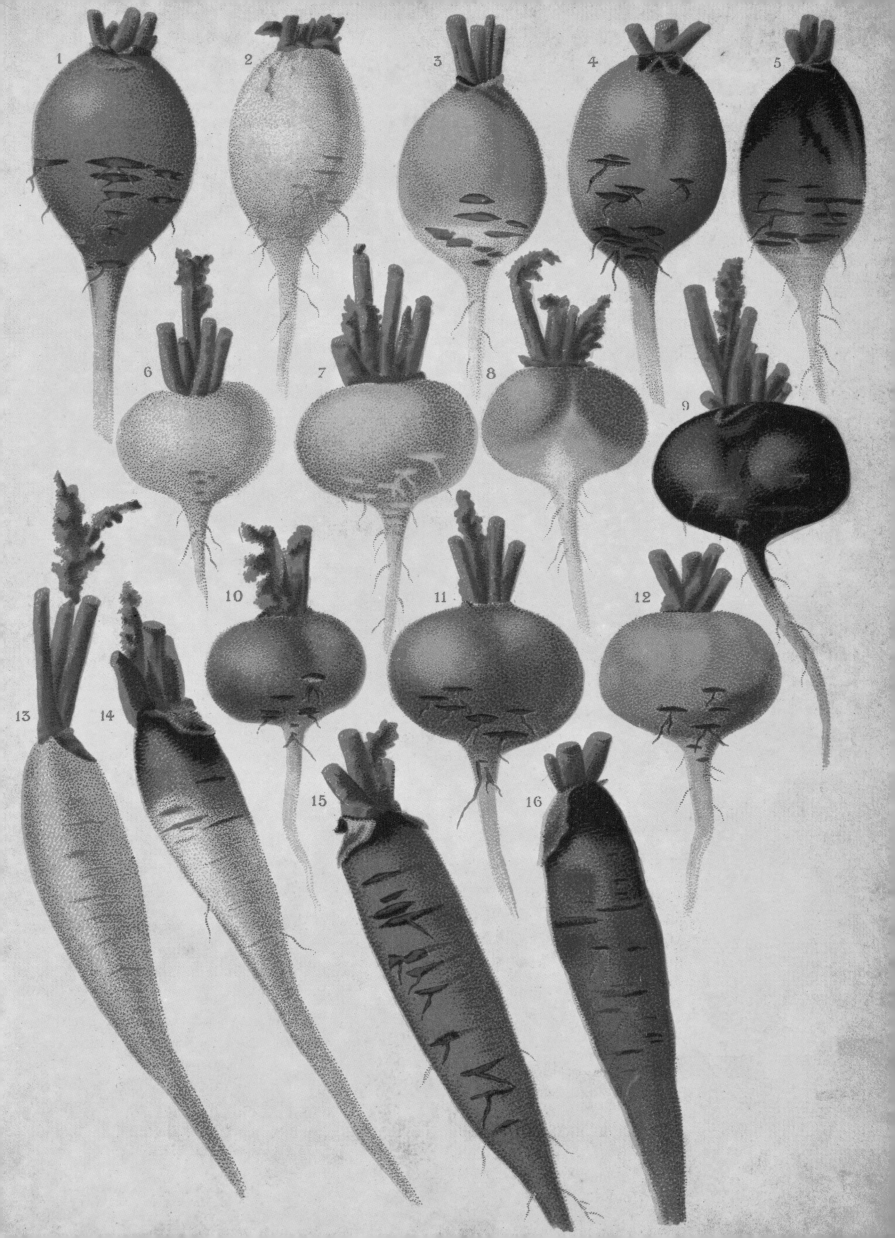

remains were also found in ancient Troy. It seems that a large, dry and coarse **pea** variety has survived from then to this day.

In the Middle Ages, this **pea** variety was so wide spread that it was the base ingredient in a stew served as part of the daily alms at monastery gates. In the Renaissance a completely different **pea** made its appearance with the **Medicis** in France. The small, delicate and sweet vegetable was well liked by **Louis XIV** and soon it became a favorite of the court. **La Quintinie**, who supervised the marvellous kitchen gardens of the king in Versailles, acclimatized it, leaving the plant unchanged. It was not until the next century that the Dutch developed its cultivation further. Today the **pea** is a widespread vegetable which has never fallen into oblivion and has not yet been completely rejected. **Peas**, fresh and tinned, are an important element in every day cooking; however, in gourmet cooking their popularity has declined.

Beans, which at the beginning of the 20th century were considered equivalent to **peas**, come from afar and have followed a very different path. In the Americas, the indigenous peoples cultivated the plant for its seeds, which, once ripe and dry, were a food that was easy to store. In the 16th century, **beans** were introduced to Europe where many different varieties were developed. Originally it was known as a dried vegetable with a high calorie content occasionally causing flatulence. Today, on the contrary, it has evolved to become a vegetable whose green, tender seedpods are consumed because they are rich in vitamins and low in calories. Fresh, they have become very stylish.

Lettuce and **corn salad** were already known in the late Middle Ages. **Lettuce** arrived in Avignon, France, with the popes in the 14th century. In the 16th century the first **cabbage lettuce** appeared and the vinaigrette was developed. **La Quintinie** cultivated **lettuces** in the royal garden because **Louis XIV** had a particular liking for them. **Corn salad** grew for a long time in the wild, and farmers collected it after mowing the meadows or weeding the vineyards. The French poet **Ronsard** praised its delicacy. In the 17th century attempts were made to breed varieties with bigger leaves without success, so it continued to be a wild plant. Some years later it became almost an industrialized product cultivated in a large way because of its popularity in Europe.

Tomatoes are a vegetable which is sometimes eaten raw and other times cooked. They are a good example of how species evolve. The Incas of the Peruvian Andes and the Aztecs of Mexico cultivated a small, yellow and bitter **tomato**. The Spanish conquistadors brought it to Europe where attempts were made to develop a breed that would better agree with the European taste. Nevertheless, the plant was regarded with suspicion as a food due to the fact that it is a close relative of poisonous plants such as mandragora, belladonna and deadly nightshade which were used in sorcery and witchcraft. Botanists would give it the name of *Lycopersicum cerasifome* (wolf peach). In the course of the following centuries, gardeners undertook different experiments, some of them with interesting results. In the 19th century, for example, **tomatoes** were grafted onto **potato** plants to harvest both fruit and tubers from a single plant; no one knows if the fruit were tasty, but the experiment was never repeated. The Italians seem to have been the first ones to adopt it as a fruit some time during the Renaissance. Soon its cultivation and consumption spread throughout Europe, and in the 19th century the plant crossed the Atlantic, back to its place of origin in the New World.

The **Chinese artichoke** is an example of a different evolutionary process. In Asia, its place of origin, it was not regarded as an edible plant until the 12th century. It was acclimatized to France, in 1882, by **Pailleux** and **Bois** in Crosne. It became a commercial product by chance: the farmers of the Somme in France, who competed in bulb cultivation with the Dutch, experienced a weather crisis and were forced to find an alternative crop which would prosper on their sandy soil. They went in search of a forgotten taste and, finally, came upon the **Chinese artichoke** which they cultivated successfully. After many years, this vegetable has slowly made its reappearance in the marketplace. Even though it is not very widespread, due to its taste, originality and quality, it has managed to capture the attention of those amateurs who prefer fine vegetables.

Broad beans belong to one of the oldest, most easily preserved food groups: cereals. It is believed that the **beans** were already being consumed in the 9th century BC. They are mentioned several times in the Old Testament: they were prepared with oil during normal times, but were treated like flour to make bread in times of need. Excavations in Gaul, France, show traces of **broad beans** dating from the Bronze Age. In the Middle Ages, they were a staple food; however, in the Renaissance, with the arrival of **green beans**, they

became less popular in Europe. In North Africa and in the Middle East they are still highly appreciated.

Wheat is not only one of the most popular cereals, it is also one of the most symbolic foods there is: a **wheat** field is almost sacred, reminding us of **Demeter**, Greek goddess of agriculture, Mother Earth, seed and fertility. At the same time, **wheat** fields have been the background of many conflicts. It is believed that **wheat** comes from a cereal originally found in Abyssinia which only had one large, hard grain. Accidentally, this grain crossbred with an unknown cereal producing an ear with multiple grains which, over the years, has been improved through selection. There are several very ancient and primitive varieties of **wheat**, and it is believed that all together there are at least 12,000 different **wheat** types. Crossbreeding must have taken place very early on; 8,000 years ago, starch **wheat** was already being cultivated in Kurdistan. In the 5th century BC, it was found in Iraq, Asia Minor and around the Mediterranean. It is frequently mentioned in the Bible: it was considered an excellent source of courage and strength. Cultivation areas for **wheat** were important to the Egyptians, the Greeks and especially the Romans who rewarded their veteran troops with "villa," properties surrounded by **wheat** fields. In the valleys of the Danube and the Rhine, a variety of wheat with stronger coated grains appeared.

The adaptability of **wheat** enables it to be grown in almost any country in the world, except tropical regions where there is not enough rainfall. In India a variety that is resistant to the tropical sun has been developed. Today, it is one of the crops with highest yields due to its resistance to disease and hardiness to cold. The most important **wheat** exporting countries are the United States, Canada, Argentina, the Ukraine, France and Australia.

Another very ancient cereal plant is **barley** which has been traced all the way back to prehistoric times. Even though this cereal was already cultivated, like **wheat** and **rye**, in ancient Egypt, bakers preferred to use **wheat**. The Greeks used unfermented **barley** to prepare a coarse bread known as *maza*, which had the shape of a big biscuit and was cooked on hot stones. It was given to slaves and disdained by wealthy people. Incidentally, it was **barley** bread that **Jesus-Christ** used in the feeding of the multitude to still the hunger of the crowd after the death of **John the Baptist**.

Millet is also a very ancient grain. Excavations prove that it was known 5,000 years before our time in China, as well as in Mesopotamia, later in Egypt, Greece and Western Europe. In France, on the banks of lake Annecey, traces have been found which date back to the Bronze Age. Today, this grain is a staple food for millions of people in Asia and Siberia. During the big

Carrot

The carrot is one of the oldest cultivated vegetables. It comes from a wild variety found in Asia. It is mentioned in the Bible and in the Koran as a valuable food source. The first traces of its culture go back at least six millennia before our time. Pliny the Elder named it the "Gallic root" (Pastinaca gallica). It appeared on the Iberian peninsula following the invasion of the Moors. It was also found in the kitchen gardens of Charlemagne.

Originally the roots were white, but for some unknown reason, in Afghanistan they spontaneously turned orange. Latter, a similar orange root was discovered in Holland which then spread to England. Since the beginning of the 19th century many different carrot varieties have been developed.

Potato

Potato has its origins in the Andean mountains where this tuber has long been known under the name of papa. Images portraying potatoes on early ceramics dating from before Inca times have been found. The Spanish conquistadors brought the potato to Spain where it was first cultivated as in its place of origin. In 1534 the potato arrived in France, later spread to Italy and soon to the rest of Europe where it was used as livestock feed. At that time, the tubers were still small, bitter and indigestible. The military pharmacist Antoine-Auguste Parmentier, while living under captivity in Germany, was forced to survive on potatoes. He discovered that potatoes were not harmful and that they had a high nutritional value. When he was freed and under the patronage of Louis XVI, he began to cultivate potatoes, improving their taste.

famine after the October Revolution in Russia, it was for many the only source of nourishment. Today, in the western world, it has fallen into oblivion and it is only processed in bread mixtures. Germinated **millet** grains are used in the vegetarian kitchen. However, the grains are mostly used as bird food.

When **Christopher Columbus** arrived in the Americas and saw **corn** for the first time, he thought it was **rice**, the plant so many other navigators had described before. On the 5th of November 1492 he wrote in a letter that these ears had a good taste and that all the inhabitants of the region survived on this plant. In 1519 when **Cortés** arrived in Mexico, he also noted that the cultivation of this plant was particularly simple requiring only superficial fertilizing of the ground. Both navigators were impressed with the density of the crop and its extraordinary yield. They also pointed out that the native people never seemed to suffer from hunger. At the time, food in Europe was scarce. **Columbus** brought **corn** seeds to Spain to be planted. Soon **corn** cultivation had spread throughout the Mediterranean region; it was used

in Italy to make polenta and in Turkey to prepare a national dish. The flour obtained from this new cereal was also mixed with other flours to make bread, but due to its yellow color it was never very successful in Europe.

Corn, which was also known as Turkish, Indian or Spanish wheat was cultivated in France during the 17th century where it was used for both human and animal consumption. Today **corn** is one of the most widely distributed food plants ranking third in world cereal production. The main producing countries are the United States, China, Russia and France.

Rice is one of the oldest of foods. Its development and its longevity are striking. There are more similarities than differences between rough **rice**, which for many years has been the basic ingredient of the Asian diet, and more refined and elaborate **rice** varieties sold in gourmet stores. The origins of **rice** cultivation can be traced back to China in about 2,800 BC and to India in about 2,300 BC. It was also known by the peoples of Egypt, Persia and Macedonia, but it only arrived in Europe during the 8th century with the invasion of the Moors in Spain. From there it spread onto the Camargue and the Po Valley where it is still cultivated today. **Rice** arrived in North America in 1615, when an English ship caught in a storm took refuge in Charleston on the coast of South Carolina. In appreciation for the way he and his crew had been treated, captain **James Thurber** gave **rice** plants to the distinguished people of the city. These plants are the ancestors of the **rice** plants we find today in South Carolina.

The **soy bean**, formerly known as *Dilochos soja*, is a herbaceous plant native to the warm regions of the earth. It is grown predominantly in China, but it is also cultivated in Japan and other Asian countries. The plant was not introduced to Europe until the 18th century as a botanical curiosity. By the end of 19th century it gained

considerable importance not only in the food industry, but also in the medical field. It was introduced to France in 1740 by missionaries who brought it from China. **Soy milk** was produced for the first time in Paris in 1910. In the United States **soy beans** have been cultivated since 1880 quite successfully.

Earth almond now brings us close to the valley of the white Nile and Sudan where it grows in the wild. Tubers of this plant have been found in the tombs of the Pharaohs. **Theophrastus** describes it as an edible plant which grows near water, and he even offers us an interesting recipe: tubers should be cooked in boiling beer. Today, this oil plant is cultivated in Spain, Italy, Hungary, the United States and Russia.

Sorghum takes us to the tropics. In Egypt, during the times of the Pharaohs, **sorghum** was not used for human consumption but was given to livestock instead. It was introduced to France under the name of "broomcorn," and was used for centuries to manufacture brooms and brushes. The *Sorghum saccharatum* variety comes from China where it is known as **kaoliang**. It is rich in sugar; therefore, it is used to produce sugar and alcohol. Because of the different properties possessed by each variety, the one providing fodder and the other sugar, producers decided to crossbreed them. The result was **sorghum bicolor**, a grain cereal of great importance throughout the world. It is a staple food in India, Africa and China. Researchers have also produced a fodder variety called "Haygrazer," which is used to promote the fast growth of pasture land.

We end our journey with a very unusual edible plant: **nettle**. This plant, whose properties were ignored for a very long time, has followed man since the Neolithic period. In the Bible, this peculiar companion is the symbol of laziness, idleness, desolation and ruin; fields which were badly maintained were depicted as being covered with **nettles**. It was regarded as harmful

to agriculture and injurious to man when touched, causing a burning sensation and leaving scars on the skin. In the Middle Ages, it was used to treat a number of different ailments. In France, for example, a **nettle** bouquet was given to the bridegroom so he would rub it on his bride, if on their honeymoon she did not show enough passion. A beating with **nettles** was also used as a punishment for naughty children. Soon, in the northern part of Europe, especially in Sweden, the plant was exploited in a different way. It was cultivated and became a fodder plant resistant to drought with the advantage that it developed quickly. Since then, in the north, the young seedlings are used as a potherb. **Nettle** leaves are used to feed bovine animals, pigs, ducks and geese, and the seeds to feed birds. The fibers found in its stem are used to produce fabric and paper. For a long time it was used only in certain regions, while it was ignored throughout most of the world. Today, thanks to advances in technology, we are beginning to discover the medicinal and nutritional properties of this prehistoric and wild plant which has never been well liked.

After the great famine of 1770, potatoes began to be more popular and by 1785 they had become a staple food. In the mid-19th century, Irish potato crops were damaged by late blight fungus causing potato famines. As a result of this, many Irish people emigrated to the United States taking some potato plants along with them. This time the plants were attacked by an insect known as the Colorado beetle. This insect was transported in trading vessels back to Bordeaux from where it spread throughout Europe. Late blight disease was no longer a threat because it had been brought under control by using copper sulphate; however, there was nothing that could help fight the Colorado beetle. Many solutions were tried without success. Finally, the plants were bred to make them resistant against this insect. Today potatoes are a staple food in many countries.

Jerusalem Artichoke

Samuel de Champlain brought the tubers of this plant to Europe, after he discovered that the Indians used it as food. The plant, which comes from Canada, has experienced short waves of rejection. It was very popular during the war, but soon it was to disappear from the marketplace. Today the tubers are considered a luxurious extravagance.

VEGETABLES AS REMEDIES

CARDIO-VASCULAR SYSTEM

ANAEMIA - SORGHUM seeds, germinated WHEAT kernels, COW PARSNIP vegetable leaves, MILLET seeds and porridge, whole and ground DRY BEANS.

ARTERIOSCLEROSIS - germinated WHEAT kernels, SOY BEAN seeds and flour.

BLOOD CLOTS - infusions of COW PARSNIP leaves and seedlings, CARDOON stems, ARTICHOKE heart and leaves, JERUSALEM ARTICHOKE tubers, GREEN BEANS, raw or grated RADISH roots, SCORZONERA root and juice, infusions of LADY'S MANTEL, decoction of CHICORY roots.

BRUISES - COW PARSNIP leaves in a compress or in infusions.

CHOLESTEROL - SORGHUM seeds, germinated WHEAT kernels, germinated CORN KERNELS, OAT grains, and SOY BEAN seeds and flour.

CIRCULATION - SNAKE GOURD pulp, COW PARSNIP infusions.

HAEMOPHILIA - infusions with CORN SPIKLETS.

HAEMORRHOIDS - wild CUCUMBER balm.

HEART - germinated WHEAT kernels, ONION, germinated BARLEY kernels, green BEANS, AUBERGINE pulp, germinated SORGHUM roasted like COFFEE in infusions.

HIGH BLOOD PRESSURE - fresh ORACH leaves, EARTH ALMOND oil, MILLET seeds and flour, raw SPINACH.

LOW BLOOD PRESSURE - infusions of GERMINATED BARLEY.

MEMORY - BEETROOT, SOY BEAN seeds, PEAS.

MENOPAUSE - infusions with LADY'S MANTEL, FRESH CARROT roots, SOY BEAN grains seeds, germ and flour, ALFALFA leaves in salads, decoction of RHUBARB roots.

UREA - SALSIFY roots to promote perspiration, infusions with BAOBAB leaves.

DIGESTIVE SYSTEM

ABDOMINAL COLIC - poultice with POTATOES, decoction of CARROT seeds, cooking water of RICE, cooked CUCUMBER and SQUASH.

AEROPHAGIA - FENNEL, seeds and cooking water.

APPETITE STIMULANTS - fresh SPINACH leaves in salads and in juice, fresh CELERY stems and roots raw and grated, raw PEPPER, ENDIVE salad, fresh WATERCRESS, TOMATOES.

APPETITE SUPPRESSANTS - ground CORN salad, cooked TANIA pulp, flour made of from TANIA tubers.

COLITIS - infusions with LADY'S MANTEL leaves, infusions with CARROT seeds, raw ONIONS, raw RADISH, and whole RICE.

CONSTIPATION - cooked SPINACH leaves, whole WHEAT, AUBERGINE, CHINESE ARTICHOKE, CHARD, ONION, LEEK, POTATO, TOMATO, JERUSALEM ARTICHOKE, MALABAR SPINACH, SEA KALE, CARDOON, CHICORY salad, PUMPKIN soup.

DIARRHOEA - infusions with NETTLE, LADY'S MANTEL in warm wine, BAOBAB, CABBAGE, PUMPKIN PULP, MILLET, BARLEY, RICE, CHINESE CABBAGE, ORACH and RHUBARB.

DIGESTION - decoction of COW PARSNIP roots, infusions with PARSLEY seeds, LEEK, SWEET PEAS, LETTUCE, FENNEL, MANIOC, GOURD.

INDIGESTION - infusions with FENNEL seeds, cooked ASPARAGUS, GOOSEFOOT salad, RHUBARB wine.

STOMACH - infusions with RHUBARB roots, CARROT, BARLEY, POTATO, PUMPKIN, GOURD, FENNEL, LENTILS.

VOMITING - HONEY with BELL PEPPER powder.

MUSCULO-SKELETAL SYSTEM

ARTHRITIS - NETTLE, BAMBOO seedling, RADISH, LEEK stock, CORN salad.

GOUT - CABBAGE, CORN, SALSIFY, SCORZONERA, TOMATO, decoction of ARTICHOKE leaves.

LUMBAGO - poultice with boiled CABBAGE leaves.

OSTEOPOROSIS - WHEAT, SOY BEANS, raw SPINACH leaves, ALFALFA SPROUTS, RADISH, BEETROOT, BAMBOO seedlings.

RHEUMATIC PAIN - SORGHUM, PUMPKIN, GREEN BEANS and CELERY juice, decoction of SALSIFY roots, BURDOCK leaves, poultice with cooked BURDOCK LEAVES, raw and crushed CABBAGE leaves, chopped raw ONIONS.

RICKETS - germinated WHEAT, SPINACH, PARSLEY, CUCUMBER, QUINOA, MILLET, SOY BEANS.

SCIATICA - poultice with raw CABBAGE leaves, massage with fresh NETTLE.

RESPIRATORY SYSTEM

ASTHMA - COW PARSNIP seeds in liqueur, infusions with CORN salad roots, RADISH syrup, infusions with SCORZONERA roots.

BRONCHITIS - TURNIP ROOTED CHERVIL: infusions with the whole plant, decoctions of LEEK, CARROTS, SCORZONERA, ONION, BARLEY, CELERIAC, CABBAGE, BLACK RADISH syrup, poultice of BARLEY flour.

COUGH - infusions with ONION, decoctions of CARROT and LETTUCE, LEEK and BLACK RADISH syrup, decoctions of SCORZONERA roots.

DRY MOUTH - TURNIP ROOTED CHERVIL roots crushed or in a decoction.

INFLUENZA - decoctions of CARLINE THISTLE ROOTS, with ASPARAGUS and with MILLET, COW PARSNIP, fresh ground RADISH ROOT.

LARYNGITIS - LEEK juice, decoction of LADY'S MANTEL leaves used as gargle.

TONSILLITIS - infusions of LADY'S MANTEL, infusions with RAMPION roots, gargles with BARLEY SEEDS, CELERY juice, cooked LEEK poultice.

URINARY AND REPRODUCTIVE SYSTEMS

AMENORRHOEA - STINGING NETTLE juice, decoction of LADY'S MANTEL, ground CORN salad root, infusions with germinated BARLEY seeds.

IMPOTENCE - PARSLEY, OATS, germinated WHEAT, COW PARSNIP ground and diluted in wine.

INFERTILITY - OATS, WHEAT, ARTICHOKE, POTATO, LEEK.

IRREGULAR MENSTRUATION - infusions with CARROT leaves and seeds, decoction of COW PARSNIP root, infusions with LADY'S MANTEL, fresh PARSLEY juice.

LEUCORRHEA - douche with decocted PARSLEY leaves, fresh NETTLE juice, NETTLE flower infusion.

SEXUAL FATIGUE - CELERY, CELERIAC and FENNEL as vegetables, COW PARSNIP infusion.

NERVOUS SYSTEM

ANXIETY, NERVOUSNESS, SPASMS - WHEAT, SOY BEANS in all its their forms, TURNIP, GOURD, decoctions of LETTUCE.

CEREBRAL FUNCTION - BEETROOT and SOY BEAN in all its forms.

INSOMNIA - fresh LETTUCE or decoction of the leaves, cooked ASPARAGUS, PARSNIP.

MIGRAINE, NEURALGIA - decoction of CORN and LADY'S MANTEL.

MOUTH PROBLEMS

ABSCESSES - fresh GARDEN CRESS and WATERCRESS.

BLISTERS - decoctions of NETTLE.

CAVITIES - chew WHEAT as a preventive measure.

CHAPPED LIPS - rub with a fresh slice of CUCUMBER.

TOOTH PAIN - CORN infusions.

LIVER PROBLEMS

BILE DUCTS - ARTICHOKE, ASPARAGUS, AUBERGINE, BEETROOT, CARDOON, CARROT, CHERVIL, CHICORY, CABBAGE, GARDEN CRESS, CHINESE ARTICHOKE, GREEN BEANS, RADISH, SALSIFY, SCORZONERA, decoctions of CARLINE THISTLE and ARTICHOKE leaves.

GALL BLADDER - decoction of ARTICHOKE leaves, fresh RADISH juice.

GALLSTONES - CELERY decoction, CORN and BURDOCK.

JAUNDICE - infusions with CHERVIL, decoctions of CHICORY.

HAIR AND NAIL PROBLEMS

ATHLETES FOOT - drink the cooking water of SCORZONERA.

HAIR GROWTH - BURDOCK root ointment, decoctions of BURDOCK and NETTLE roots, GARDEN CRESS juice and fresh NETTLE leaves.

HAIR LOSS - eat raw GARDEN CRESS or drink its juice.

PALE, GROOVED NAILS - cooked ONION poultice, WHITE LEAK leaves cooked, ONION juice in a compress, CABBAGE leaves.

SHINY BLOND HAIR - decoctions of RHUBARB FLOWERS.

SHINY BRUNETTE HAIR - LEEK juice.

SPLIT, BRITTLE NAILS - germinated WHEAT, SOY BEAN, fresh NETTLE or GARDEN CRESS juice in a compress.

SKIN PROBLEMS

ABSCESSES - burdock root in a poultice, fresh POTATO pulp, fresh LEEK juice in a compress, ground CARROT, RAW CABBAGE leaves, cooked LENTILS, ONION, RHUBARB.

ACNE - compress with NETTLE and CABBAGE juice, decoctions of CARLINE THISTLE and LETTUCE leaves, PARSLEY, RADISH, TOMATO, CABBAGE and SPINACH juice.

BLOTCHY COMPLEXION - decoction of LETTUCE leaves in a compress.

CHAPPED SKIN - raw ONION plaster.

CHILBLAIN - decoction of whole CARROT and CELERY leaves in a poultice.

CONGESTED SKIN - fresh CUCUMBER juice.

ECZEMA - fresh BURDOCK leaves in a poultice, fresh CABBAGE juice in a compress, decoction of CARLINE THISTLE.

ERYTHEMA - fresh CUCUMBER juice.

GRAY SKIN, DULL COMPLEXION - decoctions of BURDOCK root, CARROT, CHICORY, SALSIFY, LEEK juice, infusions with nettle leaves.

HARSH, DIRTY SKIN - to clean the skin, mix fresh CARROT juice, CUCUMBER and GARDEN CRESS, decoction of SCORZONERA, CHERVIL and NETTLE lotions.

HIVES - NETTLE decoction.

IMPETIGO - poultice with fresh BURDOCK leaves, compress with fresh CABBAGE juice.

IRRITATION - poultice with RICE flour, decoction of CARLINE THISTLE in a compress, germinated WHEAT, CAULIFLOWER, on blisters apply wild CUCUMBER balm.

ITCHING - decoction with SWEET PEAS, mask with DRY BEAN flour.

PSORIASIS - decoction of NETTLE used in a compress.

RASHES - *decoction of* BEET, CORN *infusions*, PUMPKIN.
RED SPOTS - PARSLEY *juice*, ONION *paste with vinegar*.
SCABIES - *cream with cooked wild* CUCUMBER *roots*.
STRETCH MARKS - *decoction of* LADY'S MANTEL *used in a compress*.
SUN BURN - *sliced* POTATOES, ALFALFA SPROUTS
and ground RADISH *in a compress*, TOMATO *salad*.
ULCERS - ONION *vinegar, poultice with raw, crushed* CABBAGE *leaves*, CARROT, BURDOCK.
WARTS - RAMPION *leaves crushed into a plaster,*
compress with fresh ONION *juice*, SALSIFY.
WOUNDS, CUTANEOUS BLEEDING - *plasters with* POTATO *pulp, wild* CUCUMBER,
compress with crushed LADY'S MANTEL *leaves*, BURDOCK, CABBAGE *juice*.

KIDNEY AND GLANDULAR PROBLEMS

ALBUMINURIA - *in the evening*, ONIONS, *decoction of* CELERY *roots, dried* BEANS, CORN,
infusion with LEEK *seeds*.
CYSTITIS - *infusions with* STINGING NETTLE, BAOBAB,
CORN, FRESH TOMATOES.
DIURESIS - *decoction of* ASPARAGUS, LEEK *seed wine*, PARSNIP *or* LEEK *porridge*.
ENURESIS - *in the evening*, WHEAT *and* NETTLE *cookies*.
KIDNEY STONES - CHARD *decoctions*, CORN.
NEPHRITIC COLIC - *warm plasters with* CABBAGE *leaves*.
NEPHRITIS - *infusions with wild* CUCUMBER *pulp raw or cooked*.
RENAL INSUFFICIENCY - LEEK, SPINACH, ASPARAGUS, CARDOONS, CELERIAC *and* CELERY.

EYE PROBLEMS

CONJUNCTIVITIS - *compress and rinse with a decoction of* LADY'S MANTEL *leaves*.
NIGHT BLINDNESS - *decoction of* CARROT *root*.
OPHTHALMIA - CHERVIL *or* PARSLEY *juice applied as eye drops*.
SWOLLEN EYELIDS - *thin, raw* POTATO *slices*.

OTHER AILMENTS

ACOUPHENE - ONION *juice in on cottonwood balls in the ear, roasted*
MILLET *seeds with coarse salt on gauze in the ear*.
APHONIA - LEEK JUICE.
BREAST FEEDING DIFFICULTY - LENTILS, JERUSALEM ARTICHOKE,
FENNEL, *infusions with germinated* BARLEY.
BURNS - *poultice of cooked* SPINACH *leaves*, ORACH, CARROT,
crinkled CABBAGE *leaves, fresh* PUMPKIN *pulp,*
cooked BEAN *puree, raw* ONION *juice, fresh* POTATO *leaves*.
OEDEMA - NETTLE *decoctions*, CORN, PARSLEY *infusions, raw wine* ONION, LEEK *seed wine*.
EXHAUSTION, FATIGUE, CONVALESCENCE - *raw* ONIONS, CARROT, CABBAGE, TOMATO, BELL
PEPPERS, GARDEN CRESS, *as a vegetable cooked* LENTILS, CELERY, BEETROOT, SALSIFY, OATS,
SOY BEAN LEEK, MILLET, PEAS.
FEVER - *infusions with* BAOBAB *leaves*, CARLINE THISTLE.
IMPOTENCE - *eat* OATS, *germinated* WHEAT,
drink the wine of COW PARSNIP *root and leaves*.
MICROBIAL AND VIRAL AILMENTS - BEETROOT, CABBAGE *in all its forms,*
fresh BELL PEPPERS, GARDEN CRESS *salad*.
OBESITY - AUBERGINE, CELERY, CORN SALAD, PARSNIP, LEEK, TURNIP, CHINESE ARTICHOKE,
OKRA, CUCUMBER, *drink* ARTICHOKE *infusions*.
PHYSICAL AND INTELLECTUAL EXHAUSTION - BEETROOT *juice, eat* GREEN PEAS.
SCURVY - *fresh* CABBAGE *juice*, GARDEN CRESS, ALFALFA SPROUTS, RADISH.
WEANING - *poultice wit fresh* PARSLEY *and* CHERVIL *leaves*.

GLOSSARY OF MEDICAL PROPERTIES

ANTISCORBUTIC : *fights scurvy.*
ANTISEPTIC : *stops infections and destroys microbes.*
ANTISPASMODIC : *see calmant.*
APPETITIVE : *stimulates the appetite.*
ASTRINGENT : *diminishes the secretions*
of glands and mucous membranes.
BALSAMIC : *stimulates the digestive and respiratory tracts.*
CARMINATIVE : *favors the elimination of gas and calms stomach pains.*
DIURETIC : *increases the excretion of urine.*
EMETIC : *favors vomiting.*
EMMENAGOGUE : *provokes, facilitates menstrual flow.*
EMOLLIENT : *soothes and calms inflammation of tissues.*
EXPECTORANT : *eases the bringing up of phlegm*
and mucus from the respiratory tract.

FEBRIFUGE : *lowers fevers.*
GALACTOGENIC : *favoring milk production.*
HEMOSTATIC : *stops bleeding.*
LAXATIVE : *loosens the bowels and relieves constipation.*
PURGATIVE : *cleans the intestines.*
PURIFIER : *cleanses the blood from impurities.*
SEDATIVE : *soothes and calms the nervous system.*
STIMULANT : *augments energy*
of the vital functions.
STOMACHIC : *excites the appetite.*
SUDORIFIC : *favors perspiration.*
TONIC : *strengthens the organism.*
VULNERARY : *externally, heals wounds;*
internally, combats physical weakness.

GLOSSARY OF TECHNICAL TERMS

ALTERNATE : *leaves arranged at different levels on the stem;*
one leaf to a node.
BERRY : *fleshy fruit with pips.*
BIPINNATE : *leaves formed of pinnate divisions, themselves formed*
of pinnate leaflets.
BRACT : *leaf at the base of a flower, usually much reduced in*
size.
CARPEL : *female organ of the flower.*
CORDATE : *heart shaped.*
COUMARIN : *a greasy, fragrant substance.*
CUPULE : *a series of closed bracts that form a cup beneath the*
fruit.
DECOCTION : *a preparation made by putting the plant in cold water*
and heating to a boil.
DIOECIOUS : *having male and female flowers on separate plants.*
EVEN-PINNATE : *compound leaf with an even number of leaflets.*
INFUSION : *an herbal tea prepared by pouring boiling water on*
the plant and allowing to stand for 5 to 10 minutes.
LEAFLET : *division of a compound leaf.*
MELLIFEROUS : *producing honey.*
MONOECIOUS : *a plant bearing both male and female flowers.*
MONOSPERMOUS : *having only one seed.*

ODD-PINNATE : *leaf having an uneven number of leaflets*
with a terminal leaflet.
PEDUNCLE : *small ramification of the stem ending in a flower.*
PERENNIAL : *said of a plant that survives several years and that*
flowers every year, the aerial parts disappearing each
winter.
PINNATE : *feather-like; leaflets arranged along a central leaf*
axis.
PUBESCENCE : *the soft down that covers the surface of many plants.*
RHIZOME : *perennial subterranean stem.*
ROSETTE : *a radiating leaf cluster at or near the base of the plant.*
SELF-POLLINATION : *pollen is transferred from the anthers to the stigmas in the*
same flower.
SESSILE : *attached directly to the stem without a peduncle.*
SILIQUE : *dehiscent fruit opening in four parts.*
SPADIX : *inflorescence surrounded by a large bract.*
STALK : *also petiole, the main stem or axis of a plant.*
STEM : *the main upward-growing axis of a plant.*
STOLON : *creeping aerial or subterranean stem by which the*
plant propagates.
VERTICILATE : *an almost circular arrangement of leaves or flowers at the*
same level of the stem.

THESE NATURAL REMEDIES ARE NOT BY ANY MEANS INTENDED
TO REPLACE MEDICINES PRESCRIBED BY A DOCTOR.

VEGETABLES FROM A TO Z

ABELMOSCHUS ESCULENTUS   *Okra*
Fruit vegetable
Family: *Malvaceae*
Origin: *tropical Africa*
Height: *3 to 6.5 feet (1 to 2 m)*
Flowering: *late spring*
Properties: *digestive, laxative, stomachic*

ADANSONIA DIGITATA   *Baobab*
Leaf vegetable
Family: *Bombaceae*
Origin: *African Savanna*
Height: *6.5 feet (2 m)*
Flowering: *summer*
Properties: *anti-diarrhoea, febrifuge, sedative*

Okra arrived in Egypt, where the Pharaohs began to successfully cultivate it, from Africa. Later, it spread to tropical and subtropical Asia and America where it is still grown today.

It is an herbaceous, annual plant with long, ramified, erect stems. Its alternate, very lobed leaves, which are smooth on top and hairy underneath, have a long petiole. Its splendid solitary flowers, measuring about 3 inches (8 cm) in diameter, appear on the ends of superior leaves. They are generally yellow, sometimes white or reddish, like those of the Syrian **okra**, with a violet-blue center. They render an edible fruit or pod, hairy at the base which is a capsule, measuring about 4 to 10 inches (10–25 cm) in length, that contains numerous oval, dark colored seeds. This fruit has a sweet, delicate flavor.

Okra is grown from seed at a minimum temperature of 59 °F (15 °C). Once the pods have been harvested, the seeds are sown on plain soil. Harvesting is done while the fruit is still tender and unripe, because ripe **okra** is very fibrous with several hard grains which are not pleasant to the palate. To preserve the fruit, it is dried in the sun and later pickled or frozen. **Okra** is rich in mucilage, vitamins, and mineral salts. Due to its high mucilage content, it is recommended for weight loss and stomach problems. Its roots are used in the manufacture of paper.

Its unique size and longevity make this tree the giant of the vegetable kingdom. It was named after the French botanist **Adanson** who spent time studying it in Senegal, the tree's place of origin. Even though it is a tree and not a plant, the **baobab**, due to its medicinal and nutritional properties, is considered to be a great vegetable and a very useful plant.

Although the tree spreads itself out, it does not have many branches. It has a short, deformed, stalky trunk that can reach 30 feet (9 m) in diameter. Its large digitally compound leaves, with long leaflets sprout on the young branches, fall during the dry season. The solitary terminal flowers hang from a long peduncle. They are formed by a calyx of five white petals with a long pistil and numerous stamens that bear fruit in the shape of oval-pointed capsules which can be almost 12 inches (30 cm) long and 6 inches (15 cm) wide. Their woody bark has a very thick green covering. This fruit, known to the native people of Senegal as "bread of the apes," is divided in several segments containing various kidney shaped seeds enclosed in a floury, fibrous sweet-and-sour pulp.

The **baobab** contains alkaloids, tannin, sugar, oil, vitamins and minerals. Its bark is used to extract an alkaloid which serves as an antidote for curare poison. Its leaves regulate breathing allowing the elimination of

Okra

This vegetable is used fresh in salads or cooked in ragouts. When cooked in salted water, with or without spices, this clear, viscose preparation is known in the Creole kitchen as Calalou. It can also be boiled like green beans, fried in a pan, baked in the oven or used as an ingredient for a gratin. When dried, okra must first be soaked. The powder obtained from drying and crushing the ripe vegetables is also used to thicken sauces. The grains can be roasted to obtain a drink similar to coffee. They also contain an oil used in certain drinks and perfumes.

toxins. An infusion of the leaves is used to alleviate diarrhoea, fever and urinary problems.

The leaves are prepared like any other green vegetable: fresh, in salads; cooked in baked pies, stews and gratins accompanying both meat and fish. *Lalo*, as it is known to the local people, is a nutritional supplement made by drying the leaves in the shade and crushing them to a powder.

AEGOPODIUM PODAGRARIA	Goutweed
Leaf vegetable	

Family: *Umbelliferae*
Origin: *Europe and western Asia*
Height: *31 inches (80 cm)*
Flowering: *May to July*
Properties: *astringent, mineralizing, tonic*

Goutweed is a perennial plant renowned in antiquity for its medicinal properties. It thrives easily in a shady underground with rich humid soil. Its characteristic scent resembles that of the **carrot**. This wild vegetable is propagated through its strongly ramified rhizome which has alternate, feather-divided leaves that are sheathed at the base. Its leaflets are pointed, lanceolate and dentate. Its trunk is hairy, branched, hollow, angular and channelled. The flowers, white or pink, are usually arranged in conspicuous umbels. They bear an achene fruit that is ovoid and flat on the sides.

Goutweed is propagated through the new rhizome shoots which are planted in the shade in a humid, fertile soil that is rich in nitrogen; this plant is rarely propagated from seed. Seedlings which have not yet bloomed are harvested, as are the leaves during the entire growth period of the plant. **Goutweed** is rich in mineral salts. Its leaves contain carotene and are rich in vitamin C. Because of its medicinal properties, it is used in health spas and during convalescence for its invigorating and revitalizing effect on the body.

Goutweed

The leaves and young shoots can be used in salads, or cooked in stews. The leaves can also be cooked in oil with onions, garlic, a pinch of nutmeg, salt, potatoes, and whipped cream, and served as a side dish for meat, eggs or fish.

ALCHEMILLA XANTHOCHLORA	Lady's mantel
Leaf vegetable	

Family: *Rosaceae*
Origin: *Europe, western Asia, North Africa and Canada*
Height: *about 12 inches (30 cm)*
Flowering: *May to September*
Properties: *anti-inflammatory, astringent, laxative, digestive, diuretic, emollient, emmenagogue, stomachic*

In former times, alchemists collected the rose beads that lay on the leaves of **lady's mantel**, for it was believed they possessed special curative powers. It was also well liked in folk medicine.

This perennial plant has a rosette of basal leaves. It thrives in damp areas near streams and marshes. Its straight growing trunk is branched at the top with relatively broad leaves that have shallow, rounded lobes and toothed edges. Their lower blades have a velvety, grey green surface, while those on top are smooth and light green. The pale yellow flowers, which bear an achene fruit, are grouped in cymes forming loose panicles appearing in terminal clusters.

The leaves, which do not have a specific scent, are harvested before the flowering period. They have a slightly bitter and astringent taste. **Lady's mantel** is very conducive to good health because it is rich in vitamin C (five times more than lemon), carotene, mineral salts (calcium, magnesium and phosphorus), mucilage, saponin, bitter substances, salicylic acid and contains up to 8% tannin.

Lady's mantel stimulates digestion, prevents gall bladder obstruction and kidney pain, and also stimulates the production of urine. It is also used to regulate the menstrual period and to relieve menopausal problems. An infusion of the leaves used in a compress helps heal wounds; used as a gargle it soothes swollen glands. In former times, German alchemists believed that a decoction of **lady's mantel** leaves had a rejuvenating effect. The fresh leaves can be used in stews and vegetable dishes. They can be added to a pea puree or served as an accompaniment to meat dishes. A rich beverage can also me made by soaking the fresh leaves in hot water.

ALLIUM CEPA	Onion
Root vegetable	

Family: *Liliaceae*
Origin: *Asia*
Height: *from 12 to 24 inches (30 to 60 cm)*
Flowering: *July to August*
Properties: *anti-scurvy, antiseptic, cardiotonic, diuretic, emollient, laxative, stimulant*

Onions, relatives of the garlic plant, are amongst the oldest of cultivated plants, and have long been used as a vegetable and a seasoning. The Ancient Egyptians were fond of it, as were the Greeks who blamed it for

being the cause of bad breath. During the Middle Ages, **onions** were found in every kitchen and are still widely used today.

This biennial plant has a largely developed bulb. Its dark green, hollow, tubular leaves swell at the base to form the underground, fleshy bulb. The green or pink flowers are clustered in spherical, terminal umbels on stalks that can reach up to 31 inches (80 cm). The roots of the bulb are poorly ramified appearing in numerous tiny white filaments.

Onions are grown from seed and sown directly onto the field, or raised in greenhouses, and require a soil which is both porous and nutritious. The bulb is usually harvested the same year as the seed was sown, although it is possible to overwinter the plants and thus achieve a second year's cultivation. Once the bulbs are pulled out, they are left to dry in the air for a few days, which facilitates their preservation.

There are two types of **onions**: those large bulb varieties, some of which are pungent and others which are mild, with colors ranging from yellow, to red or white, and which include the small onions often used for pickling; and the small spring **onions**, or scallions, which are eaten whole while they are still young and tender. The taste of **onions** is more or less sweet or pungent, while the characteristic scent results from the sulphur-rich volatile oil they contain which, when released, is an irritant and often brings tears to the eyes of whoever is preparing them.

Because **onions** contain a lot of water, carbohydrates, sugar, mineral salts, lipids, trace elements, vitamins A, B, C, E, and bioflavonoids, they stimulate the cardio-vascular system, fight infections and prevent scurvy. They cleanse and tonify the organism, and alleviate coughs.

A raw **onion** cut in half is used to eliminate the smell of a freshly painted piece of furniture or surface, to remove the rust from a kitchen knife or to reanimate someone who has fainted.

Onion

Onions can be eaten raw in salads, where the addition of nuts and oranges provides a contrast in aroma, and sweetens their taste while reducing their pungency. Cooked onions are used to make delicious toppings for soups, juicy purees, and savory pies and tarts. They can also be stuffed and served as a light dish. Sliced and sautéed, they are used to accompany both red meat and poultry. Peeled and whole, they make a wonderful garnish for roasts. As a chutney or simply pickled, they are often served warm or cold to accompany grilled, sautéed or cold meats. The pungency also offers an interesting contrast to various cheeses. Nevertheless, they can sometimes be difficult to digest.

ALLIUM PORUM **Leek**

Stem vegetable
Family: Liliaceae
Origin: Mediterranean area
Height: about 19 inches (50 cm)
Flowering: May to July
Properties: apéritif, diuretic, emollient, purgative

Leeks do not actually have a genuine bulb, but rather a leaf tuber. The plant has been cultivated since ancient times and is most probably the descendant from another variety of **leek** known as *Allium ampeloprasum.* It was widely used by the Athenians and the Romans for to its beneficial health properties. In the Middle Ages, a very popular soup made with **leeks** was served at just about every table.

Leeks have a white, fleshy compressed stem plate; the thick leaf bases overlap and are arranged concentrically in a nearly cylindrical bulb. A tuft of fibrous, shallow, white roots grows from the base of the stem plate. As the plant develops, a tall solid stalk arises bearing light or dark green, sometimes slightly violet, leaves and a large globular umbel with many white, pink and violet, star shaped flowers. The plant has a sweet fragrance that attracts insects; thereby, promoting pollination of neighboring species. **Leeks** are propagated from seed in deep, rich and permeable soil; this is done either in March in the greenhouse or in May in the open field. The young plants are then replanted in rows. Their roots and leaves are, however, first cut back in order to promote growth. Plants sown in March are harvested in August (**autumn leeks**), while those sown in May are harvested from autumn until winter (**winter leeks**). **Winter leeks** are biennial since they only bloom the following spring. However, some shoots are left untouched in order to promote seed production.

Leeks contain only a few calories, but much water and many mineral salts such as iron, magnesium, calcium, potassium, phosphorus and sulphur. Furthermore, they are rich in mucilage, cellulose, as well as vitamins A, B and C, which are to be found in the green parts of the plant. This vegetable stimulates digestion, soothes inflammations of the larynx, tracheitis, and bronchitis. Its juice clears the voice. This vegetable has become the national emblem of Wales. It is known to have been displayed as a Welsh emblem in 1536 and in **Henry V, Shakespeare** acknowledged this as an ancient custom. One legend tells of a battle between the Welsh and the Saxons fought in a field of **leeks**. At some time in the past, the **leek** was an important part of the diet but it is not commonly eaten today. It is delicious when part of the traditional **leek** and **potato** soup.

AMARANTUS CAUDATUS   **Amaranth**
Fruit vegetable
Family: *Amaranthaceae*
Origin: *Latin America*
Height: *3 to 8 feet (1 to 2.50 m)*
Flowering: *late spring*
Properties: *nourishing, invigorating*

A very old herbaceous plant, **amaranth** was already grown as a cereal more than 4,000 years ago on the high plateaus of the Andes; in Africa and Asia it is still considered a nutritional plant. There are about 60 varieties which are cultivated as vegetables and cereals in tropical and subtropical regions of the world.

This hairy, strong, fast growing plant has a well ramified foliage with alternate, oval, leaves. Its very small, monoecious, reddish to magenta-red flowers appear in long hanging clusters which can reach up to 12 inches (30 cm) long. They bear numerous very small, reddish brown seeds rich in starch. **Amaranth** is propagated from seed on well permeable, light soil. Containing starch, proteins, sugar, vitamin A and mineral salts, it is a very nutritional vegetable and very easy to digest.

Its crushed seeds are used to produce a starch used in porridges, pastries, crepes, and biscuits flavored with ginger. Its leaves are used as any other green vegetable in soups, gratins, herbal pâtés, stuffings and omelettes. They are also used as a side dish for meat or fish. Its flowers, which keep their color when dry, are used to make dried bouquets. **Amaranth** is considered a symbol of immortality.

AMORPHOPHALLUS CAMPANULATUS   **Elephant's foot or Hottentot bread**
Root vegetable
Family: *Araceae*
Origin: *Africa and tropical Asia*
Height: *6 feet (1.80 m)*
Flowering: *spring*
Properties: *nutritional, mineralizing*

Elephant's foot, also known as **hottentot bread**, belongs to the family of the *Araceae*, and is cultivated in the tropics because of its enormous edible tuber. It is grown mostly in tropical Asia and the Pacific region.

It is a herbaceous, monocotyledon, twining plant with a few gigantic petioled leaves. It has a hardy, large, woody and partially exposed tuber covered with voluminous tubercules resembling an **elephant's foot** and weighing about 55 lbs. (25 kg). The flowers, generally small and inconspicuous, are surrounded by a spathe. There is another variety *Amorphophallus titanum* which has the largest flowers of the vegetable kingdom: its leaves can reach a length of 6.5 ft. (2 m) and a diameter of up to 4 ft. (1.20 m). Fruitage is insignificant due to the fact that the fruit very rarely develop to full maturity. The tubers have a very mild, slightly pungent taste. Its culture takes place by planting the tubers in damp, rich soil in tropical regions. Harvesting is done very carefully because both plant and tubers contain calcium oxalate which causes skin irritation. The tubers are stored dry and in the dark. The large amount of calcium oxalate contained in the tubers is removed by soaking or cooking. **Elephant's foot** is rich in starch, fiber, carbohydrates, proteins, mineral salts (calcium, potassium), and vitamins A, B and C. It is a very nutritious vegetable which provides the organism with the necessary minerals and vitamins.

Elephant's foot must be peeled using gloves. After that, the tubers are soaked for a whole day in water that is constantly changed. Subsequently, they can be cut into pieces and fried, mashed into a puree, or simply cooked in water. They can be used to prepare porridges, ragouts and soup stocks. A starch is extracted from the

Leek
Young leeks have a sweet taste and are eaten raw with salt. Cooked, they are delicious with a vinaigrette. Leeks are used to prepare vegetable pies, purees, soufflés and stews. They can also be cooked in water, rolled with ham, topped with a béchamel sauce, covered with cheese and baked in the oven like a gratin. They can also be cut in slices and sautéed in butter to accompany meat, game or fish.

tubers and used in desserts, cakes, and soup vermicelli. The young leaves are steamed and eaten like **asparagus**. Tubers and leaves are also used as animal fodder.

APIUM GRAVEOLENS VAR. DULCE   *Celery*
Stem vegetable
Family: Umbelliferae
Origin: Mediterranean basin
Height: 20 to 24 inches (50 to 60 cm)
Flowering: summer (from the second year)
Properties: apéritif, purifier, digestive, diuretic, tonic

Celery was used as a flavoring by the ancient Egyptians, Greeks and Romans. The ancient form resembled smallage or wild **celery** and it was used among other things in funeral ceremonies. Over time, the quality and taste of smallage was improved through cultivation. In the 17th century, it became a very popular nutritional plant known in Italy as **celery**. During the Renaissance, **celery** made its way to France where the new vegetable with its juicy, tender leafstalks began to be cooked as a vegetable and used as a flavoring. Today, there are several varieties of **celery**, like the Pascal, whose fleshy, succulent leaves are used in salads.

Celery is a plant with strong branches and bright green foliage. The plant has large, fleshy, upright leafstalks, also known as petioles, which are grouped on one unique stem with small roots. The white, umbel flowers appear once the plant is two years old.

Celery is cultivated in rich soil in open land with a good irrigation system. The seeds are sown in April, and in June the seedlings are replanted leaving a space of 12 inches (30 cm) between each one. After the fresh young shoots have been harvested in summer the plant is blanched (i.e., deprived of light) to produce light tender shoots. There are, however, varieties that blanch naturally. The last shoots must be pulled before the frost begins; **celery** does not prosper in the cold. They should be stored in a cellar, where they will keep for a longer period. **Celery** leafstalks are crisp, juicy, slightly peppery with a characteristic strong aroma.

The nutritional value of **celery** is low, hardly containing any fat and proteins. The water content amounts to approximately 90%, and it is rich in fiber. It also contains carotene, vitamins A and C. Because it contains vitamin E, it is said to be an aphrodisiac. Its essential oil strengthens the digestive system. It is also a vegetable that helps the body eliminat toxins. The juice

of the pressed leaves also have a soothing effect on rheumatism.

The seeds have a strong aroma and a slightly bitter taste. They can be used whole, or ground to a powder and used as a seasoning for salads, soups and stews, fish dishes, various sauces or **tomato** juice. In Scandinavia they are used to season bread dough. **Celery salt**, a mixture of ground **celery** seeds and salt, has a brownish color and a rather intensive taste, and should therefore be used sparingly when seasoning food. **Celery** also keeps for a long time when stored in the fridge (particularly when wrapped in aluminium foil).

APIUM GRAVEOLENS   *Celeriac*
VAR. RAPACEUM   *or Celery root*
Root vegetable
Family: Umbelliferae
Origin: Mediterranean basin
Height: 12 inches (30 cm)
Flowering: summer (from the second year)
Properties: apéritif, aromatic, diuretic, stimulant, stomachic, tonic

---

In contrast to celery, **celeriac** has little foliage and a voluminous root tuber. **Celeriac** is the result of several attempts to improve wild celery by reducing the number of flowers and further developing its stalks and roots.

Even though **celeriac** was already known in Italy during the 16th century, it took almost two centuries for it to make it to the tables of the rest of Europe. In England it was only introduced in the 19th century via Alexandria.

Essentially, it consists of a large, white, relatively smooth edible root tuber which can weigh more than 2.2 lbs. (1 kg). The plant is crowned by bright green leaves with hard, thick stalks. On the base of the tuber there are small radicles. Its taste is very strong and slightly peppery. It is cultivated from seed, initially indoors at the beginning of the spring, and later in the open, in temperate regions on neutral soil; too much fertilizer easily causes the tuber to dry up. It should, however, be watered regularly. In the middle of summer, the first still tender and sweet tubers can be harvested. However, the real harvest takes place in late August before temperatures drop. To protect the plants from frost, they are covered with a layer of straw. **Celeriac** can be stored in a cool, dry, dark cellar for a long time.

Celery

Celery is eaten raw in salads such as salad niçoise. It can also be served as an hors d'œuvre, raw, cut into small pieces and served along with a dip. Its strongly aromatic leaves are used in preparing stocks and soups. It can be pickled in vinegar and used as a seasoning. It can be boiled in water or steamed to accompany meat, or prepared as a gratin with béchamel sauce and grated cheese on top. Celery is also used in vegetable soups, with fish and seafood.

In contrast to celery, **celeriac** is poor in vitamin C, but contains numerous trace elements such as bromine, copper, iron, iodine, manganese, magnesium and zinc, as well as carbohydrates and great amounts of cellulose. It has hardly any fat or proteins. It is a nutritional vegetable which provides lots of energy and has important medical properties. It increases the synthesis of certain hormones, it stimulates the metabolism and digestion, and is also a diuretic.

ARCTIUM LAPPA **Burdock**
Leaf and root vegetable
Family: Compositae
Origin: Europe and Asia
Height: 5 to 6 feet (1.60 to 1.80 m)
Flowering: July to August
Properties: anti-poison, bactericide, purifier, diuretic, regulates blood sugar, stomachic, sudorific

---

In Antiquity, **burdock** was only used for its medicinal properties. During the Middle Ages, the plant was said to help the growth of hair. It is also said that **Henry III of France** was cured of a terrible skin disease with its leaves. Once it had spread throughout Europe and Asia, it made its way to America.

This hardy biennial plant is easily recognizable due to its seeds which tend to hook onto the fur of animals and people's clothing. It has a pivotal, fleshy, ramified root, outside brown and inside white, which becomes fibrous with maturity.

Burdock thrives on ground rich in nitrogen in temperate and northern subtropical regions. During the first year, a rosette of large basal leaves appears. In the second year, a tall, hairy, ramified, cottonlike, reddish trunk develops. Its entire, oval, alternate, leaves with basal petioles, are covered on the underside by a light grey fuzz. Its purple-red flowers appear in loose corymbs with large, globular peduncles surrounded by green bracts provided with tiny pointed hooks that adhere to rough surfaces. These flowers bear brown-red to black achenes arranged in several rows.

The root has a sticky, slightly bitter, sweet-and-sour taste. The leaves also have a sticky taste, but they are more sweet and herbaceous. The leaves are harvested during the entire growth period, while the roots are harvested young in the autumn of the first year or in the spring of the following year. **Burdock** is highly perishable; therefore, it must be consumed immediately.

Because its leaves contain a lot of vitamin C, they are an excellent tonic; they are used during convalescence and in health spas. The root contains inulin, a substance which replaces sugar in the cases of diabetes, as well as proteins, carbohydrates, mucilage, tannin, resin, bitter substances, ethereal oil, and minerals such as calcium, potassium and phosphorus. In traditional medicine, **burdock** is used to treat kidney problems, urinary tract infections, digestive problems, gastritis, stomach ulcers, eczema, and wounds. Applied in a poultice, the leaves soothe the pain and inflammation caused by insect bites. Steeped in oil, they are used in the manufacture of hair care products.

ASPARAGUS OFFICINALIS **Asparagus**
Stem vegetable
Family: Liliaceae
Origin: the Middle East, Mediterranean basin
Height: 3.5 to 5 feet (1 to 1.50 m)
Flowering: spring
Properties: mineralizing, diuretic, purifier, sedative

Asparagus was prized as a vegetable by epicures in Egypt, Byzantium, Greece and Rome. It was introduced to France as late as the 16th century by the **Medicis**. Later **Louis XIV** hired an agronomist, **La Quintinie**, to supervise the gardens of Versailles where fruit and vegetables were grown to please the king. From then on, **asparagus** became quite popular in Europe. Around 1805 it began to be cultivated intensely in the area of Argenteuil which soon became the French **asparagus** capital, producing a white **asparagus** prized for its delicate flavor. Today, **asparagus** is cultivated in almost all temperate regions of the world.

Asparagus is an erect or climbing, dioecious, perennial plant. Its tuberous or rhizome-like roots give rise to a conspicuous, fleshy, feathery spray of branchlets whose true leaves are reduced to small scales gathered in bundles of three or four enclosed by several stipules. Its flowers are small and greenish. Only female flowers bear fruit; small berries, at first green but turning red with maturity, enclosing the seeds. Male plants are stronger and more productive.

Asparagus has a fresh, mild and delicately sweet taste. It is grown in deep, loose, light clay soils with much organic matter, and light, sandy loams which should be broken up regularly with compost and fertilizer. The **asparagus** field is prepared by heaping up

Burdock

The fresh leaves are used to prepare mild and delicious salads. They are also used as an ingredient in spicy, juicy vegetable stews, herbal pâtés and green vegetable gratins. The raw roots can be grated and added to salads and hors-d'œuvres. They are also mixed into various vegetable dishes, stuffings and sauces. In Japan and China the roots are cut into pieces to accompany several fish or meat dishes. They are also crystallized in honey to make a type of confectionery.

earth to form long ridges on top of which narrow shallow trenches are made. **Asparagus** is propagated from seed in early spring directly into the trenches or in May through root division. Harvesting is done three years later in May and June when the seedlings just break through the heaped up earth. They are dug out and cut off at a depth of about 6 inches (15 cm) from the top. Afterwards the earth is reheaped over them. In order for the plants to be productive for about 15 years, they must be fertilized annually. Once cut, **asparagus** can be stored for several days in boxes, or covered with dry peat in a well aired, cool and dark place. It can also be pickled.

Asparagus contains plenty of water and is rich in fiber which makes it easy to digest. It also contains essential oils, sugar, mineral salt (potassium and magnesium), amino acids and trace elements (iron, iodine and copper); however, it is poor in vitamins. It is reputed for its sleep-promoting and sedative effect. Its active substance, asparagin, makes it an excellent diuretic. **Asparagus** slows heart rhythm. In ancient times it was used to prepare a diuretic known as "syrup of five roots." Near Cahors, in the south of France, there is a wild variety of **asparagus**, *Asparagus acutifolius*, which is harvested in April. It has a delicate, stronger taste than that of cultured **asparagus** and it is prepared in the same way.

Asparagus

Before cooking it, asparagus must be peeled with caution because it is very fragile. It can be eaten hot, lukewarm or cold. There are white, purple and green varieties. This last one is the most popular. Asparagus contains many vitamins. Steamed or boiled in salt water, asparagus is served fresh as an hors-d'œuvre or in a spicy aspic as a garnish. It can be prepared with chopped hard boiled eggs, parsley, or with melted butter and covered with bread crumbs. Cooked whole, it can be prepared with eggs, or cut into pieces, it provides a good filling for an omelette.
It can be used to make a gratin covered with bread crumbs, cream, and paprika or Mornay sauce and parmesan cheese. It can also be served as a vegetable alongside white meat and fish. Asparagus is also good in soufflés, purees and soups. Its foliage is often used as a fragrant foliage in floral bouquets.

ATRIPLEX HORTENSIS　　　　　　　**Orach**
Leaf vegetable
Family: Chenopodiaceae
Origin: central Asia
Height: 5 feet (1.50 m)
Flowering: July to September
Properties: purifier, diuretic, laxative

Wild orach, like *Atriplex astata* and *Atriplex patula*, are very ancient, aromatic, edible plants which propagate in dry areas. In antiquity the people of the Mediterranean ate **orach** as a vegetable. In the Middle Ages it was considered an ornamental plant. **Wild orachs** are the true ancestors of three current varieties: one with pale green leaves, another with dark green leaves, and the third with reddish-violet leaves. **Garden orach** was widely grown from the Middles Ages up to the 19th century. Today, it is becoming fashionable once again.

Orach is a splendid herbaceous plant with a somewhat branched stem. Its alternate leaves, triangular and angular, are covered with minuscule glandular hairs which give it a pubescent appearance. The red or yellow flowers appear grouped in numerous interrupted bunches bearing a multitude of flat fruit. It self-propagates from seed, in rows, on fertile, damp soil in the full sun at the beginning of spring or autumn. The young leaves can be harvested three months later and throughout the season; if the shoots grow higher than 20 inches (50 cm) the leaves become too hard. Blanched and frozen, the leaves can be stored for up to a year. Although reminiscent of **spinach** its taste is milder and more delicate because the leaves contain less oxalic acid. **Orach** is rich in calcium, phosphorus, magnesium, iron, vitamin C, carotene, proteins, carbohydrates and anthocyanin (a coloring substance present only in the red variety). It facilitates digestion, purifies the blood, helps cleanse the kidneys and the gall bladder.

Its leaves are prepared like **spinach**: raw, in salads; cooked, in soups and purees. They can also be served as a vegetable sautéed in butter as an accompaniment to meat. The leaves are also used to prepare pies and soufflés. In the garden, it is a very decorative plant.

AVENA SATIVA　　　　　　　**Oat**
Fruit vegetable
Family: Gramineae
Origin: western Asia, the Middle East and Northern Europe
Height: 4.3 feet (1.30 m)
Flowering: spring
Properties: emollient, regulates blood sugar, nutritious, sedative, stimulant

---

Oat is an annual cereal, cultivated since antiquity, which is probably a descendant of **wild oat** (*Avena fatua*) known for the quality and size of its grains. It reached Middle Europe from Asia Minor during the Bronze Age. Although **oats** are used chiefly as livestock feed, some are processed for human consumption. There are two varieties: *Avena nuda*, which has small grains; and *Avena orientalis* with big, white starchy grains, which is usually preferred for cultivation. The plant thrives in the cool, temperate regions of Northern Europe and it is also grown in Canada and the United States.

The **oat** plant is a tufted annual grass with a hairy, rounded stalk that contains nodes. Its alternate leaves are long, thin and erect. The seeds appear in loose clusters of numerous branches, each bearing florets (ears) that contain the seeded fruit which do not fall off when mature. Its cultivation is done in temperate, humid regions in moist, fertilized soil; the plant does not prosper in dry, arid lands. **Spring oats** are sown in March, while **winter oats** are sown in September.

This cereal is very nutritious. Its grains are high in starch, lecithin, proteins, lipids, sugar, mineral salts such as phosphorus, calcium, magnesium. They are also a source of vitamins A and B. The grain husks contain saponin and its straw is rich in silicon and vitamin A. The whole plant can be used.

Oatmeal is a popular, digestible food for children and during convalescence. The grains have an anti-inflammatory effect, lower cholesterol level and stimulate the metabolism.

In former times, the husks were used as filling for pillows and mattresses, and the starch was used to starch collars and garments. **Oats** are used by dermatologists in a variety of skin products because of their soothing properties.

Oat stalks can also be used to decorate dried flower arrangements. The grains are used to feed fowl, rabbits and horses. **Oats** are used to feed cows because they stimulate milk production.

also surrounded by sepals. The leaves of the **Malabar-spinach** have an insipid, sticky and slightly sour taste. The first harvest takes place six months after sowing on rich, moist soil. The plant is also propagated through its aerial roots which can take root in the earth producing an offspring that is later separated from the parent plant.

This vegetable is a good source of vitamin A, carotene, carbohydrates, starch, mineral salts like calcium, magnesium and iron as well as vitamins B1, B2 and E. **Malabar-spinach** soothes the stomach, strengthens and invigorates the organism. Thanks to its mucilage content, it is a good aid to digestion.

Malabar-spinach is eaten raw, in simple salads, or cooked. Like **spinach** it can be used to compliment other foods. The leaves can be prepared in stews, gratins and soufflés.

BENINCASA HISPIDA   *Wax pumpkin*
Fruit vegetable
Family: Cucurbitaceae
Origin: Asia
Height: 6.5 to 10 feet (2 to 3 m)
Flowering: summer
Properties: soothing, laxative, sedative, vermifuge (grains)

This herbaceous plant is a strong climber which, unlike most species of its type, is consumed as a vegetable in tropical regions.

Wax pumpkin is covered by a soft fuzz with thin ground tendrils divided into three parts growing from the bottom of its stalk. Its large, round, palmately lobed leaves are velvety on the top side and covered with tiny bristles. Single, yellow bell-shaped flowers with five lanceolate, dented sepals, appear on the axiles of the leaves. They bear big fleshy, elongated oval, bluish grey to greenish fruit which can reach up to 16 inches (40 cm) in length and about 4 inches (10 cm) in width. They are covered by a waxy substance and filled with flat, oval grains.

The pulp of the fruit is delicious, very light, slightly floury, somewhat like a cross between a **cucumber** and a **pumpkin**.

In Europe the culture of the **wax pumpkin** is difficult because it does not tolerate temperatures below 59 °F (15 °C); nevertheless, in the south of France, it is grown in open fields near the Loire. The plants need a rich, well irrigated soil and sunny exposure.

Oat

Oats are processed to produce flour and several breakfast foods made from rolled oats and the groats. Oat flour is used to make cakes, biscuits with dried raisins, crepes with orange flower, and vanilla or chocolate puddings. Oat semolina cooked in milk is used to prepare desserts with fruit or caramel sauces. Rolled oats are used, when cooked in milk, to prepare porridge which can be served with sugar, almonds, honey, or fruit such as apples, bananas, and oranges cut into pieces. This preparation makes an excellent and very nutritious breakfast. The groats are used not only to make sweet desserts, but also savory and hearty sauces which can be used warm or cold with meat, fish and seafood.

BASELLA RUBRA   *Malabar-spinach*
Leaf vegetable
Family: Basellaceae
Origin: tropical regions, India
Height: 3 to 20 feet (1 to 6 m)
Flowering: spring
Properties: soothing, purgative, refreshing, mineralizing

The **Malabar-spinach** is an herbaceous vine which prospers only in moist, warm climate zones. Today it is cultivated extensively as a green vegetable in South-East Asia and Africa.

It is acopious perennial climber which branches out widely. Its alternate leaves are thick, oval or round, pale green with a hint of red. The tiny white or pink flowers are hermaphrodite; their cupshape calyx has five stamens attached to the spathe from the base. They bear small, drupe-like, black, smooth, fleshy fruit which are

Plants must be propped in order to ventilate the fruit. Once harvested, the fruit can be kept for a up to a year when stored in a cool, dry place.

Wax pumpkins are also known as English winter melons. They contain a lot of water, but few fatty acids and sugar. They are also a good source of vitamins A and C and trace elements. It is a very nutritious and easily digestible vegetable. Its grains are used to treat worm infestation.

Wax pumpkin is used to prepare soups, purees, gratins and soufflés. Cut in cubes and sautéed, it is a good accompaniment to meat dishes. It is also used in beef, pork and fish stuffings.

BETA VULGARIS VAR. CICLA
Chard or Swiss chard

Leaf vegetable
Family: *Chenopodiaceae*
Origin: *Europe*
Height: *28 inches (70 cm)*
Flowering: *summer*
Properties: *soothing, anti-anaemia, emollient, laxative*

Swiss chard is a variety of the **beet** from the Mediterranean region and the Atlantic coast, also known in India. It was first discovered by the Assyrians at around 700 BC. Later, the Greeks and the Romans consumed its leaves just like those of **spinach**; hence its name: **Roman spinach**. In the Middle Ages, **Swiss chard** was used as an ingredient for soups and purees.

Swiss chard has greatly developed leaves and leafstalks. The leaves, which have a fleshy texture and are slightly pleated, are smooth, dark green, and veined. The small flowers develop numerous irregularly formed fruit with several hollow cavities, each one containing a seed.

Swiss chard has a juicy and refreshing taste. It is grown from seed between April and May on rich, moist soil. Harvesting takes place two months later and continues well into the autumn. The stems have a delicate flavor. Cooked and chilled stems are very good with salad dressing or mayonnaise.

Chard is a very nutritious vegetable and a good source of iron and vitamins A, B2 and C. It is low in calories and protects against infections of the digestive system and stimulates the metabolism.

Beets

Before preparing this vegetable, the stems must be cut into pieces in order to eliminate the hard fibrous parts. Then they can be boiled in salted water and prepared in a gratin, covered with béchamel sauce and sprinkled with parmesan cheese on top. Cooked in butter, they can be served as a vegetable alongside meat or fowl. The leaves, like spinach, are used in salads, soups or purees. They are also suitable for making soufflés, cakes, gnocchi, stuffing or to be used as a filling for an omelette. They are an ingredient in the poitevin-herbs stuffing which is typical of French cuisine. There is a variety of beet with shiny red and pink stems which is used as an ornamental plant in the garden. In the kitchen they are used in the same way as the white variety, they tend however, to lose their intense color with cooking.

BETA VULGARIS VAR. ESCULENTA
Beetroot or Garden beet

Root vegetable
Family: *Chenopodiaceae*
Origin: *Europe*
Height: *8 to 12 inches (20 to 30 cm)*
Flowering: *summer*
Properties: *apéritif, laxative, mineralizing, stimulant, tonic*

There are three different types of **beets** cultivated for different purposes: **sugar beet**, **chard** and **beetroot**. The last was already consumed in the Middle Ages in Germany and France, where it quickly became a basic ingredient for many dishes. In the 19th century, it arrived in Russia where it immediately became popular. Today **beetroot** is cultivated in the north of France and in England. **Beetroot** is highly prized for its sugar content and the intense red color.

Beetroot has globular and somewhat conical taproots which can be red to red-purple and flat toward the bottom. The fine, smooth purple red rind encloses a thick flesh, of the same color, covered with concentric ring fibers around the root axis. The tall, branched reddish-brown stems bear clusters of minute green flowers and carry splendid entire, shinny green, red veined leaves. The fruit, or seedballs, contain two to four seeds that appear clustered together. The red color of **beetroot** comes from the anthocyanin pigment it contains and its characteristic pleasant sweet taste is from the active substance, beta carotene. **Beetroot** is cropped in rows from the end of March until May in rich, well fertilized soil. The young plants are thinned out at a distance of 12 inches (30 cm) well protected from the cold which causes them to germinate too early. The harvest takes place in October and November. The roots should be harvested before the frost period and stored in a dark, cool place.

Beetroot is a very nutritious vegetable. It contains a lot of water and fiber. It is relatively poor in vitamin C, but is a good source of vitamins B1, B2, B3, B6 and E, carotene, iron, sodium, calcium, magnesium, phosphorus and potassium.

Because **beetroot** contains glutamic acid and beta carotene, it strengthens the functioning of the brain and stimulates the balance of hepatic cells. Because of the vitamins it contains, it helps prevent viral infections.

BRASSICA CHINENSIS — **Bok choy or Chinese mustard**

Leaf vegetable
Family: Cruciferae
Origin: the Far East
Height: 12 to 20 inches (30 to 50 cm)
Flowering: summer
Properties: anti-diarrhoea, anti-inflammatory, stimulant, tonic

Bok choy is relatively new to Europe. In Asia, this **cabbage** of the **mustard family** is more popular than **cabbage** itself. It is one of the least common **Chinese cabbages** and the one with the most atypical characteristics.

There are two kinds: **bok choy** which resembles a **leek**, and the **tientsin** with its big, fleshy, almost unveined leaves.

The plant is formed by a rosette of entire leaves with slightly undulated edges which are glossy dark green. It has thick, crisp white stalks in a loose head. The root is small and delicate. It is usually cultivated in humid, warm regions, but there are a few varieties which are suitable for cultivation in temperate zones because they are rather more tolerant of cold temperatures. The sowing takes place from February to March in the greenhouse. Later the seedlings are replanted at intervals of 5 inches (15 cm) from each other. At the end of September, the rosettes are harvested by cutting them at a height of less than an inch (2 cm) from the ground. New rosettes will then sprout from the rootstock. In Asia Bok choy is stored in sand, salt or vinegar. In Europe it is either stored in the cellar or soaked in water and kept wrapped in a moist cloth in the refrigerator.

Bok choy is rich in vitamin C, carotene, potassium and proteins. It has a invigorating effect on the organism. It helps fight anaemia and relieves inflammations and diarrhoea.

Beetroot

Small, young beetroot can be eaten raw. It can also be pickled and used as a relish or grated into a salad. Boiled and cut in small cubes, it can be served with a vinaigrette as an hors-d'œuvre. Beetroot is the ingredient in the typical Russian soup known as borscht. It can also be used to prepare jams and a sweet wine. Cooked in sweetened water, it is a great side dish for game and fowl dishes. Beetroot leaves are used as livestock fodder.

BRASSICA JUNCEA — **Brown or Indian mustard**

Leaf vegetable
Family: Cruciferae
Origin: Asia
Height: 8 to 12 inches (20 to 30 cm)
Flowering: June
Properties: aromatic, purgative, emetic

This **Himalayan mustard** was introduced approximately one hundred years ago to Europe, appearing first in Hungary and later in other central European countries. Its smooth leaves are pale green, dark green or colored purple, plain or slightly crumpled with fleshy petioles arranged in the form of basal rosettes. The yellow flowers stand in a pedicel which rises approximately 5 feet (1.5 m) above the ground. They bear fruit, or siliques, which contain numerous light brown to dark brown seeds of a bitter, sharp taste.

In order to cultivate **Indian mustard**, seeds must be sown very early in the spring or from July onwards, because when it is sown at the beginning of the summer the plant germinates too early without forming rosettes. In hot regions, it can be cultivated in the open during winter, harvesting the leaves on demand. If the plant has bloomed, the floral peduncles can be harvested as a vegetable. Once the fruit ripens, the seeds are harvested to produce **mustard**. The leaves can be eaten fresh or pickled in vinegar or brine. **Indian mustard** contains mucilage and alkaloids. It improves digestion, invigorates the organism and stimulates all vital functions.

The fresh leaves can be used to prepare a pungent salad, or they can be cooked like **spinach**. Pickled in vinegar, they make a delicious accompaniment or side dish. The fresh flowers can also be used in salads, or cooked and served with a vinaigrette as an accompaniment to other dishes.

BRASSICA NAPUS VAR. NAPOBRASSICA — **Rutabaga or Swede turnip**

Root vegetable
Family: Cruciferae
Origin: northern hemisphere
Height: 12 to 16 inches (30 to 40 cm)
Flowering: spring
Properties: nutritious, stimulant, tonic

Rutabaga, also known as **swede turnip,** or more commonly just **swede**, is one of the oldest vegetables of the northern hemisphere. Before the introduction of the **potato**, this root was an important ingredient in the European diet. During the 19th century, **swede** was grown in most kitchen gardens throughout the south of France. Thus, it became a synonym for "bad times." Today, **swede** is gaining back its popularity and is once again being sold on markets.

This annual, hardy plant carries big, petioled, bluish leaves which are smooth and glaucous. They are strongly lobed all the way up to the central vein, and appear in a rosette-like bunch at the top of the yellow root. The latter bears a distinct neck with well marked leaf scars and is surrounded by numerous radicles. The yellow flowers have four, cross-shaped petals and four free sepals equal in size which open upon maturity in order to release the seeds. **Swede** has a sweet and slightly pungent taste.

Sowing takes place from March to April directly onto the field. While the plants are developing, they are banked up with soil because the roots tend to come out of the ground. **Swede** is hardy to cold, so harvesting can be done in late autumn. Once harvested, it is piled up and covered with straw and soil in order to preserve it for a longer period of time.

This vegetable is very nutritious and a good source of proteins and carbohydrates. Besides, it contains vitamins B and C as well as traces of sulphur which give it its characteristic pungent taste.

Swede is extensively cultivated, often as a cattle fodder crop.

BRASSICA OLERACEA VAR. ACEPHALA   Kale
Leaf vegetable
Family: Cruciferae
Origin: Europe
Height: 12 inches to 4 feet (30 cm to 1.20 m)
Flowering: late spring (from the second year)
Properties: anti-scurvy, vulnerary, purifier, diuretic

Kale was already cultivated by the Teutons and Celts. The Romans used **kale** for its healing and nutritious qualities. **Kale** is still a widely used vegetable today.

It is a hardy biennial, which, in contrast to most other **cabbages**, does not form a cabbage head. The plant produces a strong growing rosette of long petioled, elongated leaves with wavy to frilled margins. The yellow flowers and the small fruit resemble those of most crucifers. The small, and shallow root makes the plant very fragile. For this reason, dwarf and semi dwarf varieties have been developed.

Kale is one of the hardiest and most undemanding vegetable crops. It can tolerate temperatures as low as –59 °F (–15 °C) and prospers in almost any soil.

Kale

Kale boiled in water or sautéed in butter is used to accompany both meat and fowl. It can also be used to make purees, soups and gratins. Cooked in the pressure cooker with spices, cream, and hard boiled eggs, it makes a delicious stuffing for fowl. Raw, it is wonderful in a salad with olive oil and lemon juice.

Cauliflower

Cauliflower has a delicious nutty taste when used raw in a salad. It can be pickled in vinegar and used as a condiment. In this way, it is used in the preparation of salad niçoise. It forms part of the popular mixed pickles made in Great Britain. Steamed cauliflower is prepared in a vinaigrette or covered with a light cheese sauce and gratinated. It is also prepared as fritters, purees, and of course, it is used to garnish several meat dishes.

The sowing takes place from April to May directly onto the field. The plant may be harvested by cutting off the entire rosette before the stem has elongated, or (especially in areas with long, cool growing periods) the individual lower leaves may be removed progressively as the main stem elongates.

Kale which is harvested after the first frost is slightly sweeter in taste. The leaves of **kale** contain

protein, sugar, fiber and are a good source of vitamin C, particularly during the winter. Besides, **kale** is rich in iron and mineral salts.

It is a mineralizing vegetable which detoxifies the body and improves digestion. **Kale** juice is an excellent healing agent for external wounds and its high content of vitamin C helps the body fight against all sorts of infections and fatigue.

BRASSICA OLERACEA VAR. BOTRYTIS

Cauliflower

Flower vegetable
Family: *Cruciferae*
Origin: *the Middle East*
Height: *16 to 24 inches (40 to 60 cm)*
Flowering: *summer*
Properties: *soothing, anti-scurvy, antiseptic, purifier, diuretic*

Cauliflower is one of the oldest vegetables known in France, which is one of its main producers. It is grown in the regions of Brittany, the Nord-Pas-de-Calais, Normandie and Bouches-du-Rhône.

Cauliflower has a big, thick, woody stem with bluish-green leaves and crisp leaf stalks. Enormous, compact flower peduncles form an imposing white terminal head made up of uniform white, tight bouquets. This infertile inflorescence is, in fact, a vegetable monstrosity.

Cauliflower is grown from seed. Once developed, the young plants are replanted at a distance of 16 inches (40 cm) apart from each other. They must be watered and fertilized regularly if they are to form magnificent heads. Harvesting takes place from late spring until winter. Cauliflower can be kept covered with a moist cloth in the refrigerator for a few days. It can also be frozen once it has been blanched. The vegetable is not very nutritious; it contains a lot of water and some sulphur, vitamins A, B and C. However, cauliflower is rich in fiber and mineral salts. It has small amounts of carbohydrates and mucilage and very little fat.

Cauliflower is good for the skin, the bones, the liver and the nervous system.

BRASSICA OLERACEA VAR. CAPITATA **Cabbage**
Leaf vegetable
Family: Cruciferae
Origin: the Middle East
Height: 16 inches (40 cm)
Flowering: late spring (from the second year)
Properties: antibacterial, anti-scurvy, diuretic

It is said that this vegetable was already bred in Antiquity from the wild, or **sea cabbage,** found on the coasts of the Atlantic Ocean and the Mediterranean Sea. The aim was to obtain a greater number of leaves which were even more serrated. After several rigorous selections, common **cabbage** and **savoy cabbage** were developed. These **cabbages** have smooth leaves and come in two different shapes and three different colors.

The heads of horticultural varieties of **cabbage** range in shape from pointed, through globular, to flat; from soft to hard in structure; through various shades of green, grey-green, and magenta or red. In Alsace there is a **green cabbage**, which is pickled to make choucroute,

or as it is known in Germany "sauerkraut." These are very ancient herbal plants.

All these forms of **cabbage** have a hard head formed by the grouping of entire, smooth, grossly veined leaves and a compact voluminous head with a few external leaves. The entire structure is supported by a deformed stem. The young flowers have four petals and four opposing, cross shaped sepals. They bear fruit known as siliques with two valves which open upon maturity releasing the seeds. There are of course some differences among these **cabbages**: **red cabbage** is the smallest one with a more pronounced and pungent taste than that of **white cabbage,** which has a sweet taste. Both are eaten raw in salads or pickled.

Cabbage is easy to cultivate and is a major table vegetable in most countries of the temperate zone. It can be kept fresh in the refrigerator or frozen after being blanched. Cabbage has a high water content and is rich in carbohydrates, nitrogen and fatty acids. It has few calories and a lot of vitamin C, which is why it is used to prevent scurvy, viral infections and anaemia. Because it contains sulphur derivatives it also has antibacterial properties.

BRASSICA OLERACEA VAR. CYMOSA **Broccoli**
Leaf vegetable
Family: Cruciferae
Origin: Asia Minor
Height: 16 to 20 inches (40 to 50 cm)
Flowering: from autumn to winter
Properties: anti-scurvy, purifier, diuretic

Broccoli cultivation is fairly recent. It was first cultivated in Italy, and then spread to Great Britain where it is consumed in great amounts. This close relative of **cauliflower** is an annual plant. It is fast growing, upright and bears tight, dense green clusters of flower buds at the ends of the central axis and the branches. Harvesting takes place before the Flowering while the buds are still on the compact, grey-green head. Like **cauliflower**, **broccoli** also has a thick, woody trunk with several fleshy pedicels which end in the floral clusters. Its leaves are fleshy, deeply scalloped and bluish-green. However, **broccoli** has a longer growth period than **cauliflower**.

It demands a well-irrigated, rich soil, but is hardy to temperature fluctuations and air humidity. The flavor

Broccoli

Broccoli is eaten cooked, in a vinaigrette, in gratins, with light sauces, in fritters and purees. In Italy and Asia it is particularly used as an ingredient for cheese omelettes and for sweet-and-sour pork. On the photograph, broccoli is the vegetable that appears between the peppers.

of **broccoli** resembles that of **cabbage** but is somewhat milder. It has a high water content and is rich in vitamins C and E. It is used to prevent scurvy and its invigorating effect is beneficial during convalescence. It helps cleanse the organism from toxins and improves the digestion.

BRASSICA OLERACEA   **Brussels sprouts**
VAR. GEMMIFERA
Leaf vegetable
Family: Cruciferae
Origin: Belgium
Height: 2.5 to 3 feet (0.80 to 1 m)
Flowering: late spring (from the second year)
Properties: anti-scurvy, diuretic, nutritious, mineralizing

Brussels sprouts appeared on markets around 1820 after a careful cultivation and selection process. They are the smallest type of **cabbage** of the **mustard family**.

The plant's main stem is quite tall with a not very deep flat root. When cultivating the plant care must be taken that it takes root well, because the small heads of the plant, once developed, can pull the plant out of the ground with their weight. To avoid this the plant has to be constantly banked up with earth and sheltered from the wind. The stem has axillary buds along its length which develop into small heads or sprouts similar to heads of **cabbage** but measuring 1 to 2 inches (25 to 40 mm) in diameter.

Brussels sprouts are a slow growing vegetable. It is sown in April in plant beds and transplanted directly onto the field once it is strong enough. **Brussels sprouts** endure neither aridity nor heat. They need a rich soil containing little nitrogen to avoid the heads opening.

Once they are long enough, **Brussels sprouts** heads are separated from the stem, from bottom to top. Harvesting is done during the plant's entire growth period. If they are not harvested regularly, the heads on the lower part of the stem begin to turn yellow. The tops of the plant can also be cut in order to accelerate growth. In order to avoid diseases, yellow leaves should be removed.

Brussels sprouts are hardy to cold and are generally best when harvested before the first frost. There are also red-purple varieties which are less productive, but more tasty. **Brussels sprouts** are the most fragrant and tasty of the **cabbages**. They are also very nutritious containing high amounts of water, vitamin C, mineral salts, carbohydrates and fatty acids.

BRASSICA OLERACEA   **Kohlrabi**
VAR. GONGYLODES
Stem vegetable
Family: Cruciferae
Origin: the Far East
Height: 16 to 20 inches (40 to 50 cm)
Flowering: summer (from the second year)
Properties: invigorating, nutritious

Kohlrabi's most distinctive feature is the greatly enlarged stem just above the soil which is the part of the plant harvested for food. It was developed by gardeners after being crossbred several times.

Its white-green stem is rounded, fleshy and flat at the ends. The length of the stem is covered with long leafstalks with green, pinnately lobed and fragile leaves. The fine, rather narrow root is not anchored very deeply in the soil.

The tuber has, on average, a diameter of approximately 4 inches (10 cm), but it can also reach 12 inches (30 cm) and weigh up to 4.4 lbs. (2 kg).

Kohlrabi can be purple, red-purple or white. It is sown directly onto the field in the spring and must be watered regularly to ensure that it does not become fibrous. Harvesting takes place from early summer until autumn.

The harvested **kohlrabi** is easy to store and keeps fresh very long without losing its properties. It is rich in fiber, mineral salts, trace elements and vitamin C; therefore, it is very nutritious. It is a stimulating and invigorating vegetable. It is a very popular seasonal vegetable which facilitates digestion.

The peeled tuber is boiled in water that is changed several times to eliminate the nitrogen it contains which makes it difficult to digest.

Kohlrabi is used to compliment sausages and pork. Because of its fragrance and flavor, **kohlrabi** can be used in purees and vegetable soups. When raw, because of its sweet mustardy taste, it is an excellent ingredient for salads. It can also be stuffed with meat and prepared as a gratin.

Red cabbage
Raw red cabbage, finely cut, adds color and aroma to salads and raw fruit and vegetables dishes. It can be cooked in a pot with apples or red wine and served as an accompaniment to meat, fowl and game dishes.

BRASSICA OLERACEA VAR. SABAUDA — Savoy cabbage

Leaf vegetable
Family: Cruciferae
Origin: Italy
Height: 12 to 16 inches (30 to 40 cm)
Flowering: summer (from the second year)
Properties: antibacterial, anti-scurvy, diuretic, tonic

Savoy cabbage was discovered towards the end of the Middle Ages. This head **cabbage** has a green head, more or less dense, formed by frilled, wavy leaves that due to their waffle like structure are surmounted and folded one on to the other. It has a deformed stem with a small root. The small yellow flowers bear tiny fruit or siliques containing numerous seeds.

It has a delicate flavor. It is cultivated the whole year long from seed. When it is sown in January / February harvesting takes place before the summer. When grown in the nursery, it is sown in April and harvested from autumn until winter. **Savoy cabbage** is available during the whole year thanks to the different varieties that exist. It is hardy, but requires a soil rich in nutrients which must be well irrigated in the summer because the plant is not tolerant of heat. Storage should be in a dark, cool place.

Savoy cabbage is best when stewed with **carrots** and **potatoes**. Its leaves can be used to make a delicious herbal stuffing for meat or cooked and prepared as a gratin. It is also used in stocks and soups, often served with bacon and croutons.

BRASSICA PEKINENSIS — Chinese or Celery cabbage

Leaf vegetable
Family: Cruciferae
Origin: the Far East
Height: 12 to 20 inches (30 to 50 cm)
Flowering: summer
Properties: anti-anaemia, anti-inflammatory, anti-diarrhoea, mineralizing

Chinese cabbage
Raw Chinese cabbage gives salads a very crisp, refreshing taste and a fine aroma. It is used in soups, broths and ragouts. It can also be sautéed and served to accompany various meat and other vegetable dishes.

Chinese cabbage is the result of the careful crossbreeding of a Chinese garden variety. It was introduced to Europe in the 18th century and soon became one of the most popular **Chinese cabbages**.

Its root is fine and thin; its head pale green and fleshy. Its interlocked leaves have a powdery appearance. They are formed by a large white side with numerous veins and are slightly crinkled and wavy on the edges. **Chinese cabbage** blooms in the summer. After being exposed to too much light, it does not form a head and germinates too early.

Chinese cabbage is a crisp, digestible vegetable with a delicate mustard taste. It is sown in February in the nursery on moist soil. It is harvested at the end of September by cutting off the heads roughly 1 inch (3 cm) from the ground to clear the way for new rosettes. Even in the refrigerator or the cellar, it can be kept for only a short period of time. In Asia it is preserved in salt, in vinegar or dried.

This vegetable contains plenty of water and is rich in vitamin C, carotene, proteins and potassium. Therefore, it works against anaemia and diarrhoea, and helps relieve inflammations.

BRASSICA RAPA — Turnip

Root and leaf vegetable
Family: Cruciferae
Origin: northern hemisphere
Height: 20 inches (40 cm)
Flowering: summer (from the second year)
Properties: tranquilizer, diuretic

Before **potatoes** arrived in Europe, **turnip** was for many years considered to be the vegetable of the poor. Today, it is a fashionable vegetable. It is widely used in England, and in Scotland it is regarded as the national vegetable.

The **turnip** root is formed by the thickening of the primary root of the seedling together with the base of the young stem immediately above it. The leaves, forming a rosette-like bunch at the top of the root, are grass-green and bear rough hairs. In the second season the bud in the center of the rosette forms a strong, erect, branched stem bearing somewhat glaucous smooth leaves somewhat like those of the **swede**. Their color varies according to the species: early ones are generally white or violet around the high part of the tuber; others are yellow, greyish, orange-yellow or even black. Stem and branches end in clusters of small, bright yellow flowers, which are succeeded by smooth, elongated, short-beaked pods containing brown pungent seeds.

Turnip is a vary undemanding vegetable to cultivate. It is sown directly onto the field during the whole

season from March to September. The first tiny **turnips** are so mild and tender that they can be quickly harvested and eaten raw. They can also be harvested once they have fully developed, and are then ready to be cooked.

Turnip is very low in calories, but it contains a lot of water, fiber, essential oils, sugar and mineral salts. It is not very nutritious, but it is used for its diuretic and tranquilizing properties. It is also of use in weight loss diets.

CAMPANULA RAPUNCULUS   *Rampion*
Root and leaf vegetable
Family: *Campanulaceae*
Origin: *Europe, Asia, North Africa*
Height: *20 to 31inches (30 to 80 cm)*
Flowering: *summer (from the second year)*
Properties: *antiseptic, astringent, tranquilizer, mineralizing*

Rampion was eaten in medieval Europe during times of famine. Very soon its nutritional qualities were discovered and it became part of every day menus.

Rampion grew mostly as a weed in vineyards, but was soon also cultivated in kitchen gardens as a vegetable. Today it is cultivated particularly in the south of France and in Italy. It is a beautiful plant with a white, fleshy root which resembles that of the **carrot**. It propagates through numerous, tiny, secondary root tubers. In the course of the first year, it produces narrow stem leaves and untoothed, broadly oval basal leaves that form a rosette around the stalk. During the second year, it produces ascending clusters of long-stalked lilac bells bearing capsules which contain in each case numerous seeds. The root has a soft, sticky, slightly sweet taste. This hardy perennial plant is cultivated by laminar sowing or plantation of the root tubers. It is harvested in autumn and stored in the cellar. The young leaves can also be consumed; they are harvested before the inflorescence forms.

Rampion contains inulin, a sugar substitute. Therefore, it is often used in special dietary foods for diabetics.

In addition, it contains iron, calcium, phosphorus, vitamins, mucilage, cellulose, rubber resin, choline, and mineral salts. This plant also has medicinal properties: it strengthens, invigorates and purifies the organism and is used to treat angina.

The root is used as a vegetable for soups and as an accompaniment to meat dishes. It is also often eaten raw in salads. The leaves can be cooked in the same manner as spinach leaves. Its blue flowers are also very decorative in ornamental gardens.

CAPSICUM ANNUUM   *Bell pepper*
Fruit vegetable
Family: *Solanaceae*
Origin: *South and Central America*
Height: *24 to 32 inches (60 to 80 cm)*
Flowering: *May*
Properties: *anti-fatigue, anti-stress, apéritif, digestive*

Bell peppers arrived in Hungary from the New World around 1585. However, the plant which is a spice and a vegetable at the same time, was not introduced into other European countries until about a century ago.

There are more than 200 different species of **peppers**, varying not only in form and color, but also with a wide variety of aromas and tastes. **Bell peppers** are one of the milder variations, and are available in several different colors: red, green, yellow, orange and violet.

This herbaceous plant has branched, woody stems equipped with simple leaves that alternate in gentle colors of green. Its white, self-pollinating flowers bear generally elongated or rounded fruit which are green at first, gradually turning red, orange, yellow, purple or black once they have reached full maturity. The fruit appears in the shape of big smooth, inflated, round or elongated berries. Their interior is formed by lobes which enclose numerous seeds. Their skin is hard, smooth and glossy. Their thick, juicy, sweet or pungent pulp is endowed with a gamut of different flavors. The plants are grown from seed on rich, humid soil and in sunny fields. The plants require warm temperatures and a lot of water. They are sown from February to March in sheltered beds. The young plants are transplanted from the outset of the flowers directly onto the field. Harvesting is mainly done by hand three months later from June until the autumn.

Bell peppers are rich in vitamin C and have a high water content. Ripe **bell peppers** are rich in vitamin A, fiber, carotene, mineral salts, essential oil which give it their characteristic flavor, and coloring substances. This vegetable is beneficial during child-

---

Turnip

Not only the root of the turnip is used in the kitchen. There are some varieties which are cultivated for their fleshy leaves. Cooked in salted water, the young shoots are seasoned in different ways. The leaves can be used in stews or as green vegetables. Raw, they are added to salads to give them a pungent taste. Young turnips with their delicate taste are eaten raw. Cooked and cut into pieces, they can be served with butter to accompany various meat dishes, being an especially good companion for roast duck. They are a delicious ingredient for gratins and purees, and can be used in preparing chicken stew, vegetable and oxtail soups.

hood. It stimulates the appetite and gastric secretions. Furthermore, it aids during convalescence and protects against viral infections.

CARLINA ACAULIS

Carline thistle or Stemless caroline

Flower vegetable
Family: Compositae
Origin: Central Europe
Height: 0.4 inches (1 cm)
Flowering: May to September
Properties: antibacterial, astringent, emollient, vulnerary

This now largely forgotten vegetable, which in some countries is registered as a protected species, was in former times, renowned for its medicinal properties. The plant was named either after **Charlemagne** or **Charles V**. According to the legend an angel appeared to him displaying the plant. The angel then explained that the plant could be used to cure his people of the plague.

Carline thistle is a hardy perennial plant related to **thistle** and **burdock**. This self-propagating plant, with its spiny almost non existent stem, thrives in dry, sandy ground and in sunny locations. **Carline thistle** has a dense head of small, usually pink or purple flowers and green, prickly leaves. It also has spiny stems and flower heads without ray flowers. The flowers bear achenes covered with yellow hairs which open up in feathery umbels double in size. Its thick, red-brown, root contains latex and has a fetid smell. The root is harvested in autumn; the flowers are picked before they bear fruit.

When there is a lot of moisture in the air, the sepals around the flower close up forming a conical capsule that protects the flower. The plant contains inulin, a sugar substitute for diabetics, as well as essential oils, tannin, resin, carlinen (an antibiotic substance) and saponine. It is applied to cure eczema, acne and other skin diseases. Its antibiotic property makes it effective against influenza and feverish viral infections.

Its unripe fruit can be prepared like an **artichoke** – either steamed in salted water and served with vinaigrette, or sautéed in butter with parmesan cheese and garlic, and served with grilled or toasted bread and other vegetables. It can also be stuffed with other vegetables covered with a béchamel or other light white sauce, and then baked in the oven as a gratin.

Bell pepper

Bell peppers are generally added raw to salads. They are also used with other raw vegetables to prepare salad niçoise or a variety of seafood salads. Cooked and cut into pieces, they are an ingredient for several dishes like Ratatouille as well as other Mediterranean dishes made with meat, pork, chicken, crab or squid. They are also used in making minestrone soup, and are a real delicacy when braised with ricotta cheese. Bell peppers lend a special aroma to omelettes and several Spanish dishes such as Paella, while Basque cuisine would be unthinkable without them, their colors reflecting those of the Basque national flag, red and green. They are highly regarded as an ingredient for many Chinese dishes, and are an ever present topping for Italian pizzas. Whole, deseeded peppers, stuffed with meat, vegetables or fish and baked in the oven, are served as a main dish, either warm or cold, right across the Mediterranean basin.

CHAEROPHYLLUM BULBOSUM

Turnip-rooted chervil

Root vegetable
Family: Umbelliferae
Origin: eastern France, Central Europe
Height: 47 inches (1.20 m)
Flowering: June to July (from the second year)
Properties: apéritif, nutritious, stomachic, tonic

The **turnip-rooted chervil,** an ancient vegetable which is becoming more and more popular again of late, is found in Europe, Asia and North America. In the 19th century it arrived in Germany from Hungary and soon spread to Spain where it is cultivated not for its root, but for its aromatic leaves. Depending on the region where it is grown, it is a biennial or a perennial. In the wild, it grows in shady, moist soil, mostly on meadows and in vineyards. During the first year, a rosette of very pinnate leaves, reminiscent to that of **parsley**, appear on the short, yellowish, tuberous, very fleshy, **carrot**-shaped root. During the second year dense, close umbel clusters of white flowers appear on the flower stalks which can reach up to 8 inches (20 cm) in length. The flowers bear double, pointed achenes.

The root of the **turnip-rooted chervil** has a rather floury consistency, and is reminiscent in taste of the chestnut. The plant is grown from seed from September to October in cool, airy but not too moist soil. The first leaf shoots appear in February; the root is harvested as soon as the leaves fade and turn yellow, in July. Once the leaves have been removed, the freshly harvested roots are left out on the field to dry for a couple of days. They are then stored in a cellar or silo, where they will keep until the following spring.

The root of the plant is rich in sugar, vitamins B and C, as well as mineral salts. Raw, grated, or sliced with a vinaigrette, it is delicious and nutritious. The fragrant leaves are used to add aroma to stews and salads.

CHAMAEDOREA ELEGANS

Mountain palm tree

Leaf vegetable
Family: Ceroxyloideae
Origin: Mexico and Colombia
Height: 10 feet (3 m)
Flowering: summer
Properties: nutritious, purgative, mineralizing, tonic

Like other palm trees, the mountain palm tree is also harvested for its **cabbage** palm (that is, the large bud that is formed by the flowers and the leaves at the top of the palm). The **mountain palm tree** forms big bushes of approximately 8 feet (2.50 m) in diameter. The short, tightly packed, trunks grow up to 10 feet (3 m) high. The long, light green, pinnate leaves carry from 20 to 40 oblong, pointed leaflets. Its dioecious flowers are borne on long stems of up to 1 yard in length (1 m). They bear small, round, berries the size of a pea which become black as the leaves of the tree turn orange, a characteristic which accentuates the beauty of this palm tree.

The **mountain palm tree** is propagated through its shoots from which new palm trees develop rapidly. Leaf buds are harvested in the spring, once the plant begins to produce sap; the flower buds are harvested during the Flowering.

Palm **cabbages** are highly perishable, and must be either consumed immediately or preserved. They are mostly available canned. They contain a lot of water, fiber, carbohydrates, some oil and mineral salts.

They are cooked in water and served alone or together with other vegetables to accompany meat and fish. Although highly recommended in the form of vegetable fritters, they can also be served cold with a vinaigrette, as an hors-d'œuvre, or simply mixed in a salad.

CHENOPODIUM QUINOA　　**Quinoa**
Fruit and Leaf vegetable
Family: *Chenopodiaceae*
Origin: *the Andes (Peru, Bolivia and Ecuador)*
Height: *5 feet (1.50 m)*
Flowering: *spring*
Properties: *anti-anaemia, emollient, mineralizing*

Quinoa is a very old plant cultivated for over 3,000 years on the high plateaus of the Andes. In contrast to other members of its family, the plant has not spread beyond this region.

It was a basic food source for the Incas. Competition came when the Spanish tried to replace it with **barley**, but the experiment was unsuccessful as the climate of the high plateau turned out to be too harsh for the European grain. **Quinoa** is still consumed today in Latin America and the United States where it is highly prized, and recently it has even been introduced to Europe.

It has an upright, poorly branched-out trunk and alternate, long-stalked, very lobed, triangular, pointed leaves. The small simple flowers appear in terminal clusters around the stem. The monospermous fruit resemble small nuts. Today more resistant and more productive new varieties which do not contain saponine are cultivated, thus removing the necessity to soak the grains.

Quinoa is sown in the spring. Shortly before the grains have reached full maturity, about five months later, they can be harvested. If done later, the seeds would fall to the ground as the stalks were cut. The stalks are first left to dry, then they are threshed. Finally, the grain are removed from the husks as are other impurities. The leaves, which are eaten like **spinach**, can be harvested throughout the entire growth period while they are still young and green.

The grains contain much carbohydrate and protein, small amounts of lipids, cellulose and minerals salts like calcium, phosphorus and potassium. The leaves contain a lot of cellulose, proteins and sugar as well as minerals salts and vitamin C, and helps improve digestion.

Quinoa grains are a rich and nutritious food source which, as part of the daily diet helps prevent rickets. **Quinoa** flour mixed with **wheat** is used to make pastries, biscuits, crepes, porridges and soups. The fermented grains are used to prepare an alcoholic drink known as chicha, very popular among the Indian population. The leaves cooked in boiling water and seasoned are served with butter as an accompaniment to meat dishes. They are also used to make herbal pâtés, omelettes and stuffings. In agriculture, the leaves are also used as fodder.

CICHORIUM ENDIVIA　　**Endive**
Leaf vegetable
Family: *Compositae*
Origin: *Western and Central Europe*
Height: *4 to 8 inches (10 to 20 cm)*
Flowering: *summer (from the second year)*
Properties: *apéritif, purifier, diuretic, stomachic, tonic*

The Greeks and Romans used **endives** for both their pharmacological and their culinary properties.

However, tastes have changed with time and **endives** are nowadays only prized by those amateurs who prefer crisp salads with a bitter flavor. This tendency has been emphasized by those producers who concentrate on the cultivation of other types of lettuce.

This biennial plant produces rosettes of leaves without forming heads. The foliage is dense, refreshing and delicately bitter. The green, more or less large leaves have white borders and are gathered together at the neck of the root. Its many varieties form two groups, the curly, or narrow leaf, and the Batavian, or broad leaf, **endive**. The small whitish flowers stand in panicles and bear achenes with a small, silky crown.

Endive thrives in loamy soil; the sowing takes place on a well prepared field which must be regularly watered during the whole growth period. When the required size has been reached, the heart is covered with plastic film which has the effect of reducing the bitterness, producing a milder and more tender lettuce. The same results can be achieved by placing the roots in glass containers. Because **endives** do not keep for long, they must be used right after being harvested. They are very rich in vitamin A and C and contain vitamin B, cellulose, a few carbohydrates, and bitter substances. They have diuretic and purifying properties. Prepared in salads, they form part of a well balanced diet. **Endives** stimulate the appetite and aid digestion and the elimination of toxins. They also stimulate and tonify the organism.

Endive salads

Endive can be eaten raw. A delicious salad can be made by adding diced bacon, garlic or finely grated Gruyere cheese. The leaves can also be prepared in the same manner as with a green vegetable. They can be boiled in salted water and sautéed in butter. They are also good when braised with cream, and are suitable for use in gratins, fritters, vegetable pies and soufflés.

CICHORIUM INTYBUS   **Chicory**

Leaf and Root vegetable
Family: Compositae
Origin: Western and Central Europe
Height: 12 to 56 inches (30 to 90 cm)
Flowering: from July to September (wild Chicoree); other varieties after the second summer
Properties: apéritif, laxative, diuretic, purifier, stomachic, tonic

---

Chicory was mentioned as long as 4,000 years ago in the Ebers papyrus, an Egyptian compilation of medical texts and one of the oldest known to date. It was known to the Romans and eaten by them as a vegetable or in salads. **Chicory** is still prized today for its culinary and medicinal properties.

This perennial plant, which has been cultivated since the 17th century, has a rigid, branching, hairy stem. Its long, brown, fleshy taproot contains a white latex resin. The basal leaves are divided while the superior ones are lobed, elongated and toothed. The shining blue flowers of several petals appear in big terminal clusters and bear simple achenes.

Chicory is sown in July. Leaves are harvested from the following July up until the flowering starts, while the roots are harvested in the autumn.

Wild chicory has given way to a number of different varieties: **witloof** and **carla chicory**, **barbe de capucin**, **red chicory** from Vérone, **trévise chicory**, **sugarbread chicory**, and a number of other hybrids. **Witloof chicory** is a variety whose white leaves stand together so closely that it looks almost like a spindle. When exposed to direct light, **chicory** turns green and becomes even more bitter. The **carla** variety has red-rimmed leaves and is sweeter. **Chicory** is juicy, refreshing and crisp. It is grown from seed in the open in the spring. In autumn, the roots are dug out, and after the leaves are cut back to less than an inch (2 cm) from the neck they are stored over the winter in the cellar. From December to March the roots are stored in the darkness of the cellar, two thirds covered with damp sand at about 57–68 °F (14–20 °C).

Harvesting is done by hand three weeks later by cutting the lettuce head at the base of the leaves. The **barbe de capucin** variety is sown in July. Its long, blanched, green to pale yellow, loose leaves have a very indented stem. The leaves are soft, sweet, juicy and refreshing. Harvesting is also done by cutting the leaves less than an inch (2 cm) from the neck. The **red chicory** of **Vérone**, the **trévise**, and the **sugarbread** varieties form a type of head. **Red** and **trévise chicory** are crisp, with large white leaves and red stalks. Their flavor is less bitter and more pleasant. **Sugarbread chicory** has a moderately tight foliage with a long and wide green stem. It has a slightly bitter taste and is a great appetite stimulant. These varieties are generally sown in July in the open and are later thinned out and replanted 12 inches (30 cm) apart from each another. **Chicory** can withstand temperatures down to 18 °F (–8 °C). After the first head has been harvested, the stem can produce new heads to take its place.

Chicory contains a lot of water, cellulose, fiber, vitamin A (carotene), vitamins B, C and K, mineral salts (calcium, magnesium and phosphorus), amino acids, inulase as well as bitter substances. **Chicory** stimulates both the appetite and the digestion. It adjusts the metabolism, thereby detoxifying the organism. Because it is so rich in vitamins it is used in spring diets, and curative diets to cleanse the organism.

COLOCASIA ESCULENTA   **Taro or Eddo**
Root and leaf vegetable
Family: Araceae
Origin: Burma, tropical Asia
Height: 24 to 28 inches (60 to 70 cm)
Flowering: summer (seldom)
Properties: nutritious, mineralizing, stimulant

Taro is a very old plant which was already being cultivated in China about 2,000 years ago. Today there are approximately 1,000 different cultivated varieties worldwide, growing on damp as well as on dry soil. Taro can therefore be grown in Asian floodlands, on the Amazon delta, and in the relevant agricultural areas of Australia, Africa and India. In India it is known as **eddo**; in Hawaii, where it is consumed cooked, mashed and fermented, it is known as *poi*.

This plant with its creeping rhizome produces, depending on the variety, one large or several smaller

Taro
These tubers can be cooked and used in various salads, purees or fritters. They can be sliced and sautéed in hot oil. The leaves and the leaflets provide a highly prized green vegetable used to accompany a variety of meat and fish dishes.

edible tubers. It has very long stalks which carry oval or pointed leaves that tend to hang loosely when mature. Some species may have leaves as large as 20 inches (60 cm) in length and from 24 to 28 inches (60 to 70 cm) in width. The flowers, surrounded by a white spathe, appear deep between the leaf stalks, and bear very small shining berries. **Taro** is cultivated in hot climate zones. The tubers are planted in the spring in a well prepared, always damp soil. In Asia, the dachine and macabo varieties are widely cultivated. The tubers, which are harvested in late autumn, can only be stored for a short period of time because they perish quickly. For this reason there are numerous early and a late varieties, to ensure that fresh **taro** is readily available throughout the year.

Taro contains a lot of carbohydrate, carotene, vitamins B and C, as well as mineral salts such as calcium and magnesium. In the raw state, **taro** leaves, tubers and stems contain calcium oxalate which can cause severe skin irritation; they must therefore always be cooked, as heating destroys the irritant concerned. Nevertheless, it is a very nourishing and healthy vegetable. The tubers are cooked and served in salads, purees, as fritters, or sliced and sautéed in oil. The leaves and leaflets provide a very nourishing leaf vegetable which is a good accompaniment for meat and fish dishes. **Taro** tubers can be germinated in a glass of water, thus obtaining a very decorative tropical plant.

COPERNICIA
MACROGLOSSA   **Caranuba wax palm**
Leaf and Stem vegetable
Family: Coryphoideae
Origin: northeast Brazil
Height: 13 to 16.4 feet (4 to 5 m)
Flowering: spring
Properties: purifier, invigorating, stimulant, tonic

This **wax palm** tree is named after the Carnaubeira indians who inhabit the area where the palm grows. This tree is very important for the economy of the region, providing the native population with numerous products such as wax, palm **cabbages**, sago, syrup and timber. The roofs of their huts are thatched with palm leaves, which also supplies the material for their hammocks. It is a small palm whose fanlike leaves appear in a spherical crown. Its trunk, which reaches

only a diameter of about 8 inches (20 cm), is surrounded by a velvety mat of dead leaves that, with increasing age, cover only the top part of the tree leaving behind numerous stigmata on the rest of the trunk. The tree has approximately fifteen splendid greenish-blue leaves, which spread out, on a span of about 7 feet (2 m), approximately sixty fanned segments each of about 5 feet (1.50 m) in length. The small hermaphrodite flowers appear in ramified inflorescences and bear green, egg-shaped fruit.

This variety of palm tree is quite useful; it produces vegetable, edible substances which are rich in sugar, starch and mineral salts. The leaf buds are consumed as a vegetable similar to palm hearts. After the woody fibers of the trunk have been rinsed several times, sago, a very nutritious food starch is extracted. A sugar syrup is obtained from the juice of the trunk which is used to make an alcoholic beverage known as Arrak. And finally, this decorative palm tree is a welcome addition to any tropical garden.

CRAMBE MARITIMA — Sea kale

Leaf vegetable
Family: Cruciferae
Origin: north and west coasts of Europe
Height: 12 inches (30 cm)
Flowering: May to July
Properties: purifier, diuretic, anti-scurvy, antiseptic

Sea kale is a shrub which loves salty soil; therefore, it is to be found on the seashores and cliffs of both the Mediterranean Sea and the Atlantic Ocean. **Sea kale,** the taste of which resembles **cabbage,** has been around for quite a time. That renowned vegetable expert **Louis XIV** knew of it, and ordered its cultivation in the gardens of Versailles. The plant has a thick, woody, pale green trunk with large, bluish-green, fleshy, lobed, waxy, coarsely toothed leaves. Honey fragrant, clustered sprays of white, four petaled flowers rise from the basal leaves. They bear small, round, split fruit containing the seeds. **Sea kale** thrives in cool, deep and salty soil and a sunny location in mild, damp climate zones. It's cultivated from seed directly onto the field from March to June, through division of shoots in the spring, or through division of the root into pieces of 4 inches (10 cm) long with at least two buds. The young, fleshy, white shoots with pink leaf buds are harvested. The young, external leaves are also edible; however, to ensure they lose their bitter taste they should be blanched before hand. When harvesting the leaves, care should be taken not to damage the heart of the plant which can remain for several years. **Sea kale** perishes quickly, so it should be consumed immediately. However, the blanched leaves can be frozen or preserved. **Sea kale** is rich in vitamin C, mineral salts, sulphur and iodine. It has a metabolism-stimulating effect, thereby detoxifying the organism. Because of its high vitamin C content, it is used to prevent scurvy as well as viral infections.

Blanched in boiling water, the sprouts may be served as an entrée with a vinaigrette or mayonnaise. It is also delicious when coated in meat juices, covered in béchamel sauce, baked in the oven and served as a side dish with meat.

CUCUMIS SATIVUS — Cucumber and Gherkin

Fruit vegetable
Family: Cucurbitaceae
Origin: probably western Asia
Height: About 8 feet (2.50 m)
Flowering: May to July
Properties: diuretic, emollient, refreshing, tonic

This annual, creeping plant is widely cultivated in temperate regions for its fruit. **Cucumbers** have a rough, succulent, trailing stem which bears branched tendrils by which the plant can be trained to supports. Its hairy, very serrated leaves have three to five pointed lobes and a conspicuous palmate vein on their edges. The trumpet-shaped yellow flowers are unisexual because they can sometimes be male (five stamens on three entities) and sometimes female. Fertilization occurs through self-pollination, but not necessarily through cross-pollination. **Cucumbers** cultivated in greenhouses only bear fruit through parthenogenesis. The more or less large fruit are very succulent, elongated berries. According to the species the skin is green, yellow or white, bright and smooth or covered with spines. Their flesh is crisp, light green and enclosing manyl seeds arranged in six rows.

Raw **cucumbers** have an insipid, watery, sometimes bitter taste. Gardeners have managed to create less bitter hybrids by eliminating cucurbitacin C, the substance responsible for such bitterness.

Cucumber

Raw cucumbers make a refreshing salad or appetizer simply sprinkled with lemon juice and olive oil, or with a creamy dressing of yogurt, cream cheese and herbs. Cooked it is used as a side dish accompanying meat, fowl, fish and mussels. It can also be chopped or cut lengthwise, removing the seeds and stuffing it with rice, olives, minced meat or fish – seasoned with a pinch of garlic – and then baked in the oven. In England it is used to prepare a soup. Mashed, seasoned with green aniseed and chilled, it is a delicious accompaniment for cold cuts. Small cucumbers can be pickled. After rubbing them thoroughly with a dry cloth, they are marinated in either brine or vinegar and herbs. Larger cucumbers can be cut and preserved in the same way.

Gherkins are small immature **cucumbers** which are regularly used in pickles. Some varieties are the "small green of Paris," short, crisp and very thorny; the large **gherkin** of "Massy," and the "Kerby," which has an intense green color and is picked when it is very young. **Cucumbers** are extensively grown in frames or on trellises in greenhouses; in milder climates they are cultivated as a field crop and in home gardens in moist, well drained soil sheltered from humidity and cold. An excess of seed is sown in March or April, and the seedlings are thinned out to the number desired in May. The shoots are pinched off and when the stems appear, three or four leaves are picked off, leaving a leaf on top of the fruit. **Gherkins** are cultivated in the same way, but they are not pinched.

Even though **cucumbers** contain a lot of water, they are not diuretic. They contain magnesium which promotes growth and the development of bones, iodine, and trace elements necessary for hormonal and cellular metabolism. **Cucumbers** are used to soothe the skin, eliminate blotchy complexions, freckles and wrinkles.

Pumpkin and Squash

For pumpkins and squash there are numerous recipies, according to which they may be used for sweet or savory dishes. They can be cooked with onions in purees, gratins or in soups. Cut into pieces, cooked in the pressure cooker and seasoned with parsley and garlic they are served as a vegetable to accompany meat dishes. Sweet, they are used to make pies and vanilla desserts. They can be used to prepare souf-flés, added to pancake batter, and pureed as a side dish. They are also used to make rissoles, brioche, and ice cream. Raw and cut into pieces they are served as an hors-d'œuvre, and grated they are added to salads with lemon-juice, raisins and roasted almonds. The seeds are boiled or roasted. They are rich in amino acids and proteins. Spaghetti pumpkin is cooked in boiling water until the fibers in its flesh take on the consistency of noodles. This vegetable spaghetti is used as a garnish for meat dishes or served as a main dish with cheese, ham and basil. Because of their different colors and shapes, pumpkins are also used as a household decoration.

CUCURBITA MAXIMA	**Winter squash or Pumpkin**

Fruit vegetable
Family: *Cucurbitaceae*
Origin: *North and South America*
Height: *10 to 13 feet (3 to 4 m)*
Flowering: *May to July*
Properties: *soothing, tranquilizer, laxative, vermifuge (seeds)*

The original cultivators of the **Winter squash**, the largest most popular variety of **pumpkin** due to its characteristic form and color, were the American Indians. The European colonists considered it at first to be an oversized melon; whereas, centuries later, the jack-o-lanterns with their grotesque grinning faces, first cut by Irish immigrants to North America, have become the epitome of Halloween.

On All Saints' Eve, children dressed up as ghosts, witches, demons, monsters and other such scary beings go from door to door collecting sweets – but always with the threat that if refused, they will play a trick on the householder (trick or treat).

It is an annual plant that climbs by a simple, sometimes branched, spirally coiled tendril. It has long stalked, palmate, velvety and soft leaves that alternate

along the stem. Most species have unisexual flowers, which are borne in the leaf axils and have five white or yellow petals; male flowers have five anthers, and female flowers have five carpels. The fruit in most species is a fleshy, round, many-seeded berry with a tough rind, often attaining considerable size and growing close to the ground. It can weigh, according to the species, between 6 and 110 lbs. (3 and 50 kg).

Pumpkins generally have a smooth and usually lightly furrowed or ribbed shell with a thick, sweet flesh and a large amount of edible seeds. Among the favorite **pumpkin** varieties are: red **pumpkin of Etampes**, a scalloped and flattened fruit with strikingly red flesh; the great yellow of Paris, a big fruit with a thick, yellow flesh; the **Alençon pumpkin** with its oblong shaped, ribbed and shinny fruit which can weigh up to 44 lbs.

(20 kg); the **golden hubbard**, an orange, woody variety with a sweet, fine, compact and very aromatic flesh. There is also the **autumn queen pumpkin** which can weigh up to 33 lbs. (15 kg) and which has an elongated, round shape with a dark green shell and a pinkish yellow flesh that is quite mediocre. The most well known **pumpkin** is the **turban pumpkin** with its decorative orange, green, yellow and red fruit weighing from

6 to 9 lbs. (3 to 4 kg). It has a high quality floury, sweet flesh. There is also the "**Giraumon Galeux d'Eysines**" **pumpkin** weighing about 4.4 lbs. (2 kg) with a thin pink shell which is covered with small excrescencies when ripe. The **Hokkaido pumpkin** has a delicate orange flesh and is rich in vitamins, mineral salts, amino acids, fatty acids, fiber, sugar and carotene. Its taste is similar to that of chestnuts. Its shape and color vary according to variety: the "**chestnut bush**" has a grey blue, tasty flesh; the 8.8 lbs. (4 kg) "**golden delicious**" is yellow with an orange flesh and very rich in vitamins; the "**kabocha**" is a medium-sized, spherical, dark green **pumpkin** with bright orange, sweet, starchy flesh used in soups or roasted. "**Delicata**" and "**sweet dumpling**" **pumpkins** have green striped fruits with an exceptionally sweet, orange flesh whose taste is similar to that of chestnuts. The "**nice**" variety has a firm pulp that is extremely delicious; and the "**spaghetti pumpkin,**" native to Manchuria, has oblong fruit the delicate flesh of which has long fibers that are highly digestive and light. Finally, there are a few dwarf varieties like the "**sugar pie**" **pumpkin** whose very sweet flesh is used to make **pumpkin pie**; and the "**pepper**" and "**gland**" **pumpkins** whose flesh is sweet and nutty.

Pumpkin is enjoyed in both sweet and savory dishes; as a puree, a gratin, fritters or in soups. It makes an excellent vegetable side dish when diced, steamed, and then seasoned with garlic and parsley. It is suitable for many sweet dishes, ranging from cakes to jam. The **dwarf pumpkin** is used in soups, chestnut soufflés and as a puree for meat dishes, but also in biscuits and desserts. Pumpkins are also prized for their decorative value in the household, whether it be for Thanksgiving or for Halloween, or simply as charming piece of natural decoration. The decorative properties of the **pumpkin** in the garden is not to be overlooked, whether it be the large-leafed plant with its pretty yellow flowers, or the ripe colored fruit that provide attraction.

Moschata pumpkin

Nutmeg and butternut pumpkins are used as ingredients for cakes, pies and soufflés as well as aromatic soups served with cream. They are also used to prepare warm or cold sweets, desserts flavored with vanilla, cinnamon or chocolate. Other varieties are used in purees, fritters, and vegetable gratins. The roasted, salted seeds are served as a snack with apéritifs.

CUCURBITA MOSCHATA   *Moschata pumpkin*

Fruit vegetable
Family: *Cucurbitaceae*
Origin: *North and Central America*
Height: *10 to 13 feet (3 to 4 m)*
Flowering: *June to July*
Properties: *soothing, laxative, nutritious, vermifuge (seeds)*

The **moschata pumpkin** differs from the other plants of the *Cucurbita* type by its very short calyx and its soft leaves. It often bears only a single, firm-fleshy fruit. The **moschata pumpkin** is generally medium sized, except for the **portemanteau** variety cultivated in Italy whose fruit can reach up to 3 feet (1 m) in length and weigh 44 lbs. (20 kg). Even though, the **moschata pumpkin** has the same characteristic features and quali-

ties of other **pumpkins**. The most popular varieties are the "**sucrine**" and "**butternut**" **pumpkins** due to their sweet flavor. The "**trompe d'Albanga**" stands out because of its long, twisted shape. Like most **pumpkins**, the **moschata pumpkin** also needs rich, well drained soil and plenty of sun. The fruits are harvested when they are ripe – usually in autumn. Stored dry, they keep fresh for three to six months.

CUCURBITA PEPO **Zucchini, Courgette, Gourd, Summer squash**

Fruit vegetable
Family: Cucurbitaceae
Origin: Central America
Height: 10 to 13 feet (3 to 4 m)
Flowering: May to July
Properties: soothing, laxative, mineralizing, sedative, vermifuge

Popular among the natives of Central America, the *Curcubita pepo* arrived in Europe during the 16th century. Today, they are prized in the United States and Eastern and Southern Europe alike. This perennial plant differs in its appearance according to the variety: some have long, trailing stems and others have short hairy ones. The large, more or less lobed leaves have a long, spiny leaf stalk. The orange flowers can reach a diameter of up to 6 inches (15 cm); they bear more numerous and smaller fruit than those of the *Cucurbita maxima* variety. The elongated, green **zucchini**, also known as **courgette**, which has a white juicy flesh, is attached to the stem by a short and angular peduncle. **Gourds** are mostly round. **Summer squash** have a flesh similar to that of the **artichoke**; flat and round, they have scalloped, smooth, ridged, or warty surfaces with ten horn-like outgrowths and a white, yellow, star shaped flesh. All of these **pumpkins** contain in their thick flesh numerous seeds that are small and soft when young, and hard when mature.

The rind which is often smooth becomes hard with age. **Zucchini** and **summer squash** can be eaten with their skin, but they must be harvested before they are ripe. **Gourds,** which are usually peeled before being prepared, are harvested when they are ripe. The following are some of the most popular **gourds** worth mentioning: the **acceste**, the **aurore**, the **tamarino**, the **d'Altai-Kaja**, and the **nice** variety with its aniseed taste and without a doubt the most succulent one of all. Finally, there is, of course, the **spaghetti gourd** which has a white flesh whose fibers resemble noodles. These fruit contain a lot of water, a few lipids, and sugar; therefore, they are not very nutritious. Nevertheless, they are healthy, easy to digest, and recommended in diets designed to lose weight. They contain a lot of vitamin C, vitamin A, and trace elements.

Cultivation is done from seed. The plants require a rich soil, plenty of sun and a lot of water. The plant responds badly to dryness, so care must be taken to ensure it is well watered. The harvest begins in July which allows the growth of another generation of fruit. Because the **courgettes** are harvested before maturity, they are highly perishable, however, they can be blanched and frozen.

As most of the fruit have a rather watery taste they should be prepared with care. They are generally eaten in purees and soups seasoned with garlic, thyme or mint. Sliced or cut in cubes and sautéed with garlic and parsley, they are a delicate accompaniment to meat dishes. Stuffed or in a gratin, these vegetables can be served as a main dish. Peeled and without seeds, **summer squash** can be cooked in boiling salted water, seasoned and served warm or cold in a vinaigrette or with mayonnaise.

CYNARA CARDUNCULUS — **Cardoon**
Stem vegetable
Family: Compositae
Origin: Central Europe, North Africa
Height: about 3 feet (1 m)
Flowering: early summer
Properties: rich in inulin (a sugar substitute for diabetics), apéritif, laxative, diuretic, tonic

---

This thistle-like vegetable, closely related to the **artichoke**, has a great chard with long, fleshy stalks. There are two types: the original, very prickly wild form and the vegetable **cardoon**, a new variety without prickles. The **wild cardoon** has been used since ancient times in the kitchens of North Africa and northern Egypt. Once forgotten, it has become fashionable once more thanks to those great chefs who fell in love with its fine, delicate taste. Today, it is a very popular vegetable. The variety without prickles is cultivated mostly in the southeastern part of France.

This biennial, fast growing shrub is however, generally cultivated annually. It has a milky, bitter sap and big, long-stalked, lobed, thick, and fleshy leaves. The wild varieties have prickly leaves, which the newer cultivated varieties do not have. Contrary to the popular saying "there's no good **cardoon** without prickles," these latter ones are quite tasty and tender. The purple flowers appear during the second year on long stems reaching about 4 feet (1.20 m).

The most famous popular varieties are the **thornless simple white**, the **Tours** or **Spanish cardoon** which is very thorny, and the "red-stemmed" **cardoon**. **Cardoon** thrives in sunny locations and require a deep and moist soil. It is sown in May. Once the seedlings are strong enough, they are replanted at about 1 yard (1 m) intervals to give them enough room to grow. Three weeks before the harvest, which can take place according to demand from August up to the beginning of the winter frosts, the **cardoons** are blanched, to reduce their bitter taste, make them sweeter and tender.

Cardoon

Cardoons, like celery, are peeled in order to remove the fibrous threads. Immediately after that, they are rubbed with lemon juice, to prevent their discoloring. They are then cooked for two hours in boiling water in which previously a little bit of flour was added. Prepared in this way, they can be served with butter, meat juices, or sprinkled with chopped herbs to accompany white meat. They can also be fried and used in gratins.

In order to do this, the leaves are tied together or they are covered with cardboard or black plastic leaving the tips of the plant exposed to the light so that it continues to grow. Earth is also banked up around the roots. Harvesting is done by cutting the leaves at the base of the stem or pulling out the seedlings with the sod. These are then stored in the dark with the leaves tied together. In this way they keep fresh the whole winter long.

If the winter is not too rough (**cardoons** are not hardy), the seedlings can remain outside, well protected from the cold. **Cardoons** are rich in inulin, a sugar substitute for diabetics. Due to their high mucilage content, they are laxative and refreshing. They also contain mineral salts and carbohydrates.

CYNARA SCOLYMUS — Artichoke

Flower vegetable
Family: Compositae
Origin: Mediterranean region
Height: 4 to 4.5 feet (1.20 to 1.40 m)
Flowering: late spring (every two years)
Properties: apéritif, laxative, purifier, diuretic, tonic

It is believed that **artichokes** originated in Ethiopia from where they spread to Egypt and the rest of the world. Today they are cultivated all over Europe. Unknown in the wild, it is likely that they are descended from the **cardoon** which is the single known wild form of this type of vegetable. Not until the Renaissance, after numerous breeding attempts, did the **artichoke** appear in the kitchen gardens of southern Europe. Even though at the time it was already clearly different from the **cardoon**, it was developed further during the following centuries becoming the **artichoke** known to us today. Nowadays it is extensively cultivated in California, France, Belgium, and the Mediterranean countries. The **artichoke** is a large, coarse, herbaceous, thistle-like perennial plant with a big, closed and fibrous root full of radicles. The deeply cut, large, woolly leaves are white on the top, whitish on the underside and appear in loose rosettes. During the second year, sturdy, branched flower stalks rise giving way to purplish flowers which are formed by a big calyx with fleshy, pointed scales that cover one another. Inside they are covered by silky, hairy, oval seeds. The seeds ripen in September and are very popular among birds. During the flowering, these flowers are very decorative.

Artichoke

Young artichokes can be eaten raw with salt, paprika sauce or in a salad. After cutting the stems back from where they join the fruit and breaking off the very tough leaves, the artichokes are marinated in lemon juice and olive oil. Cooked artichokes must be rapidly consumed because they develop toxins that can cause digestion problems. To prepare artichoke hearts, they should be carefully washed, cut off down to where the heart begins while pulling out the spiny choke that lies on top of the heart, and cooked in boiling salted water. Upon cooling they are served with a vinaigrette or mayonnaise as an hors-d'œuvre or main dish. They can also be stuffed with vegetables or meat and cooked in the oven. Artichokes can also be quartered and cooked with stock or parsley and garlic. They can be prepared in a gratin with béchamel sauce and grated cheese, or simply in an omelette. In Italy, artichokes are used to produce an apéritif.

The **artichoke** has a delicate, nutlike taste; it is starchy and at the same time sweet and slightly bitter. It needs light, deep, airy, acid soil rich in humus, and a warm sunny location. The French varieties are a little bit more resistant than the more demanding Italian ones. The **artichoke** is planted in the spring, by planting divisions of the crown or rooted offshoots. It can also be propagated by sowing, but it tends to degenerate.

Harvesting is done before it blooms, once the heart has reached its full size, approximately 3 to 4 inches (8 to 10 cm) in diameter. The parts of the plant above ground are cut back before winter and it is covered with hay or soil. After four years, the plants are no longer harvested because they begin to degenerate. It is a healthy vegetable, rich in vitamins B and C and containing mineral salts and inulin, a substitute sugar for diabetics.

CYPERUS ESCULENTUS **Earth almond or Chufa**

Root vegetable
Family: Cyperaceae
Origin: southern Europe, Asia and North Africa
Height: 8 to 24 inches (20 to 60 cm)
Flowering: summer
Properties: soothing, hypotensive, laxative, nutritious

The **earth almond** is to be found wild in the basin of the White Nile, in Upper Egypt and the Sudan. Its cultivation was known in Ancient Egypt, as tubers have been found in the graves of Pharaohs from the 2nd and 3rd millennia BC. **Theophrastus** acknowledged it as an edible plant, to be found growing on the banks of rivers, the tuber of which could be cooked in beer.

Earth almond is cultivated mostly as an oil plant. Its oil is comparable in quality to olive oil and is used extensively by the food industry. For this reason a variety of bigger tubers providing greater yields has been developed. This hardy shrub has leaves with parallel veins. Its straw colored terminal flowers bear shinny reddish-brown seeds.

In Europe, **earth almond** rarely blooms. It is propagated through its reddish, oval or globular tubers which appear by the thousands at the end of the short rhizome of any given bush. The plant thrives in sandy, damp soil with plenty of sun. The tubers are planted in April and harvested in October by pulling the whole plant from the earth. The tubers are collected and washed. Containing about 20% oil, **earth almonds** produce a high quality edible oil which is used to fight against cardio-vascular diseases. In addition, it contains 30% fiber, 15% carbohydrates and up to 10% protein, as well as vitamins A and B. These tubers are quite nutritious.

The oil with its almond like taste is used to season salads and to roast meat and fish. The tubers themselves are consumed like **almonds,** fresh or dried, but can also be roasted like peanuts. From the roasted tubers, a flour is obtained which can be used to make pastries and cakes. It is also used to prepare a hot drink similar to cocoa. Cooked in salted water, the tubers are a tasty vegetable accompaniment for meat, fowl, rabbit and lamb. They are also deliciously nutritious when prepared as a puree or in soups. The raw tubers are used as fodder for pigs.

The **carrot** is known throughout Europe, growing on the pathside and in meadows. The distant ancestor of the **carrot** was a wild species to be found in Eurasia, and when humans first discovered it, the root was white. For some unknown reason a new variety with an orangey-yellow root spontaneously developed in Afghanistan.

The **carrot** is a biennial plant that produces an edible fleshy taproot. The root is generally white or orange and bears an erect rosette of doubly compound, finely divided leaves above ground. During the second year, large, branched flower stalks arise. They are hollow, have a circular cross section and can reach up to more than 30 inches (80 cm) high. The ends of the main stalk and branches bear large compound umbels of tiny white flowers formed by approximately 20 rays in the center of which a sterile, dark purple flower is formed. The flowers bear small elongated, oval, dented, spiny seeds. **Carrots** have a characteristic sweet, herbal fragrance; their taste is soft, sweet, and slightly bitter. **Carrot** is grown from seed at the end of March directly onto the field, and harvested three months later. Late varieties are sown from the end of May to mid-June and harvested six months later. Once the seeds have germinated, the plants are thinned out at intervals of a little more than an inch (3 cm) apart from each other. The tiny **carrots** seen during this procedure can already be eaten. **Carrots** can be harvested upon demand during the whole season. Autumn **carrots** keep longer if they are left two to three days to dry in the sun.

Carrots are rich in beta carotine which the body transforms into vitamin A, an essential vitamin for the development of children. It supports the intake of minerals and the regeneration of the skin by stimulating melanin production and facilitating the absorption of proteins. It also helps prevent night blindness and improves vision. **Carrots** contain B vitamins, a lot of vitamin C, as well as vitamins D and E. Moreover, they supply the body with trace elements and amino acids.

Carrot

These attractively colored roots are eaten both in a raw and a cooked state. Raw and grated with some lemon juice and olive oil, they render a delicious, refreshing hors-d'œuvre. The juice is useful against spring tiredness. Steamed or cooked in salted water, they are served tossed in meat juices or butter as an accompaniment to other dishes. They taste delicious prepared with cream, and are a traditional combination with peas. Carrot puree goes well with white meats such as roast veal. They are used as an ingredient for soufflés and sweet and savory pies. Sliced, they can be sautéed in butter with parsley and garlic. Carrots are a very healthy and easy to digest vegetable. Their popularity is due to the fact that they are easy to prepare in a variety of different ways.

DAUCUS CAROTA	**Carrot**
Root vegetable	
Family: *Umbelliferae*	
Origin: *Eurasia*	
Height: *8 to 12 inches (20 to 30 cm)*	
Flowering: *summer (from the second year)*	
Properties: *soothing, anti-anaemia, improves vision, laxative, mineralizing, regenerates tissue*	

DIOSCOREA	**Yam**
Root vegetable	
Family: *Dioscoreaceae*	
Origin: *all tropical regions of the world*	
Height: *according to sort 6 to 10 feet (2 to 3 m)*	
Flowering: *spring (inconspicuously)*	
Properties: *nutritious, purgative, stimulant, tonic*	

Worldwide there are at least forty different varieties of **yam** whose tubers serve as food and animal fodder. They are an important agricultural commodity in Africa, especially in Cameroon and Togo where they are part of the everyday diet. They were successfully introduced in France in 1853 by **Monsieur de Montigny**. Today **yams** are cultivated in the Loire valley and consumed mainly by people of Asian, African and South American origin living in Paris. The world's biggest **yam** producer is Nigeria, followed by the Ivory Coast and Brazil.

The plant is a woody vine with thick tubers from which protrude long, slender, annual, climbing stems which are reinforced with a sort of hook. The alternate or opposite leaves are either entire or lobed. The greenish white and very fragrant flowers, generally small and individually inconspicuous, though collectively showy, appear in clusters on the leaf axils. They bear three-celled, three-winged dry berries containing an ovary which when ripe liberates numerous flat seeds. The underground taproot carries several black or purple edible tubers which can reach magnificent sizes.

Dioscorea alata and *rotundata* are the most widely cultivated white **yam** varieties. Native to West Africa, they are highly tolerant of long dry seasons. The *Dioscorea batatas* is an Asian **yam** with white or reddish flesh whose tubers can measure up to a yard (1 m) in length and weigh 44 lbs. (20 kg). Globular tubers of *Dioscorea globosa* variety also have a white flesh and a very sweet taste. They are cultivated predominantly in India. Finally, there are the *Dioscorea esculenta* and *bulbifera* varieties which form large tubers on the leaf axils and which can also withstand periods of drought.

The cultivation of **yams** is relatively easy provided the climate is warm and humid. The tubers are planted, like **potatoes**, in loose earth with good drainage. They are harvested approximately ten months later. All **yam** varieties are rich in fiber and starch. There are also a few that contain dioscorin, a toxic alkaloid which dissipates with cooking. Furthermore, they supply vitamins B and C, as well as different minerals.

Yams are a very nutritious vegetable which tonify the organism. Before being cooked, they must be washed with plenty of water, in order to reduce the dioscorin content as much as possible. They are cooked in boiling water and served as an accompaniment to meat and fish.

Palmetto

Once the exterior cover is removed, palmettos can be eaten either raw or cooked, and are a delicious addition to salads. They are crisp and tender with a slight nutty taste, and can also be sliced and added to other vegetables or served as an accompaniment to sweet-savory dishes. In Brazil a creamy, brown beverage is prepared with the pulp obtained from pressing the fresh palmetto. Because palmettos do not keep for long, they are usually only found canned.

EUTERPE EDULIS	**Palm hearts, Palmetto**
Stem vegetable	
Family: Arecaceae	
Origin: tropical and subtropical regions	
Height: about 131 feet (40 m)	
Flowering: spring	
Properties: purifier, mineralizing, tonic	

Like most palm trees, the *Euterpe edulis* produces **palmettos**. This palm tree is an important source of food in tropical countries where it is also cultivated as an export product. Seeds were found on the coasts of Costa Rica which date from 2300 to 1700 BC.

This big palm tree of upright growth has a slim trunk with ring-shaped stigma left behind by dead leaves. It has a bright grey-green coloring. Its long leaves, 6 to 10 feet (2 to 3 m) long, are stalked and pinnate. They appear at the head of the trunk forming a hanging tuft. The leaf stalk flows into the central vein of the leaf which can have forty to eighty thin, pinnate, linear or lancelike leaflets. The flowers appear in groups of three (two male ones and one female). They have white sepals and dark-purple petals. The cone that grows at the very top of the tree is known as the **palm heart** or **palmetto**.

The cultivation and harvest of this plant are simple. When the fruit become ripe, the heart, or **palmetto**, is cut off. After this, the tree dies quickly leaving at its base some shoots from which a new tree will grow. These shoots can also be harvested; however, they are regularly left untouched in order to preserve the species.

Palmettos contain fibre, iron, magnesium, calcium, and lipids, but only a few carbohydrates. They are a healthy and nutritious vegetable. Because they contain trace elements, they help fight against anaemia and have a mineralizing effect on the organism.

FOENICULUM VULGARE	**Fennel**
Family: Umbelliferae	
Origin: southern Europe, Asia Minor	
Height: about 5 feet (1.50 m)	
Flowering: June to August	
Properties: antispasmodic, carminative, digestive, diuretic, expectorant, galactagogue, stimulant	

Fennel is a vegetable with an inflated base or false bulb and an aniseed aroma developed by improving the basal leaves of aromatic **fennel**. During the 17ᵗʰ century the Italians transformed this aromatic plant into the fragrant, juicy vegetable highly prized nowadays.

The plant is quite small with a white, climbing taproot and an inflated bulb. The bulb which is compressed on the sides is formed by a petioled base wrapped around the stem. It forms a head that becomes round when ripe. The bluish-green leaves have a long stalk and are divided in thin, filiform straps which form a dense tuft emerging from the centre of the bulb. The hollow, branched stem, which appears during the second year, carries yellow, terminal flower umbels that bear fruit, or seeds, which are split in two thin and elongated achenes. The part of the plant that is consumed is the inflated base of the leaves. There are four main varieties: the "bologne," the "sicilie," the "palerme" whose large, round and short petioles are eaten raw, and the "florence" **fennel** whose elongated petioles are preferred for cooking. The plant thrives in warm, sunny regions in rich, moist and fertilized soil. It is sown directly onto the field from April to July. Once the shoots have developed, the plant is thinned out and the roots are covered with hay to keep them moist.

Fennel bulbs are highly perishable; therefore, it is better to consume them quickly. Nevertheless, they can be put in dark or cold storage. They will keep tender and juicy, if the shoot has been pulled out with a piece of the root and the external leaves have been cut off. This vegetable is low in calories, but is rich in anethole. It has an antispasmodic effect on the stomach and colon. Because it prevents intestinal fermentation, it is an excellent carminative and digestive. Its seeds stimulate the secretion of milk in women. It is rich in mineral salts, vitamins A, B, and C, water and fibre. It is very nutritional and refreshing for the organism. It is also believed to be an aid against impotence.

Fennel

The raw bulbs with their sweet, aniseed flavor, are delicious in simple or mixed salads. They can be cut in slices and served as an appetizer. Sautéed in butter or braised in stock, with cream or in a gratin they compliment meat and fish dishes. The seeds are used to make licorice while the leaves are used in salads or to give aroma to cold sauces. A decoction of the roots is used to help the organism eliminate toxins; therefore, it is recommended in weight loss diets.

GLYCERIA FLUITANS	*Riccia*
Fruit vegetable	
Family: *Gramineae*	
Origin: *Europe, Morocco, North and South America*	
Height: *16 inches to over 3 feet (40 cm to 1 m)*	
Flowering: *May to August*	
Properties: *emollient, laxative, mineralizing, stimulant*	

Riccia is a strong herb which is found in the wild floating on the banks of ponds and rivers. In former times it was called "manna" and up until the 19ᵗʰ century, its nutritious seeds were sold on markets. In Poland, Silesia and East Prussia the plant was highly appreciated. In the 17ᵗʰ century it was cultivated in all free ponds and other damp areas. Today, this plant has been replaced by nobler cereals like **wheat**.

It is a hardy, aquatic, herbaceous plant with branching ribbons that carry narrow, bluish-green leaves. In the spring, a fine unilateral inflorescence, composed of pistils that will later produce fruit, appears at the top the stem. These fruit are elongated and yellow or white.

Their appearance and taste is similar to that of **wheat**. The superficial roots or ribbons often become tangled in large masses and cling to other vegetation floating in the water. **Riccia** prospers only on a soil which is always flooded with water. It is sown in the autumn or in winter. The successive harvest of the fruit, or caryopsis, begins in April and ends in October. They are gathered during rainy or foggy weather as the humidity prevents the fruit from drying up and setting free the seeds.

Riccia is a grain rich in starch, carbohydrates, amino acids, sugar and cellulose. It also contains lipids, potassium, phosphorus and calcium as well as B vitamins and vitamin E. It is a very healthy food which is used during convalescence and winter months. It promotes growth, prevents rickets and other diseases caused by mineral deficiency. It also helps calm the nervous system.

In the kitchen, the seeds are cooked in plain or aromatized milk to make cakes similar to those baked with **wheat**. Cooked in salted water, the seeds are served as a couscous-like accompaniment to meat and vegetables. Furthermore, they can also be used to thicken soups and stuffings. In agriculture its delicate and digestible hay is used as a cattle feed.

GLYCINE MAX   Soy bean

Fruit and stem vegetable
Family: Fabaceae
Origin: Manchuria and Korea
Height: 1.6 to 5 feet (0.50 to 1.50 m)
Flowering: spring
Properties: fights against fatigue, anti-cholesterol, energizing, nutritious, mineralizing

---

The **soy bean**, which is used to produce seasonings, as a vegetable, and as the source of an oil with many uses, has been cultivated in China and Japan since 3,000 BC, where it was classified as one of the five sacred crops. It was only in the 18th century however, that missionaries brought it to Europe, where it was grown at Kew Gardens for the first time. In the US, **soy beans** were introduced in the early 19th century. There, **soy** farming was expanded dramatically after World War II. **Soy beans** are one of the most widely consumed vegetables in the world.

It is a type of dwarf bean with stems that can reach up to 5 feet (1.50 m) high. Its root has numerous nodules containing bacteria known as rhizobium which have the ability to convert the nitrates in the soil into large amounts of nitrogen. The whole plant is covered with fine hairs and has odd-pinnate, lobed leaves. Its white, self-fertilizing flowers appear in clusters on the axils of the leaf and bear fruit or pods which contain three to six seeds.

The **soy bean** is grown from seed during the spring. It may be cultivated in most types of soil, but it thrives in warm, subtropical climates in humid, well drained, sandy loam. It requires at least fourteen hours of sunlight a day. Some of the beans can be harvested before they mature to be used as **peas**. However, they are really harvested when the beans are very ripe using a combine harvester. There is a greenhouse culture that is only for the production of shoots and **soy bean** sprouts.

Soy beans

Soy bean shoots are eaten raw, mostly with a vinaigrette, or also cooked as a vegetable ingredient of meat and fish dishes. They are a typical component of a lot of Far Eastern foods. The immature soy beans taste like young peas. The flour which is produced from the ripe seeds is used to prepare both sweet and savory breads and pastries. From the fermented seeds, soy milk is produced and used to make a type of cheese rich in iron and magnesium known as tofu. In the vegetarian kitchen, tofu is cut in pieces and added to other vegetables. The cooked beans can be mashed to a puree and used for both sweet and savory dishes. Soy beans are also used to produce tempe, a kind of "vegetarian meat" which is rich in vitamin B12 and calcium. It is prepared by mixing wheat flour with thick soy bean puree. This carefully kneaded dough is used to make flat pancakes that can be cooked like meat, fried in a pan or cut into pieces and added to ragouts and other braised dishes. Furthermore, soy beans produce an oil which is used mainly in the industrial production of paints, emulsions and soaps.

Soy beans produce a flour rich in vegetable proteins (35 to 40%), lipids (20%), essential and saturated fat (85%), carbohydrates (36 to 38%), sucrose and raffinose. Furthermore, **soy beans** contain mineral salts, phosphorous, potassium, iron, calcium, and vitamins B and C.

It is a balancing vegetable. Its flour contains a lot of lecithin which is a natural lipid that acts as an emulsi-

fier and helps the body dissolve fat in the blood. It also helps fight arteriosclerosis and reduces cholesterol levels due to its high levels of choline and inositol. Moreover, the phosphorous contained in the lecithin facilitates the functioning of the brain cells. Recently, isoflavones have been isolated form **soy bean** flour with estrogenic properties which can help fight against menopausal problems.

| **HELIANTHUS TUBEROSUS** | **Jerusalem artichoke** |

HELIANTHUS TUBEROSUS
Root vegetable
Family: *Compositae*
Origin: *southern Canada, the northern United States*
Height: *5 to 6.5 feet (1.50 to 2 m)*
Flowering: *April to May*
Properties: *antiseptic, energetic, galagtagogue, purgative*

The **Jerusalem artichoke** is a strong plant which was introduced to France in the 17th century by the Canadian governor **Samuel de Champlain** who noticed the nutritious importance of the tubers for the Huron and Algonquin Native Americans. He brought some tubers to Europe in the hope that this exotic vegetable could become acclimatized and be of use in times of famine. At the same time, the Tupinamba Indians from Brazil were being introduced to the French court. For some strange reason, the tubers were somehow associated with these indians and in France the tubers became known as "topinambour." The new vegetable, enthusiastically accepted by the people of the time, was completely rejected a century later.

In his "Traité de Jardinage," **de Combles** declared that the new vegetable was the worst of all vegetables. This was detrimental to the popularity of the **artichoke** which was soon replaced by the **potato**. To this day, this disliked vegetable is only found on the table in times of distress, like during World War II. However, recently it has quietly made its appearance once again on marketplaces. It is found under the names **Jerusalem artichoke** (derived from the Italian word "girasole" which means sunflower) or **Canadian artichoke**, a name which designates its true origin.

The part of the plant found above ground is a coarse perennial which can sometimes become invasive. It has a poorly branched out, hairy stem which carries big, oval, petioled leaves. The yellow, single flowers resemble in their appearance those of the sunflower, however, they are much smaller. They bear numerous achenes or fruit. The short underground root is frequently branched out with tubers growing from its end. The tubers resemble **potatoes** with an elongated shape and a yellowish or reddish coloring. Their juicy, firm, and sweet flesh is similar to that of **artichokes**.

Jerusalem artichoke

It is best to harvest the tubers always according to demand so that they are fresh and do not loose any of their aroma. Before being prepared, they are brushed thoroughly under running water to remove the dirt. After being soaked in water with lemon juice to prevent them from becoming discolored they are then cooked in salted water for approximately one quarter of an hour. There are many way to serve them: in a salad, sautéed with parsley and garlic, in ragouts, in gratins with béchamel sauce, in pies, purees and as fritters. Grated raw, they can be served with a vinaigrette or, seasoned with lemon, mixed in an endive or green salad with cheese. Jerusalem artichokes have a nutty taste similar to that of regular artichokes. In certain regions a spirit is distilled from its tubers.

Jerusalem artichokes grow on just about any soil. They are resistant to cold and thrive in the sun or in the shade. The plant is propagated by planting the tubers in the spring. Harvesting is often done in September; however, it is also possible to overwinter the tubers in the soil.

Jerusalem artichoke is rich in carbohydrates (15%), inulin (a substitute sugar for diabetics) and

fructose. In contrast, it is very low in proteins. The calorie content varies according to the length of storage. This vegetable increases the secretion of milk in nursing women and stimulates digestion.

The stems and leaves are used as a cattle feed. The tubers are also popular as pig fodder. **Jerusalem artichokes** are a beautiful decoration for gardens and their flowers can be used in floral arrangements.

HERACLEUM SPHONDYLIUM   Cow parsnip
Leaf and fruit vegetable
Family: Umbelliferae
Origin: Europe
Height: 1.6 to 5 feet (0.50 to 1.50 m)
Flowering: June to September
Properties: aphrodisiac, tranquilizer, digestive, emmenagogue, hypotensive, (slightly) laxative, stimulant

Cow parsnip is a robust, wild plant used for a long time both as a vegetable and for its medicinal properties. Its leaves resemble the paws of a bear. It grows wild on meadows and in damp forests. It is a biennial plant with a rigid, hollow, hairy stem. Its grey-green lobed leaves are covered with very large, rough hairs. They are cut irregularly and give off an unpleasant smell when touched. The white, yellow or pink flowers form a big terminal inflorescence which bears flattened fruit with a big winged border. This plant has a bitter pungent and irritating taste. It is sown in the spring in heavy and moist soil. The parts of the plant that are used are the leaves, the fruit and the roots which are dried in the sun.

Cow parsnip is rich in carbohydrates, proteins, minerals, essential oils, and vitamin C. It also contains a substance which can increase the skin's sensitivity to light causing severe inflammations. It facilitates digestion and stimulates the menstrual flow. Because it contains vitamin C, it is also a stimulant. It is used in health spa therapies and to fight influenza and lower blood pressure. The seeds are quite stimulating and are considered an aphrodisiac.

In Poland, the leaves and seeds are cooked and fermented to produce a bitter beverage whose taste lies somewhere between beer and vegetable soup. The young leaves and shoots are cooked like vegetables and are served as a accompaniment to meat. They can also be mixed with other vegetables, cooked like **spinach**, added to stews, or as an ingredient in herbal pâtés. In Russia they are used to prepare the traditional borscht, or beetroot soup. The seeds are used to make delicious, soothing liqueurs which alleviate indigestion.

Barley

Barley flour is used to make cakes, bread, milk puddings and porridges. The grain is offered finely ground, but is also crushed, or hulled and coarsely cracked as barley groats. Whole, peeled barley kernels are cooked like rice in salted water and served with vegetable dishes. To prepare desserts, they are cooked in milk. Cooked barley is used in stuffings and vinaigrette salads. Pearl barley consists of whole kernels from which the outer husk and part of the bran layer have been removed by a polishing process. A refreshing herbal tea is also made from barley. The roasted kernels are used to make a beverage similar to coffee. Most beer is made from malted barley. Furthermore, barley has a soft star used as livestock feed.

HORDEUM VULGARE	**Barley**
Fruit vegetable	
Family: *Gramineae*	
Origin: *the Middle East*	
Height: *about 16 inches (40 cm)*	
Flowering: *spring*	
Properties: *soothing, anti-diarrhoea, cardiotonic, emollient, sedative*	

Barley is adaptable to a greater range of climate than any other cereal, with varieties suited to temperate, subarctic, or subtropical areas. About half of the world's crop is used as livestock feed, the rest for malting and for food; however, rarely in the bakery. **Barley** flour, mixed with a little **wheat** flour, is however used to make an unleavened type of bread, or flatbread with a slightly bitter taste.

In former times, **barley** was easier to grow than wheat, and gave a marginally large yield per acre. However, it was neither as tasty nor as nutritious as wheat.

The plant has an upright, round hollow stem. Its hermaphrodite flowers stand in loose clusters. The unifloral ears appear in six rows having their spike notched on opposite sides, with three spikelets at each notch, each containing a small individual flower, or feathery floret, that develops a kernel. The kernels are oblong, green, open at the top with a longitudinal furrow.

There are several varieties of **barley**: **common barley** with six rows or **big barley**; six row **barley**, **square barley**, or **winter barley** with short, big ears; four-rowed **black barley**; two-rowed, **Spanish** or **Peruvian barley**; and **pyramid barley**, **German rice**, **false rice** or **Russian rice**, which is a very rare species with two-rowed, short ears.

Common barley is sown in winter, while the other varieties are sown in the early spring. Harvesting is done in the late summer.

Barley contains a lot of starch, 60% of carbohydrates, amino acids, lipids and cellulose. It is also a good source of minerals and vitamins B, D and E. The germinated seeds, known as malt, contain enzymes which transform starch into easily digestible substances. **Barley** is especially healthy for people with weak stomachs because it soothes the digestive tract. Its germ contains a protein, hordein, which accelerates heart rhythm and augments blood pressure just like adrenaline; therefore, it is a cardiotonic recommended for weak and slow hearts. Thanks to its emollient and sedative properties, a poultice of **barley** flour relieves bronchitis and angina.

IPOMOEA BATATAS	**Sweet potato**
Leaf and root vegetable	
Family: *Convolvulaceae*	
Origin: *uncertain, known in Oceania for a very long time*	
Height: *climbing, about 17 feet (5 m)*	
Flowering: *spring*	
Properties: *digestive, energizer, nutritious, mineralizing*	

Known in Oceania as *kumara*, and in Peru as *kamar*, **sweet potato** is a staple food in these regions. It was introduced to Europe by **Christopher Columbus** and acclimatized by the Portuguese in Africa where it is also widely cultivated. Arab traders introduced it into Southeast Asia where it forms part of the everyday diet due to its nutritional properties. **Sweet potatoes** are considered to be one of the important food crops in the world. It has been theorized that the hard coat of the **sweet potato** seed enabled it to remain floating on the long passage from the coasts of Central America to the islands of the South Pacific.

Sweet potato stems are usually long and trailing and bear alternate, long stalked, spherical, generally green sometimes dark red leaves. The flowers, borne in clusters in the axils of the leaves, are funnel shaped and tinged with pink or rose violet. The fruit, or capsules, contain three or four black, dark seeds. The edible part is the much-enlarged tuberous root, varying in shape from fusiform to oblong or pointed oval. The tubers have a smooth, fine, dark yellow to violet rind and a white, yellow or orange, juicy flesh. In Europe the most popular varieties are: the pink, the white from Malaga, the purple from the Antilles, and the yellow with brown stripes. **Sweet potato** is not hardy to temperatures below 68 °F (20 °C). The plant is propagated vegetatively through sprouts arising from the roots or by cuttings of the vines which are planted in the spring. It is best adapted to light, friable soils. The plants grow very quickly and need a lot of water. They are harvested before the first frosts. One single plant yields approximately 4.4 to 6.6 lbs. (2 to 3 kg) of **sweet potatoes** which are kept in cold or dry storage.

Sweet potatoes contain many proteins, carbohydrates (10 to 15%), amino acids (5%), mineral salts and vitamins B and C. Because they have a considerable energetic value, they invigorate the organism. Moreover, they are easily digestible.

Sweet potatoes are prepared like **potatoes**. Cooked in water or sautéed they are used to make purees, gratins and soufflés. They can also be fried like French fries. In the United States they are served caramelized along with the Christmas roast. They are also used in salads. The fresh leaves, rich in vegetable proteins (like **soy bean** sprouts) are eaten raw in salads or cooked like **spinach** as a vegetable to accompany meat and fish. The remaining shoots and leaves are used as livestock feed.

Lettuce

Lettuce is usually eaten fresh in simple salads or mixed with other vegetables. The leaves can be used to garnish cold dishes, fish, meat and cheese. They are also used to prepare purees and creamy soups. They can also be stuffed with white meat and poultry. Blanched lettuce hearts can be prepared as a gratin with béchamel sauce and grated cheese.

LACTUCA SATIVA — **Lettuce**
Leaf vegetable
Family: *Compositae*
Origin: *Europe*
Height: *4 to 8 inches (10 to 20 cm)*
Flowering: *June to September (from the second year)*
Properties: *soothing, analgesic, purgative, sedative*

Lettuce as we know it today probably derived from an improvement of the wild variety originating from Europe, known as *Lactuca virosa*. This vegetable, already known in ancient Egypt, Athens and Rome, is nowadays highly prized worldwide.

There are five principal varieties of **lettuce**: **cos** or **romaine lettuce** (without a doubt, one of the oldest); **butter head** or **cabbage lettuce**; **crisp head lettuce**; **asparagus lettuce**; and **leaf** or **curled lettuce**. All of these **lettuces** are hardy to cold. Most varieties have big, undivided leaves with smooth or wavy edges. The color varies according to sort. When there is a floral pedicel, the leaves are small and folded, and the stem is thick. At the head of the pedicel, the white or yellow flowers stand in small groups which form altogether a loose panicle. They bear flattened, dark purple achenes with thick edges. The root of the plant is fusiform with hardly any branches.

For successful cultivation **lettuce** requires ample water and shade, especially in warmer regions. **Spring lettuces** are sown in March; **winter** and **autumn lettuces** in April and June; and **summer lettuces** in August. **Romaine lettuces** are also sown from March to June and the **asparagus** variety from March until the end of August. Harvesting takes place when the heart is well formed by cutting it closely to the ground. **Lettuce** contains a lot of water (95%) and is very low in calories. Nevertheless, it contains a white latex which has a comforting and hypnotic effect. In former times, **lettuce** was used to disintoxicate opium addicts. It also contains fiber and cellulose which ease digestion. It is a good source of vitamins A, B, C and E. It is also used to alleviate inflammations and promote the regeneration of body tissue.

LAGENARIA SICERARIA **Bottle or Calabash gourd**

Fruit vegetable
Family: Cucurbitaceae
Origin: Africa
Height: climbing and creeping, several feet
Blooming time: spring
Properties: soothing, laxative, sedative

The strange fruit of the **bottle gourd** were already used in prehistoric times as a vegetable and in the production of utensils and containers. They are also known as calabash, even though they are not even remotely related to this tree which is native to tropical America. In Morocco and in many other African countries, these **gourds** are a staple crop.

This creeping or climbing monoecious, vine, with a hairy stem and long forked tendrils has large, round, heart shaped basal leaves. The large, showy white flowers have an undivided calyx. Female flowers have a long cylindrical ovary, while the male ones have long peduncles. They bear edible fruit which vary greatly in size and shape. Most **bottle gourds** have a thick, shell which is tender when young and hard, water proof and very resistant when ripe. Their flesh contains numerous flat, elongated seeds. However, there is a variety whose shell is particularly soft at first and whose flesh does not become bitter, and which is eaten as a vegetable. They

are generally sown in April and transplanted in May. The plant grows very quickly and must be watered frequently. The young fruit are harvested once they reach a good size but before they are ripe.

Bottle gourds contain 90% water and very few calories. They are rich in vitamin A, some vitamin C, fiber, and minerals like calcium and potassium. This vegetable has a delicate fragrance and a pleasant flavor. It has a soothing effect on mucous membranes, alleviates inflammations and relieves anxiety. Because it is high in fibers, it facilitates digestion and the elimination of toxins.

Bottle gourds are eaten cooked in soups or purees, in gratins or rissoles. In North Africa they are an ingredient in couscous; in Japan they are cut in small pieces, dried and used to give flavor to soups all year round. When harvested ripe, almost dry, their flesh is removed and they are left to dry in order to make utensils, containers and musical instruments.

LENS ESCULENTA **Lentils**
Fruit vegetable
Family: Fabaceae
Origin: the Middle East
Height: 12 to 14 inches (30 to 35 cm)
Flowering: late spring
Properties: emollient, purifier, laxative, mineralizing

Lentils are among the oldest vegetables to have been cultivated by mankind, reaching back into prehistory. Lentils have been food at archaeological digs dating from the Neolithic Age. Their cultivation probably started at around 7,000 BC in the Middle East. **Lentil** seeds have been found in Egyptian burials from the time of the Pharaohs. The Romans let the lentils germinate before using them in order to obtain a sweeter taste.

A long time ago only two varieties of **lentils** were cultivated. Today, many different sorts are being grown and traded: the green **Puy lentil** is one of the most popular; the **blond lentil** is the biggest; and the **Egyptian orange lentil,** which does not have a husk and is consumed foremost in Italy and Germany, to name but a few.

This small annual legume forms weak, long ascending stems with pinnate, narrow alternate leaves

Lentils

Before preparing lentils, they first have to be carefully sorted out in order to remove unwanted grit and impurities, and then soaked overnight in fresh water. Usually they are cooked in salted water with baking soda, chopped onions and cloves. They can be served cold in a salad or warm with bacon and sausages, in a soup or a puree. They can be prepared in Romany style by adding pepper, cumin, vinegar, sage, mint, parsley and saffron to the cooking water.

which have six pairs of oblong, linear leaflets ending in a spine. The single, filiform peduncles appear on the axils of the leaves each one carrying one to four terminal white flowers finely striped in blue. The fruit produce broadly oblong and slightly inflated pods which contain two seeds the shape of a doubly convex lens. These seeds are consumed as a vegetable.

Lentils thrive best in dry, sandy, but fertile soil. Because they need a lot of warmth, in temperate regions they are sown directly onto the field in the late spring. They are harvested in the late summer once the shoots are almost dry. **Lentils** are a good source of protein, vitamin B, mineral salts, and a lot of iron and phosphorus. **Lentils** are a very nutritious vegetable which soothe intestinal inflammation and reduce the danger of abscesses. Germinated lentils are used in some regions as a decoration for nativity scenes.

LEPIDIUM SATIVUM **Garden cress**
Leaf vegetable
Family: Cruciferae
Origin: western Asia
Height: 8 to 12 inches (20 to 30 cm)
Flowering: spring
Properties: anti-scurvy, apéritif, purifier, digestive, diuretic, stimulant

---

Garden cress was for a long time forgotten and is now being rediscovered by vegetarians who appreciate its taste and medical properties. It is a fast growing herb which can be easily cultivated in the garden and on the balcony. This delicate annual plant with finely pinnate foliage is sown in early spring.

There are two varieties: a common variety with simple leaves and another, more original, with curly leaves. According to taste they are cultivated in two different ways. They can be deeply sown in order to quickly obtain a tuft of herbs to season salads, meat, or cheese and which are harvested once they reach a height of 2 to 6 inches (5 to 15 cm). The advantage of the close seeding is that the **garden cress** germinates more quickly. To harvest the plant all year round, the sowing can be spread out and done several times. The second method consists of sowing it in rows. Once the plants are strong enough, they are thinned out at a distance of 4 to 8 inches (10 to 20 cm) from one another. In this way, the seeds can be sown either in the spring or the summer

Cress
The peppery young leaves of the cress are a delicious garnish for salads, meat and fish. They enhance sandwiches and cold cuts. Older leaves can be cooked in soups, purees, soufflés and gratins.

and harvested in the autumn. To prosper well, **garden cress** needs plenty of water and in summer a shady place.

Garden cress contains vitamin A and a lot of vitamin C. It is a good tonic for the body, prevents viral diseases, colds, scurvy and fatigue. Its peppery taste is due to the essential oils it contains. **Garden cress** stimulates the appetite and facilitates digestion. Its juice revitalizes nails and hair.

LYCOPERSICUM ESCULENTUM **Tomato**
Fruit vegetable
Family: Solanaceae
Origin: South America
Height: over 6 feet (2 m)
Flowering: late spring
Properties: soothing, apéritif, anti-arthritis, anti-inflammatory, diuretic, laxative, revitalizing

---

Today **tomatoes** are a worldwide favorite vegetable available all year round. **Tomato** plants are annual and generally very branched and recumbent when fruiting, but a few forms are compact and upright. Its long stalked leaves are more or less hairy, strongly odorous, and pinnately compound. The flowers are yellow and disposed on terminal pending clusters. They bear large fruit or voluminous, smooth skinned berries usually red, scarlet, or yellow; which vary in shape from almost spherical through oval and elongate to pear-shaped. The thick, juicy pulp is segmented in chambers containing many cells of small, flat seeds. The whole plant releases a strong aromatic fragrance. There are at least a hundred different varieties of **tomatoes** with different shapes, sizes and colors.

Tomatoes need soil rich in humus with sufficient humidity. Light soil is preferable for early **tomatoes** and heavier soil for late ones. The plants are rather sensitive and need a warm, sunny location which is protected from the wind. In February, they are sown in beds in the greenhouse. Once the plants reach a height of 6 inches (15 cm) and there is no more danger of frosts, they can be planted in the field at intervals of 16 inches (40 cm) from each other and propped. As the plant develops, the buds that form on the leaf axils are cut off. Harvesting begins when the fruit are ripe and very colorful. Green **tomatoes** which are large enough can be set to ripen indoors.

Ripe **tomatoes** can be dried, pickled in olive oil canned, whole or pureed. **Tomatoes** contain a lot of water (90%) as well as some sugar (3 to 4%). They are rich in vitamin A, vitamin C, vitamin B9, mineral salts, such as potassium, magnesium and phosphorus, as well as trace elements. Their red coloring comes from a pigment, lycopene, which is similar to carotene. Green **tomatoes** contain the toxic alkaloid solanine.

Tomatoes have a calming effect on tissue and alleviate inflammations. They are recommended for people suffering from arthritis. They help in the production of urine, and because they contain folic acid, they promote the formation of red blood cells. Moreover, they stimulate digestion. **Tomatoes** revitalize the skin protecting it from the sun. Despite all this, it is the only vegetable whose parts are not all assimilated by the body: its skin and seeds are not digestible.

MANIHOT ESCULENTA	**Cassava, Yuca, Mandioc, Manioc**

Root vegetable
Family: Euphorbiaceae
Origin: Brazil, northern South America
Height: 1.50 to 6.5 feet (2 m)
Blooming time: summer
Properties: soothing, digestive, nutritious, mineralizing, tonic

---

This perennial shrub, also known as **mandioc** or **manioc**, is a staple food in Central and South America where it is called *yucca*, even though the plant is not related to the ornamental plant of the lily family with the same name. **Cassava** is found growing wild in Mexico and in the Amazon area. **Cassava** consumption spread to the African continent where its culture quickly developed, particularly in Nigeria, Zaire, Tanzania, Ghana, Uganda, Mozambique and Madagascar. Today, the plant is grown and consumed in most tropical regions of the world.

The **cassava** root is tuberous with a beige brown skin and a white flesh. According to the variety it can weigh between 4.4 lbs. (2 kg) and 44 lbs. (20 kg). Its petioled leaves are dark green, palmate and deeply parted into five to nine lobes. The monoecious flowers appear in terminal clusters. They have a reddish, bell-shaped calyx with five lobes and no corolla. The male flowers have ten stamens standing on the edge of a fleshy disk. The female flowers have an ovary with three chambers. They bear globular fruit with a single seed which disintegrates while splitting in three.

The fleshy roots are the parts of the plant which are harvested. These roots contain, like the rest of the plant, a cyanide-producing sugar derivative (hydrocyanic acid) which is highly poisonous. To remove the poison, the tubers must be rubbed and dried in the sun or cooked. Because the poison is highly volatile, it is not resistant to air or heat.

Cassava thrives in average, deep soil in a warm, damp region. It is planted deep in the earth, and after a year it already has root tubers the size of a big **beetroot**. From this point on it can be harvested upon demand. The roots of this plant can remain in the soil from 8 to 24 months without rotting. **Cassava** contains mainly starch and latex, but it also has some amino acids, minerals, calcium, magnesium, vitamin B and small amounts of vitamin C. When prepared in the right way, it is a healthy and very digestive food which soothes inflammations and strengthens the organism.

MEDICAGO SATIVA	**Alfalfa sprouts**

Leaf vegetable
Family: Fabaceae
Origin: Central Europe
Height: 12 to 16 inches (30 to 40 cm)
Flowering: late spring
Properties: mineralizing, stimulant

Also called lucerne or purple medic, **alfalfa sprouts** are very refreshing and appetizing. They are found in small, tight patches of germinated seeds approximately 2 to 6 inches (5 to 15 cm) high, like **garden cress**. The plant arises from a much-branched crown that is partially embedded in the surface layer of soil. As the plant develops, numerous thin stems bearing many trifoliolate leaves arise from the crown buds. Racemes of small, pale purple flowers arise from the upper axillary buds of the stems. They bear corkscrew coiled pods containing from two to eight or more seeds.

Alfalfa is grown in greenhouses, on the balcony, or in the garden. The plant needs a light soil of average quality, not too much sun exposure and plenty of water. They are sown in the spring directly in the open land or in pots. Most seeds germinate within six days and are harvested once they reach the necessary height.

Tomato
Contrary to what one might assume, it was not the Italians who invented tomato sauce, but rather the Indians living in Central America who seasoned it with different kinds of bell peppers. Today there are a multiplicity of tomato sauces to accompany pasta, meat and fish. Fresh tomatoes can be prepared in salads or stuffed with a mixture of mayonnaise and chopped vegetables. They can be cooked with parsley and garlic or stuffed with meat. Tomatoes are an ingredient in the traditional ratatouille niçoise, in gratins, in fish and seafood recipes and in different eastern dishes. Green tomatoes are used in omelettes and to prepare chutney. Tomato juice is a delicious apéritif, preferably with a dash of Tabasco sauce.

Alfalfa sprouts contain proteins (55%), amino acids, vitamins A, B and C. Other contents are mineral salts, particularly calcium, as well as trace elements (like iron, phosphorus, zinc, copper and silicon) and a vegetable estrogen.

Alfalfa sprouts are recommended for people suffering from anaemia and nervous exhaustion. They strengthen fingernails and hair. The hormonal effect of their vegetable estrogen combined with the silicon and calcium they contain, helps fight against menopausal symptoms as well as osteoporosis.

Alfalfa sprouts are eaten raw in salads. They are used to give flavor to sandwiches and as a garnish for meat, fish, eggs and omelettes.

MESEMBRYANTHEMUM CRYSTALLINUM — *Ice plant, Sea fig, Sea marigold*

Leaf vegetable
Family: Aizoaceae
Origin: South Africa
Height: 24 to 32 inches (60 to 80 cm)
Blooming time: summer
Properties: sour, laxative, diuretic, emollient, tonic

Also known as **sea fig** or **sea marigold**, this perennial plant was forgotten for a long time. Today it is again being used for its culinary, medicinal and decorative properties.

The plant has long stems with numerous fleshy, round leaves which are covered by transparent, glistening glands containing a salty liquid. Because of these glands, the plant glitters in the sun, as if it were covered with ice-crystals. The delicate ray flowers come in a variety of colors. They form hard, pentagonal fruit. The leaves, which are the part of the plant that is consumed, have a refreshing, sour taste.

The plant thrives in light, moist, sandy soil. It does not endure constant humidity, but does well in warm, arid areas, tolerating the full sun almost as a cactus does. It is cultivated either by cuttings or by superficial seeding directly onto the field from spring to summer. The leaves are harvested fresh according to demand during the whole summer. The **ice plant** has 95% water and is low in calories. However, it is rich in vitamins A, B and C, mineral salts and trace elements. Due to its sour taste, this vegetable is very refreshing a good thirst quencher. The plant stimulates liver activity, promotes the production of bile juice, and is a diuretic. **Ice plant** is consumed raw, cut in salads or cooked to accompany meat or in purees and soups. It is also a beautiful addition to any rock garden.

MOMORDICA BALSAMINA — *Wild cucumber, Balsam apple*

Fruit vegetable
Family: Cucurbitaceae
Origin: tropical regions of America and of Asia
Height: 1.6 feet (1.50 m)
Flowering: spring
Properties: emetic, purgative, purifier, rubefacient, vulnerary

---

This ancient vegetable is quite popular in India. It is a annual climber with delicate, striped stems and simple tendrils. The palmate leaves are deeply lobed in three to five lobes whose edges are roughly dented. The small yellow, single, male and female flowers bear large, oval fruit which hang from a long peduncle. Their appearance resemble that of a big, round **cucumber**. Young fruit are at first green, then shinny orange as they ripen. The ripe fruit split open lengthways into two to three segments releasing numerous seeds. Even after seeding, this is a very decorative plant.

Its fleshy rind encloses a juicy red pulp which has a particular, sour and bitter taste. To prosper well, the plant needs a lot of humidity and warmth. The seeds are sown in the spring in average soil with a support so that the plant can climb. The fruits are harvested, when they are still green and young, before their bitterness becomes too strong and while the seeds are not too hard.

Wild cucumber contains a lot of water and a bitter substance known as cucurbacine. Even though it is low in calories, the plant is a good tonic for a weak organism. Externally applied, it helps heal small wounds and bruises. It also contains fatty acids, mineral salts, and vitamins B and C. This vegetable also has cleansing effect on the organism – it removes poisons and calms inflammations. In the pharmacy it is used to prepare ointments for haemorrhoids.

The fruit are consumed cooked as a accompaniment for meat and fish. In China the seeds of a related variety, *Momordica cochinchinensis*, are used to produce an oil for burning, while the roots are used to make soap. An African variety, *Momordica foetida*, contains a substance used in the treatment of diabetes.

Cassava

There are many different ways of preparing cassava. Cassava is obtained by rubbing the fresh root and later squeezing and drying it with a cloth in order to eliminate most of the poisonous substance it contains. This puree is then spread out in the sun to dry. The paste is thinly sliced and cooked over high heat. These cookies or toasts are eaten like bread, added to soups, vegetable stews and meat or fish dishes. They can also be made into very puffy fritters. Cassava can be kept in dry storage for many years without spoiling. Tapioca, or cassava starch, is made from mashing, roasting and grinding the roots. An alcoholic beverage, known as mobi, is made by fermenting cassava water with grated sweet potatoes and molasses syrup. The latex sap of cassava cooked for several hours over low heat with salt and pepper produces a Creole sauce known as cabiou used to enhance meat and fish.

ORYZA SATIVA   **Rice**
Fruit vegetable
Family: Gramineae
Origin: India, Asia
Height: 1.6 to 5 feet (0.50 to 1.50 m)
Blooming time: spring
Properties: soothing, anti-diarrhoea, hypotensive

It is assumed that the cultivation of **rice** began in China about 2,800 BC, and in India around 2,300 BC. As contact with India increased its use quickly spread, so that by the time of **Alexander the Great** it was already being consumed by the inhabitants of Macedonia and Mesopotamia, as well as by those of Egypt and Persia. It was not untill the 8th century however, that Arab traders brought it to Spain, from where it later spread to southern Europe.

This annual grass is cultivated in the tropical, semitropical and temperate regions of the world. Its leaves are long, sharp and flattened with very rough edges and deeply split sheaths. It has a fasciculate root, i.e. without a central pivot. The hermaphrodite flowers form a more or less, terminal panicle, or inflorescence, made up of spikelets bearing flowers that produce the fruit, or grain. The grains are compact, streaked and generally oblong. These seeds can be classified in two large groups: the "indica," which is long, slim and pigmented with different hues; and the "Japonica," which is round to oval, smaller with a short stem.

There are several different types of **rice** of which the most well known are **Thai rice**, **American rice**, **Surinam rice**, **Basmati rice**, **Italian round rice**, **full grain rice**, and **perfumed rice**, among others. The **wild rice** growing in North America and India belongs to a variety known as *Zizania aquatica*. This grass is not related to **rice**, but its grain, often considered a delicacy, is rich in proteins and fiber.

Rice is cultivated from seed in the spring in wet or inundated land. In the autumn, the seedlings are transplanted to an enclosed field, or paddy, which stands under water. After 100 to 180 days, the harvest begins. Earlier **rice** was picked by hand. Today the plants are harvested mechanically from the paddy fields. Under optimal conditions, harvesting can be done three to four times per year. It is the cereal crop with the greatest yield per acre in the world. **Brown rice** is rich in starch and vitamin B1. Besides, it contains minerals, magnesium and proteins (8%). **Rice** is a good energy source

which reduces high blood pressure. **White rice** is easier to digest and is recommended for people suffering from ulcers or dyspepsia. Its cooking water soothes the stomach and prevents irritation. The seeds mashed to a powder are used as soothing poultices.

Rice flour is used in cosmetics industry to make **rice** powder. The straw is used to manufacture cigarette paper and other fine papers.

PACHYRHIZUS EROSUS   **Jicama, Yam bean**
Root, fruit or pod vegetable
Family: Fabaceae
Origin: Central America, Mexico, Eastern and South-East Asia
Height: about 16 feet (5 m)
Flowering: spring
Properties: soothing, purifier, diuretic, purgative

Jicama is a leguminous vine native to Mexico which grows in tropical regions and has been cultivated by the people of Central and South America for years. Altogether there are six varieties, three are grown for food: *Pachyrhizus erosus* is the most popular in Asia and America, *Pachyrhizus ahipa* is cultivated in Bolivia and Argentina, and *Pachyrhizus tuberosus* with its large roots is found in the whole Amazon basin.

The plant has thick roots with irregularly globular, brown-skinned, white fleshed, crisp, and juicy tubers. The leaves consist of three single, ovoid leaflets and are dented or lobed. The exterior leaflets can reach 6 inches (15 cm) in length, while the middle ones can be up to 8 inches (20 cm) long. The blue or white purple inflorescence appear in terminal clusters and are covered with numerous butterfly flowers which bear the fruit or seedpods. These are about 6 inches (15 cm) long, covered with fine, dense hairs and contain four to nine brownish seeds. The parts of the plant which are harvested are the pods and the juicy tubers.

Jicama thrives in warm, damp regions. The roots are planted in the autumn in rich soil at the base of a solid prop to enable the plant to climb. It grows fast and problem free.

The fruit are harvested once they are formed, and consumed as a vegetable immediately as they cannot be conserved. The tubers are pulled out nine months after being planted to be consumed young, fresh and juicy, or left until the following spring when used for their starch. Once harvested, the tubers are kept in dry, dark storage.

Rice

Rice is cooked in water and served as a side dish to other foods. It is an ingredient in salads and vegetable stuffings. It is prepared with tomatoes, aromatic herbs, and is the main ingredient for risotto. It can also be cooked with oil and stock. It is added to omelettes and fritters. As a dessert it is cooked in milk and an ingredient in cakes and puddings. The grains can be eaten caramelized and puffed. Rice flour is used to make noodles of different sorts and biscuits. The grain can also be distilled to prepare a spirit known as arrak, or fermented to produce the rice wine known as sake in Japan.

Jicama has a high water content (80 %) and very few calories. It contains fiber, proteins (10%), carbohydrates, vitamins A and C, minerals and trace elements. When mature the tubers become very fibrous and are very rich in starch. They are a good diuretic, sooth the stomach and are easily digestible.

The young tubers are eaten raw in salads or cooked with fish and meat, in purees, gratins, or fried with **parsley** and garlic. In Thailand they are cooked with chili peppers, sugar, and salt. The young tender pods are prepared like string-beans. The starch extracted from the old tubers is used to prepare an alternative to arrow-root which is used in soups and crêpes.

PANICUM MILIACEUM   **Millet**
Fruit vegetable
Family: Gramineae
Origin: probably India
Height: 20 to 32 inches (50 to 80 cm)
Blooming time: spring
Properties: anti-anaemia, anti-cholesterol, diuretic, nutritious

---

Millet is considered one of the oldest cereals on earth. Archaeological finds have shown that it was cultivated in China and Mesopotamia around 5,000 BC. However, today, millions of men, women and children in Central Asia and southern Siberia still rely on it for their sustenance.

This annual plant has a stem with nodules that enable it to regenerate itself quickly. Its green, alternate leaves are thin and enclosed by sheaths. The inconspicuous, hermaphrodite, green or violet flowers are borne on terminal racemes. These flowers bear fruit or caryopsis that remain enclosed in husks without releasing the small, round, yellow, white or black seeds.

Millet prospers on loose soil and is resistant to drought. The seeds are sown in April or May on dry soil. **Millet** is rich in carbohydrates, proteins and minerals. It also contains fiber and vitamins B, D, and E. Its nutritive value can be compared to that of **wheat**. The fiber content of **millet** speeds and stimulates the digestive process and the elimination of unused and indigestible foods. Moreover, it reduces the risk of cancer. Its germ contains fatty acids that protect against cardio-vascular disease.

Millet is also used as birdseed and in chicken-feed mixtures.

Millet

Millet is used to prepare tasty and digestive porridges. It is also used to make unleaven breads that are eaten either with jelly or cracked in soups. Germinated millet seeds are used in salads or to garnish sandwiches and cold cuts. Millet seed is also well known as a food for pet birds in the home, and for poultry on the farm.

PASTINACA SATIVA   **Parsnip**
Root vegetable
Family: Umbelliferae
Origin: Eurasia
Height: 16 to 24 inches (40 to 60 cm)
Flowering: July to August
Properties: purifier, diuretic, sedative

This ancient vegetable which had a high reputation among Roman gourmets was widely replaced by the **carrot** during the 11th century, although in Great Britain it remained a much loved staple food. Recently, vegetable lovers in other countries have rediscovered it and have brought it back to the table. This biennial plant resistant to cold has an upright, hollow, grooved stem, and compound leaves with oval, lobed, hairy and dented leaflets. Its yellow flowers, which appear in large umbels, bear smooth, splendid, round to oval fruit. **Parsnip** is cultivated for its large, tapering, fleshy white edible root which has a soft, sweet and aromatic taste. **Parsnip** thrives in damp, deep, rather heavy soil in sunny areas. It is sown directly onto the field from February to June. In very mild regions, it can be sown until the end of September. Harvesting of the roots is done four months after the sowing. However, the roots may remain in the soil during the winter months; exposure to low temperatures makes the roots sweeter. **Parsnip** contains water, sugar, an essential oil, proteins and vitamin C. **Parsnip** is a good source of energy while stimulating the digestive system. It is also a tranquilizer. The young roots are usually eaten raw and grated to sweeten, refresh and flavor salads.

PETROSELINUM CRISPUM **Turnip-rooted**
VAR. TUBERSOSUM **parsley**
Root vegetable
Family: Umbelliferae
Origin: Mediterranean basin
Height: 8 to 12 cm (20 to 30 cm)
Flowering: summer
Properties: anti-anaemia, anti-scurvy, apéritif, purifier, diuretic, emmenagogue, sedative, stimulant, tonic

---

There are two varieties: **Hamburg parsley** or **turnip-rooted parsley** whose root is a vegetable; and **common parsley** whose leaves are used as a flavoring and a garnish. This hardy biennial plant has a large, white parsniplike root with a delicate flavor. Its stem is branched, streaked, and full of nodules with compound, deep green, tender and curled or deeply frilled leaves. The seed stalks are topped by compound umbels of small, yellow flowers which bear oval, greenish yellow fruit. **Turnip-rooted parsley** thrives in fresh, light soil that is rich in humus and partly sunny. The young, juicy roots which were sown in the spring are harvested in the summer; while the larger ones are pulled out in the autumn.

Turnip-rooted parsley contains fiber, water, sugar, apiol – an essential oil – iron, calcium, phosphorous and high amounts of vitamins A and C. Because of its ability to ease muscle cramps it is used as a digestive aid. It is also prescribed as a mild diuretic.

PHASEOLUS VULGARIS **Bean**
Fruit vegetable
Family: Fabaceae
Origin: South America
Height: from 1 to 8 feet (0.40 to 2.50 m), depending on the variety
Flowering: late spring, summer
Properties: soothing, purifier, diuretic, stimulant, tonic

Parsnip

The raw parsnip root, grated or thinly sliced is delicious when served with a vinaigrette as a delicate, fragrant hors-d'œuvre. Cooked in salted water it can be used alone or mixed with other vegetables as a side dish. Roasted together with a joint of meat, or simply deep fried, it is a delicious addition to any meal. It can also be used to prepare delightful purees. Its intensely fragrant leaves are used as a seasoning in soups and salads.

This dwarf or semiclimbing **bean** plant has long, petioled, green leaves with three oval and pointed leaflets. The white flowers have five petals with six stamens whose long pistil covers the growing fruit or pod. These pods are formed by two valves containing the seeds which generally have a thick shell when ripe. The size and shape of the seeds vary depending on the type of **bean**.

Beans grow well in light, fresh soil without too much lime and not too humid. They are very sensitive to cold and require a sunny, warm location. They must not be cultivated too early in the season; therefore, sowing takes place at the end of spring directly onto the field. After twenty days, the shoots are trimmed and artificial supports are set up for the climbing varieties. Harvesting differs according to variety. **Green** or **string beans** are harvested when the pods are green or pale yellow and young; **haricot beans** are harvested once they are ripe when the **beans** are well formed but still tender, or, when they are very ripe and almost dry. Dried **haricot beans** can be preserved a long time in storage; **green beans** are bottled or frozen.

Green beans are low in calories and contain water, fiber, amino acids, vitamins A, B, C and E as well as mineral salts (calcium and iron). Dried **haricot beans** contain carbohydrates (11%), amino acids, fiber (5%), trace elements (iron, magnesium calcium, phosphorus and iodine), vitamins A, C, E, and all vitamins of the B group. **Green beans** have a positive effect on the digestive tract and adjust the cholesterol level in the blood. They contain a substance which balances metabolic disorders, protects the liver and strengthens the heart. They also lower the absorption of glucose in people suffering from diabetes. Dried **haricot beans** possess an element that promotes formation of new white blood cells after treatment with antibiotics. **Beans** strengthen the organism and are recommended during convalescence.

PHYLLOSTACHYS **Bamboo (Sprouts)**
HETEROCYCLA
Stem vegetable
Family: Gramineae
Origin: Asia
Height: depending on the variety, 26 to 82 feet (8 to 25 m)
Flowering: late spring
Properties: purifier, mineralizing, stimulant, tonic

Bamboo, known in China, India and Japan for its medicinal properties, is a staple food in Asia. **Bamboos** are used for a variety of purposes: the small stems are used to produce several utensils while the larger ones are used in construction; the pulped fibers are used to make fine quality paper; its leaves are a useful fodder for livestock.

Bamboos are giant, fast-growing grasses with woody, hollow, aerial stems or culms. These culms grow in branching clusters from a thick underground rhizome. The culms often form a dense undergrowth that excludes other plants. Mature **bamboos** sprout horizontal branches that bear sword shaped, small, alternate leaves on stalked blades; the leaves on young culms arise directly from the stem which is green, thick and marked with stigmata. **Bamboo** flowers are hardly noticeable. The sprouts and shoots of the plant are edible.

Bamboo thrives in rich, moist soil and is distributed in tropical and subtropical to mild temperate regions. It is hardy to cold and warm weather conditions alike. It is propagated through its spurs which are quickly replanted on rich soil. The shoots have a low calorific value, however, they contain proteins, sugar, numerous mineral salts like silicon, phosphorus and calcium, as well as different vitamins. The fine grained silica produced in the joint stems has been used as a medicine in China and India for centuries under the name *tabasheer*. Other varieties contain a toxic substance known as hydrogen cyanide which dissipates with cooking. **Bamboo** is used in medicine to treat joint and back pain. It promotes the formation of cartilage destroyed by arthritis or other articulatory diseases. It has a mineralizing effect on the body, relieving menopausal problems and preventing osteoporosis.

The shoots cooked in water are eaten in salads, soups, stuffings, sauces, and **rice**. Because **bamboo** shoots perish quickly, they are only found fresh in Asia.

There are a wide variety of **pea** plants including dwarf, half-dwarf, trailing, smooth-seeded, wrinkled-seeded which is sweet and very common, black-eyed, and **sugar peas** which produce edible pods considered to be a green legume.

The **pea** plant is a hardy, leafy annual with hollow trailing or climbing stems that end in tendrils which facilitate climbing. Its compound and pinnate leaves have three pairs of oval leaflets. The reddish or white flowers, growing two to three per stalk, are butterfly shaped. They bear a many-seeded fruit or pod that grows up to 4 inches (10 cm) long, splitting in half when ripe. Inside the pod, 5 to 10 seeds are attached by short stalks. These seeds are the edible parts of the plant.

The pods which are covered by green, juicy husks have a hard inner skin which makes them inedible. Only the sugar pea or *Pisum sativum* variety *saccharatum* is cultivated not for its seeds, but for its tender, flat sweet pods.

Peas should be planted in fertile, well drained soil in an unshaded spot. Sowing is done from February to June: early maturing **peas** are sown first, then **sugar peas** and finally wrinkle-seeded varieties which are the latest and sweetest ones. Three weeks later, the shoots are trimmed and supports are set up to facilitate climbing. **Sugar peas** are harvested first, followed by the most rounded ones, and finally the wrinkle-seeded ones. Rounded **peas** are harvested once the seeds are ripe and hard. Then their husks are removed.

Peas are rich in carbohydrates, amino acids, lipids (1.5%) and mineral salts (3%), like phosphorus and iron.

Peas are very nutritious. Fresh **peas** contain amino acids, phosphorus and vitamins A, B1, B2 and D. They also have a high nutritional value. This vegetable is recommended for people suffering from anaemia and during convalescence.

Peas

Chopped up, dried peas are used to prepare creamy soups and delicate, sweet purees which are generally served with pork and sausages. Fresh peas can be cooked with carrots, small onions, lettuce, thyme and bay leaves to be served as a side dish for meat and poultry. Sugar peas are cooked whole in water and served in a salad or sautéed with onions and tomatoes as an accompaniment to omelettes and meat.

PISUM SATIVUM   **Pea, Sugar pea**
Fruit vegetable
Family: *Fabaceae*
Origin: *central Europe and western Asia*
Height: *6.5 feet (2 m)*
Flowering: *spring*
Properties: *purifier, mineralizing, emollient, tonic*

RAPHANUS SATIVUS   **Radish**
Root vegetable
Family: *Cruciferae*
Origin: *unknown*
Height: *4 to 14 inches (10 to 35 cm)*
Flowering: *summer*
Properties: *anti-scurvy, apéritif, expectorant, laxative, diuretic, tonic*

This annual plant has a fleshy, spherical root with fan shaped, hairy leaves which are split into elongated segments the ends of which are round. The flowers, which have four white petals with a purple veining, bear fruit or siliques containing numerous small brown seeds. The **black radish** variety (*Raphanus niger*) has a large root with a rugged black rind and white flesh; it has a characteristic taste. The **Japanese radish** or **daikon** has a very long root that can weigh a few pounds; it has a very sweet taste.

Radish thrives in sunny and half-shady locations, preferably in a nourishing, deep soil which is not too stony. It is sown directly onto the field from March until the end of September according to variety. The soil must be kept moist and irrigated regularly. Generally **radishes** are harvested early before they become too large, roughly three weeks after being sown. **Black radishes** are sown onto the field from June to July, and are harvested in the autumn. After the harvest, the plant is left to dry in the sun for a day. The leaves are then cut off and the roots are placed in cool, well aired storage.

Radish contains water, aromatic oil and few calories. Nevertheless, it contains plenty of vitamins A, B and C, mineral salts (iron, iodine, phosphorus, magnesium and sulphur). **Radishes** are used to improve the hair, the skin and the nails. Thanks to their vitamin C content, they help prevent scurvy and influenza. They are diuretic and relieve bladder and liver problems. Their aromatic oil stimulates the appetite. **Radishes** are often recommended for people suffering from diabetes.

Radish

Raw radishes with salt or in a salad have a pungent, crisp, peppery taste. Japanese radish is also eaten raw in salads or grated to marinate fish. It is cooked like turnip and served as a side dish to meat and poultry. The leaves are used to season stews. Its young flowers are eaten like broccoli. The immature fruit or siliques are deliciously crisp, juicy and peppery sweet. The ripe seeds are used like mustard seeds. The whole plant can be used in the kitchen. Radish syrup is used to decongest the respiratory system.

RHEUM RHAPONTICUM   **Rhubarb**
Stem vegetable
Family: *Polygonaceae*
Origin: *probably central Asia*
Height: *about 24 inches (60 cm)*
Flowering: *late spring*
Properties: *apéritif, tonic, laxative*

The origin of **rhubarb** is unclear. Some assume that it comes from Tibet or Mongolia, others believe, it originated on the banks of the Volga. From very early times the Chinese have used the plant primarily as a cathartic. **Rhubarb** was not cultivated in Europe until it arrived via India and Asia Minor during the 18th century. However, it quickly became renowned as a healthy, delicate addition to the diet. This large, hardy perennial is one of the vegetables available early in the season. **Rhubarb** has a thick, fleshy taproot with large clumps of big, smooth leaves strongly waved at their base with a long, thick, reddish petiole. A large central flower stalk may appear and bear numerous small, reddish white flowers and angular, winged fruit containing one seed. Usually the inflorescence is cut off, so that the plant does not loose strength of growth.

Rhubarb is a very undemanding plant; it thrives without problem in partly sunny areas in deep, moist soil with good drainage. **Rhubarb** is propagated by division of the stumps in autumn which are then covered during the winter months. They can also be replanted and covered with hay and a cask. During the first year, the plant is left to grow without harvesting so that it becomes strong. During the second year, after being forced for four weeks, the oldest petioles can be harvested: they are taken from the basis and pulled away by twisting them off the plant. The plants can be harvested for up to ten years.

Rhubarb contains a lot of calcium oxalate. It is rich in vitamins and fiber. Its root contains anthracite glycosides which give it its purgative properties and its color.

Because **rhubarb** contains calcium oxalate, which gives it its characteristic grittiness, it is definitely not recommended for people who suffer from lithiasis, gout and rheumatism. Its fiber content has a mildly stimulating effect on the intestine, and its sour taste stimulates the appetite.

SALICORNIA EUROPAEA — Goosefoot

Family: Chenopodiaceae
Origin: coasts of the English Channel and the Atlantic ocean
Height: 8 to 20 inches (20 to 50 cm)
Flowering: late summer
Properties: tranquilizer, emollient, laxative, stimulant, tonic

---

This annual plant grows in salty terrain. Today, this plant is once again fashionable and can generally be found in fish shops.

This grey, green weed has thick, juicy, leafy stems with tiny, almost invisible, terminal flowers. Its root is woody. The sprouts are harvested young, tender and crisp before blooming in May, when they become woody and hard. They have a salty herbal taste.

Goosefoot is rich in mineral salts like calcium, magnesium, iodine and iron. It has few calories. It has some amino acids, sugar and fiber which have a positive effect on the digestive system. Because it contains vitamin B12, it has a calming effect on the nervous system. It is usually consumed raw, in salads or with a vinaigrette. Cooked, the young sprouts are delicious with fish.

SCORZONERA HISPANICA — Scorzonera

Root vegetable
Family: Compositae
Origin: southern and Central Europe
Height: 8 to 12 inches (20 to 30 cm) (Rosettes)
Flowering: spring
Properties: tranquilizer, diuretic, nutritious, expectorant, sudorific

---

Rhubarb

The plant's fleshy, tart, and highly acid leafstalks are used in pies, often in compotes and preserves, and sometimes as the basis of a wine or an apéritif.

The **scorzonera** grows wild in dry regions and was already known in antiquity for its medicinal properties. It was not cultivated in the garden until the Renaissance, when it became known under the name of black **salsify**. In the 18th century **La Quintinie**, lawyer and agronomist of **King Louis XIV**, described it as a root with an extraordinary taste. Since then it has become part of European cuisine.

The roots soon replaced that of **salsify**, which was less productive, woody and of lower quality. Today, vegetable lovers prize **scorzonera**. It is a perennial plant with an upright, cylindrical, taproot of approximately 16 inches (40 cm) in length. Its black rind encloses a white, firm, slightly milky flesh that tastes of sweet **almonds**.

The entire, lanceolate leaves are wrapped around the base. The beautiful yellow flowers appear in terminal clusters and bear uniform fruit or achenes which contain a feathery, hairy valve. **Scorzonera** thrives in light, deep soil rich in humus and warm, sunny locations. It is sown directly onto the field in the spring, watering it regularly during the summer. During the first year, the long roots are pulled out, but they can also be left in the soil. If they

are harvested after the blooming period of the second year, they will be much larger. This vegetable has a pleasant taste and is very nutritious. It is rich in mucilage, carbohydrates (20%), and latex. It does not have any starch, and it contains inulin which is beneficial for diabetics.

This vegetable is recommended for people suffering from stomach disorders and indigestion. It soothes the intestine and alleviates inflammations. Besides, it is a diuretic and a sudorific, it has a positive effect on the kidneys and the urinary tract; it helps the organism eliminate toxins. It also alleviates irritations in the respiratory system and acts as an expectorant.

Before being consumed, the roots must be peeled and soaked in lemon water so that they do not turn black. They can be prepared raw, cut in pieces and tossed in a salad. They can also be cooked in salted water with a little flour and milk and served as a accompaniment for meat and poultry. They are excellent in fritters and gratins. The young fresh leaves can be used in salads or cooked as a vegetable. In Spain the **scorzonera** is used as an antidote for the poison of a dangerous snake, known as *escorsu*, which is frequently found in Catalonia.

SECHIUM EDULE   *Chayote or Chocho*

Fruit, tuber, shoot and leaf vegetable
Family: *Cucurbitaceae*
Origin: *unknown*
Height: *several feet (climbing liana)*
Flowering: *spring*
Properties: *tranquilizer, diuretic, tonic*

This vegetable plant is known in Réunion as **chocho**, in India as **chochote**, in the Antilles as **christophine** and its tubers as **chinchayotes**. Unknown in the wild, this plant was already being consumed by the native inhabitants of America. It is believed that the Aztecs cultivated it and from there it spread throughout tropical America. Today it is grown predominantly in Costa Rica, the Antilles, Mexico and in the south of France, in Midi and Charente where it prospers very well.

This is a tendril bearing perennial vine with very long stems. Its leaves are alternate, entire, long, ovoid, petioled, angular and lobed with wavy edges. The very tiny white male flowers appear in terminal clusters, while the female ones appear solitarily. They bear elongated fruit, about 6 inches (15 cm) long, which are rippled at the base. Some are green and have a smooth skin, others are yellowish with more or less sharp prickles. These fruit are monosperm; that is, they contain a single seed of the size of an almond. The main root of the plant is strongly branched out with large edible tubers which can weigh about 22 lbs. (10 kg). This plant

is amazing in that it produces edible tubers and fruit. It thrives in rich nourishing soil in warm, protected locations. The fruit are planted in the spring once there is a root and a bud. The young shoots are harvested in the spring, leaving enough behind so that the plant continues to grow. The fruit are harvested from September until early October. The tubers are pulled out just before the first frost.

Chayote contains a lot of water, vitamin B and C, and only a few calories. It is also rich in mineral salts like potassium, iron and magnesium, which are useful to the organism. Because of its water and fiber content, **chayote** promotes the bowel function and stimulates the production of urine. Its tubers, which contain a lot of starch and vitamin C, are a nutritious and easily digestible food.

The fruit are eaten raw, peeled and grated with lemon juice or cut in pieces and cooked with **onions** and curry. They can also be stuffed with meat. The tubers are cooked in water and prepared like **potatoes**. Their starch is used to make cakes and desserts. The young spring shoots are eaten like **asparagus**, and the young leaves like **spinach**.

SOLANUM MELONGENA   *Aubergine, Eggplant*

Fruit vegetable
Family: *Solanaceae*
Origin: *India*
Height: *32 to 36 inches (80 to 90 cm)*
Flowering: *spring*
Properties: *tranquilizer, healing agent, invigorating, laxative, tonic*

Aubergine is native to India, where it has been cultivated since antiquity for its fleshy fruit. It arrived in Spain around the 6th century and it was later found planted in English gardens as an exotic curiosity. **Aubergines** or **eggplants** owe their name to the color and shape of their white variety. In Italy, during the Renaissance, they were considered an extremely poisonous and evil plant known as *Mala insana* (unhealthy apple) because it belongs to the family of the nightshade plants such as belladonna. **Louis XIV** asked **La Quintinie** to grow it in the gardens of Versailles. Nevertheless, it was not until the 19th century that it made its way to our tables.

Aubergine

Aubergines have conquered not only the kitchens of Greece, the Middle East and India, but also those of the entire Mediterranean area. They harmonize particularly well with tomatoes, garlic and olive oil. Just like courgettes, tomatoes, and bell peppers, they are a key ingredient in the classic ratatouille. They are used in vegetable gratins and prepared as fritters. The Greeks use it to prepare moussaka, a meat gratin. It is mashed to a puree to prepare Turkish aubergine caviar which is flavored with lemon and served cold. It is used sautéed as a accompaniment for meat. Aubergine can also be stuffed.

Today's **aubergines** differ in appearance and color from the first that arrived in Europe. This annual plant has an erect, bushy stem, sometimes armed with a few spines; large ovate, slightly lobed leaves; and pendant, violet, characteristically solitary purple flowers. The fruit is a large, egg-shaped berry, varying in color from dark purple to red, yellowish, or sometimes striped with a glossy surface.

The plant needs a warm, protected location and very nutritious soil. In summer it must be watered regularly. Its cultivation is done in plant beds where it is sown from April to May. Once the plant has five leaves, it is replanted. During their growth, they must be regularly trimmed to stimulate the formation of side branches. Four to five months after sowing, the first ripe fruit can be harvested before they become tender and allowing only five to six fruit to mature per plant. Older fruits become bitter. They are quite sensitive and can spoil during transportation.

Aubergines contain a lot of water, few calories and lot of fiber, vitamins B1 and B2, as well as some vitamin C and mineral salts, mainly potassium. Because of the B vitamins they contain, **aubergines** protect the nervous system, promote the renewal of cells, and stimulate the metabolism. Because they have vitamin C, they work as a healing agent for wounds and strengthen the nerves. The potassium in them works as a diuretic, calms the nervous system, stimulates the heart muscles and has a positive effect on the skin.

Potatoes

Famous gourmet chefs have dedicated entire books full with original and tasty recipes solely to the potato. Generally it is consumed after being peeled, cooked in water, in oil, in sauces or steamed. They can be prepared in soups, salads, purees, fritters, croquettes, soufflés, gratins, ragouts, fried and even stuffed. Potatoes are marketed whole canned, cooked, fried, and frozen. Potato chips are a common appetizer or snack. The tubers are used to produce a starch which is used to bind sauces and make desserts. Furthermore, a spirit can also be distilled from these tubers.

SOLANUM TUBEROSUM	**Potato**

Root vegetable
Family: *Solanaceae*
Origin: *South America, the Andes*
Height: *about 20 inches (50 cm)*
Flowering: *spring*
Properties: *soothing, healing agent, diuretic, mineralizing, tonic*

Germany, Poland and Russia are the main **potato** producing countries, while in Britain, **Jersey new potatoes** from the Channel Isles are renowned for their delicate flavor. The **potato** plant is an herbaceous annual with compound leaves consisting of large, oval leaflets with slightly wavy edges. The white or blue flowers have five stamens and a shining yellow pistil. They bear small greenish fruit which contain numerous tiny seeds.

Some **potato** varieties do not bloom and others are sterile. The part of the plant that is harvested are the tubers. There are at least two thousand varieties of **potato**, the **King Edward** variety being one of the most popular in Britain.

The **potato** thrives in light, moist, deep soil, but also tolerates heavier soil that is not too humid. However, it is important to plant it in a sunny location

that is well drained for it does not endure swampy soil or frost. It is cultivated by planting the germinated tubers, from April to May, whole or cut in half at a distance of about 20 inches (50 cm) from each another. When, after about ten days, the shoots appear earth is banked up around the plants. This is repeated as the plants grow. Harvesting takes place, provided there is good weather, two or three months later for early varieties, and five months later for the later ones. Once harvested, the tubers are left to dry in the sun for a day and later are kept in dry, dark storage. If the harvested **potatoes** are exposed to light, their skin tends to turn green. Green **potatoes** are inedible as they contain a poisonous alkaloid known as solanine. **Potatoes** contain 75% of water, vitamins A, B and C. **Potatoes** are a good source of vitamins and energy. They are also rich in starch, carbohydrates (15 to 20 %), proteins (2%) and mineral salts like potassium, which is essential for the body's acid-base balance and muscle function. **Potatoes** are usually recommended during convalescence. Its pulp is a great healing agent for wounds and abscesses. They also help the elimination of toxins from the body. **Potatoes** form one of the most important staple foods of the northern European diet.

SORGHUM BICOLOR   *Sorghum*
Fruit vegetable
Family: Gramineae
Origin: Africa and the Far East
Height: 12 to 20 feet (3.50 to 6 m)
Flowering: spring
Properties: anti-anaemia, invigorating, sedative, stimulant

There are several varieties of **sorghum** raised chiefly for their grain which belong to the species *Sorghum vulgare*. This species includes varieties of **grain sorghums, grass sorghums,** and **broomcorn. Grain sorghums** include **durra, milo, shallu, kafir corn, Egyptian corn, great millet,** and **Indian millet,** which is rich in flour.

This strong decorative, annual grass has green, simple leaves with finely dented edges similar to those of **corn.** The leaves are coated with a white waxy substance, and the pith, or central portion, of the stalks is juicy and sweet. The flowers are small, yellow or pink and are grouped in terminal clusters that range from lose to dense. They bear seeds that vary widely among the different types in their color, shape, and size. They have a pleasant, sweet taste, as do the young stems of the plant. **Sorghum** thrives in deep, light and rich soil. It does not like sun, but it is resistant to drought and heat. It is sown at the beginning of spring with regular watering during the first period. It grows quickly; harvesting is done mechanically at the end of the summer.

Sorghum contains plenty of carbohydrates, and starch of which 20 to 30% is amylose and 70 to 80% amylopectin, a rather sweet, jellylike substance. **Sorghum** is also rich in vitamins A, B1, B9, C and E as well as numerous trace elements such as magnesium, zinc, selenium and chrome. **Sorghum** is a healthy, nourishing and digestible cereal. It helps fight against cardio-vascular diseases by reducing the choles-

terol level in the blood. It is a laxative which helps prevent anaemia and fatigue. It also relieves pain caused by inflammations.

Cooked, it is usually used like **rice** as a side dish for meat and fish. The grain is usually ground into a flour to make porridge, unleaven breads, and cakes. The grain is also used in making edible oil, starch, dextrose (a sugar), paste, and alcoholic drinks. The stalks are used as fodder and building materials; the branches are used in the manufacture of paper; and the bark as a natural yellow dye.

SPINACIA OLERACEA   *Spinach*
Leaf vegetable
Family: Chenopodiaceae
Origin: the Middle East, Iran
Height: 8 to 16 inches (20 to 40 cm)
Flowering: summer
Properties: anti-anaemia, healing agent, laxative, mineralizing

---

Spinach was highly prized during the Renaissance thanks to the Medicis who were fond of this green, refreshing leafy vegetable. The preparation of most other leafy vegetables is generally compared to that of **spinach.** Today, this vegetable is very popular in France where it is cultivated in Morbihan, Finistère, Somme, Oise, Aisne, and the North.

Spinach is an annual plant with alternate, lanceolate, thick leaves. They are dark green, fleshy, puckered and slightly wavy on the edges. According to variety, they have a smooth or rough stem. **Spinach** is sometimes monoecious with female and male flowers grouped in clusters on the same plant and a green perianth or floral envelope; or dioecious, having male flowers and female flowers on different plants. They are pollinated by insects and the wind. The flowers bear small seeds with a smooth or prickly husk. **Spinach** requires cool weather and deep, rich, well-limed soil to give quick growth and maximum leaf area. Seed can be sown in rows every two weeks from March to October. The last sowing produce young plants that yield a crop in the autumn and then overwinter, providing leaves in early spring or even throughout the winter if the weather is not too severe.

Spinach contains 90% water, some fiber, and a few calories. However, it is rich in vitamins B1, B2, B9 and C. Furthermore, it contains carotene (vitamin A),

Spinach

Raw spinach is eaten as a salad, by itself or mixed with onions and orange slices. It can also be steamed and served with stock, butter, or cream. Spinach can be served with just about any meat, fish and with hard boiled eggs, fried eggs or omelettes. It can be pureed and used as an ingredient in gratins, soufflés, crepes and, mixed with potato puree, in fritters. Cooked, it is ideal for most forms of pies and quiches, especially when accompanying bacon and onions.

mineral salts (calcium, magnesium zinc and iron), as well as oxalic acid which is responsible for its bitter, sour taste. Because of its oxalate content, **spinach** is not recommended for people suffering from arthritis, rheumatism, gout, kidney and liver ailments, or diabetes. Invigorating, it stimulates vital functions and the digestive system.

It facilitates the elimination of toxins. It is useful to fight against anaemia. **Spinach** facilitates the regeneration of cells and stimulates growth in children. The green water resulting for cooking **spinach** is useful as a coloring agent for food or to color hard boiled eggs for Easter.

STACHYS AFFINIS **Chinese artichoke**
Root vegetable
Family: Labiatae
Origin: Asia
Height: 16 inches (40 cm)
Flowering: rarely in temperate areas
Properties: antispasmodic, laxative, digestive, mineralizing, tonic

---

This is a hardy plant with underground creeping shoots on which small, white tubers form. Its thin, hairy, aerial stem has opposite, long, oval green leaves with crimped edges and visible veins. The small flowers are pink and are borne on terminal clusters.

In temperate climate zones, the **Chinese artichoke** hardly ever blooms and only rarely bears seeds. The tubers, which are the edible part of the plant, have a white flesh and a beige rind. Measuring between 1 and 2 inches (3 and 5 cm) long, the tubers have a knobby shape and are grouped in rings. Their taste resembles that of **artichokes** or **salsify**.

The **Chinese artichoke** needs a sunny location with light, sandy, dry, airy soil. In order to propagate it, the tubers are buried at the beginning of the spring in groups of three or four. The first harvest can take place about eight months later once the shoots have withered. Once they have been dug up, the vegetables become soft very quickly; so they are left in the earth during the entire winter, and are only harvesting according to demand.

The tubers owe their taste to the essential oils which they contain. They are rich in carbohydrates, starch, lipids and cellulose. They contain few vitamins,

Chinese artichoke
Before preparing this vegetable it must be thoroughly rubbed with a cloth and washed in running water to remove the soil. The tubers can be eaten raw in a salad. Briefly cooked, so as not to become soft, they are served with melted butter, or stock. They can also be sautéed with parsley and garlic or prepared as sweet-and-sour fritters or as a gratin with béchamel sauce.

but many minerals. As they contain few calories, they often form part of weight loss diets. They stimulate bile activity, and are recommended to fight bile and liver ailments. Moreover, they have an antispasmodic and slightly hypotensive effect.

TRAGOPOGON PORRIFOLIUS **Salsify or Oyster plant**
Root vegetable
Family: Compositae
Origin: Central Europe
Height: 8 to 12 inches (20 to 30 cm)
Flowering: spring (from the second year)
Properties: purifier, diuretic, invigorating, sudorific

Salsify was already very popular among the Romans, even serving as a motive for frescoes in Pompeii. **Apicius**, the famous Roman gourmet, had several recipes dedicated to this vegetable. In the 17th century, **Olivier de Serres**, a minister of **Henry IV**, referred to it as "sersifi". However, in those times, the **Spanish scorzonera** was preferred. Today it is sold only canned; it is unavailable fresh. Nevertheless, it has become popular among some private market gardeners who grow these tasty and delicate roots in their gardens.

Salsify is a biennial herb with a thick white taproot. It bares narrow, often keeled leaves whose basis usually clasp the stem forming a tuft at the base of the plant. Together with the root they are the edible parts of the plant. The blue-purple flowers are borne in clusters on long peduncles. They bear fruit with a feathery panache forming a fluffy ball similar to that of a dandelion. The long, fleshy, fusiform taproot has a white-yellow rind.

Salsify thrives in a sunny location with light, deep, moist soil rich in nutrients. It is grown from seed in spring directly onto the field. During the whole summer, the soil must be kept moist by regular watering. The harvesting of the leaves and roots is done from October to March, before the plant blooms.

Salsify contains many carbohydrates (12%), proteins and cellulose. It has a considerably high nutritional value. It also has a white latex resin which becomes red when it comes in contact with the air. **Salsify** is also a source of vitamins A and C. It is a nutritious vegetable which helps the body eliminate impuri-

ties and toxins from the blood. Moreover, it has a diuretic and sudorific effect; thereby promoting the elimination of uric acid. Aside from its nutritional properties, this vegetable is helpful in the decontamination, purification and regeneration of body organs. The fleshy buds are harvested in the spring and are consumed raw with fruit and other vegetables.

Salsify leaves, which have a taste similar to that of **chicory**, are also used in salads, while the roots have a nutty taste and are consumed cooked alone or sprinkled with butter, meat juices or a béchamel sauce. They are sautéed with **parsley** and mixed with other vegetables, or used in omelettes, fritters or stews. **Salsify** goes well with white meat. Its cooking water is a refreshing, fragrant drink.

TRICHOSANTHES ANGUINA — *Snake gourd*

Fruit vegetable
Family: *Cucurbitaceae*
Origin: *South-East Asia, India, Sri Lanka*
Height: *about 13 feet (4 m)*
Flowering: *spring*
Properties: *soothing, purifier, diuretic, stimulant*

The **snake gourd** is a fast growing vine which, long before being cultivated, was consumed by the inhabitants of the regions where it grew wild. Today it is a rather popular vegetable used in several traditional recipes. They are generally easy to find in Asian grocery shops when in season.

It is an annual climber with more or less palmate, two or three lobed leaves with a long petiole. It has entire, notched or slightly wavy leaflets with serrated edges. Its flowers have long fringes on the petals, and while male flowers are borne in clusters, female flowers are solitary. They bear edible, oddly shaped fruit that look like coiled up snakes. They are plain green or grey-green becoming orange or red when ripe. Their rind is thin and the flesh thick and juicy. Like **cucumbers**, they contain numerous small, flat, ovoid, and tender seeds which, when the fruit is ripe, become big and hard. They have a delicate, sweet taste.

Snake gourd needs a rich, moist, well drained soil with a sunny and warm exposure. It is sown directly onto the field in the spring with a support to facilitate climbing. During the growth period, they must be watered regularly. Approximately eight weeks after sowing, the first fruits, which are tender, juicy and well developed, can be harvested.

Snake gourd contains a lot of water and fiber, but only a few calories. It is rich in proteins, vitamins A, B and C as well as minerals (manganese, potassium, iron and iodine). It is a diuretic that helps the organism by eliminating its impurities. It has a relaxing effect on the bodily tissue; thereby, soothing inflammations. It also has a positive and soothing effect on the nervous system. It stimulates blood circulation and contributes to cleansing the blood of toxins.

Just like **green beans**, **snake gourd** is cut into pieces and cooked in boiling salted water for five to ten minutes. It can be served with a curry sauce, salads, vegetable soups, ragouts, or couscous. It can also be added to other vegetables, cooked with **tomatoes** and **onions**, or mixed with minced meat or chopped fish. The young shoots and leaves are also eaten in salads or stews.

TRITICUM AESTIVUM — *Wheat*

Fruit vegetable
Family: *Gramineae*
Origin: *the Middle East, Ethiopia*
Height: *36 to 48 inches (90 to 120 cm)*
Flowering: *spring*
Properties: *anti-anaemia, reduces cholesterol, invigorating, purifier, emollient, laxative, mineralizing, stimulant*

Wheat is probably the offspring of a species originating in Abyssinia, when a single large, hard seed accidentally crossed with an unknown cereal, producing a species with multiple grains which was farther improved over the course of time by selection. To date, there have been approximately 12,000 varieties documented. From the Middle Eastern agricultural societies it spread to Egypt where it is widely grown today. **Wheat** is the most important grain of the northern hemisphere. In Africa it is also grown on a wide scale, especially in South Africa and the Maghreb countries.

Wheat, as we know it today, is an annual, herbaceous plant with flat, branching roots. The **wheat** plant has a long, thin, hollow aerial stem with nodes. The leaves are long, slender, straight and pointed wrapped around the stem at the base forming a sheath.

Wheat

Whole wheat is a grain similar to rice. It must be soaked in cold water overnight and then cooked in salted water. It can also be cooked pilaf-style: that is, sautéed in oil, covered with water and boiled. Wheat semolina is an indispensable ingredient for couscous. Cooked in milk it is used to make vanilla or caramel cakes with raisins or other dried fruit. Wheat flour is used in making cakes, bread, desserts, pasta, ravioli, and bread crumbs, as well as to bind sauces. Dried, wheat is popular as a breakfast cereal.

The flowers are grouped together in spikelets, each having two to six flowers. They bear dry fruit or monocotyledon caryopsis, which contain in each case a separate kernel.

Though grown under a wide range of climates and soils, **wheat** is best adapted to temperate regions with moderate rainfall. In general, **wheat** requires loose, fertilized, well drained soil.

Winter and spring **wheat** are the two major types of crop, with the severity of the winter expected determining whether a winter or spring type is cultivated. Winter **wheat** is always sown in the autumn; spring **wheat** is generally sown in the spring but can be sown in the autumn where winters are mild. Seeds germinate rather quickly covering the fields in winter with fresh green shoots. Spring rain promotes their growth. In July, when they are yellow and the seeds are swollen, the plant is harvested mechanically.

On average, the kernel contains 12% water, 70% of carbohydrates, 12% proteins, 2% fat, 2.2% crude fibers, 1.8% minerals (potassium, phosphorus and calcium), as well as vitamins of the B group and vitamin C. Moreover, the germ is a source of lecithin and phosphorus. The composition of the **wheat** grain is, therefore, a major source of energy in the human diet.

The lecithin it contains helps lower cholesterol levels and has a preventive effect against arteriosclerosis and cardio-vascular diseases. Vitamin E is a natural antioxidant that fights against the accumulation of toxins in the body. Phosphorus promotes the formation of bones and teeth. Potassium and calcium nourish the nervous system, regulate the activity of the heart muscle, and improve skin condition. B vitamins stimulate the activity of the stomach, transform sugar in the body, and promote formation of red blood cells. **Wheat** lowers the risk of rickets. **Wheat** is also used to calm inflammations, sooth body tissue and increase vital functions.

In all its forms and varieties, **wheat** is the most popular and most complete cereal there is. Although most **wheat** is grown for human food, small quantities are used by industry for the production of starch, paste, malt, dextrose, gluten, alcohol, and other products.

In some regions **wheat** straw is used to thatch roofs. In Tuscany it is used to manufacture excellent straw hats which are to be preferred to imitations made from synthetic materials.

Stinging nettle

Its leaves, which are previously washed and quickly blanched to remove the stinging barbs, are used in potato salads, stuffings, egg dishes, omelettes, minced meat, pâtés and as a garnish for savory pies. Steamed, they are used like spinach. Stinging nettle soup is made in the following way: first fry bacon rashers in a pan until brown. Sprinkle them with flour and mix to a roux. Add a quarter of a liter of stock, stirring vigorously to prevent lumps forming and bring to the boil. Add the finely chopped stinging nettle leaves and let simmer for ten minutes. Add a further cup of stock, heavy cream, and season with salt and pepper. Serve warm with grated cheese on top.

URTICA DIOICA ET URENS

Nettle and Stinging nettle

Leaf vegetable
Family: Urticaceae
Origin: worldwide, except in South America and equatorial Africa
Height: about 2 to 5 feet (0.50 to 1.50 m)
Flowering: June to October
Properties: anti-anaemia, anti-diabetes, astringent, laxative, diuretic, emetic

---

Nettle is a hardy plant which is able to colonize large areas within a short time by growing abundant underground rhizomes which produce the sharply edged stems covered with fine hairs, and which branch out when cut back. The opposite, elliptical leaves have dented borders and are also covered with hairs.

Inflorescences are borne on leaf axiles and are formed by long, hanging female flowers and shorter, upright male flowers which bear numerous seeds.

Stinging nettle is an annual plant of smaller size. It has a fusiform, simple root and smaller, opposite leaves with elliptical stalks and dented edges. The male flowers, which are more numerous than female flowers, are borne in clusters and bear several seeds which can continue to germinate for a number of years.

Stinging nettle has an astringent, bitter taste. Even though it prefers soil that is rich in nitrates and phosphates, it generally adapts itself to almost all conditions. **Stinging nettle** is sown in late winter, while **nettle** is propagated by rhizome division in the autumn. **Stinging nettle** leaves are harvested as a vegetable and herbal seasoning from the beginning of spring until the end of autumn. The young **nettle** shoots are harvested from April to May; the crown of the plant and the tender leaves are harvested later.

Stinging nettle contains a lot of nitrogen, chlorophyll, proteins, fat, carbohydrates, minerals (calcium, iron, silicon and zinc), organic acids, tannin, flavonoides, vitamins A, B2 and B5, as well as a lot of vitamin C. All these contents stimulate bodily functions, promote the formation of blood, work against inflammations, chronic cystitis and diabetes, and alleviate rheumatic pain.

The high levels of chlorophyll, cellulose, vitamin C, and glycogen lower the level of sugar in the blood. Moreover, the dried leaves contain 20% proteins and approximately 2% fat.

Because of its components, **nettle** is used to prevent broken nails and hair loss. Due to the fact that it contains zinc, it is also used to treat acne. It has a mineralizing effect on cartilage and relives arthritis and rheumatism. Furthermore, it is used to fight against fatigue, stimulate the gall bladder, and improve digestion.

VALERIANELLA OLITORIA   ***Corn salad, Lamb's lettuce***

Leaf vegetable
Family: Valerianaceae
Origin: Sardinia, Sicily
Height: about 4 inches (10 cm)
Flowering: spring
Properties: soothing, tranquilizer, purifier, laxative

Corn salad or **lamb's lettuce** is a vegetable that has been used as a salad since antiquity. It previously grew wild and was collected by the rural population from meadows and from between the rows of vines in vineyards.

Corn salad is a herbaceous, annual plant with elongated, characteristically veined leaves grouped in basal rosettes. The hollow stems are branched out in the shape of a fork and can reach a height of 8 to 12 inches (20 to 30 cm). The small, white or bluish umbel flowers are borne in terminal clusters. The leaves have a fresh, sticky, nutty taste.

There are more than 50 species. **Corn salad** grows best in damp, relatively hard soil in the shade. It is sown in mid-summer to be harvested in the autumn, at the end of the summer to be harvested in winter, or at the end of September to be harvested in the spring. **Corn salad** is resistant to cold. Harvesting is done once the leaf rosettes are well formed before blooming while they still have not acquired a bitter taste.

Corn salad has a higher nutritional value than that of other lettuces. It is rich in vitamins A, B and C, minerals (iron, phosphorus and calcium) as well as saccharides, proteins, and fat.

Corn salad stimulates digestion and has a soothing effect on the nervous system.

It is eaten raw by itself or mixed with other vegetables in a salad. It goes well with green salads, **beetroot** or **potatoes**. It can also be used to make herbal soups, omelettes and pâtés.

Broad bean

Broad beans can be eaten raw with salt, pickled in oil or in salads. When they are fresh, they can be cooked and served as a side dish for meat and other vegetables. They can be sautéed in butter with scallions and served with pork or sausages. When dried they must first be soaked overnight before being cooked. They are then boiled in order to remove their coarse husks. They can be cooked to a puree, in a gratin or in a ragout. Fava bean flour mixed with wheat flour is used to prepare biscuits and cakes to which it adds a nutty flavor.

VICIA FABA   ***Broad or Fava bean***

Fruit vegetable
Family: Papilionaceae
Origin: the Middle East
Height: about 3 feet (1 m)
Flowering: spring
Properties: antispasmodic, diuretic, purifier, sedative

Broad bean is a perennial legume. It has erect stems and branches crowded with compound leaves with four leaflets. The flowers are borne on terminal clusters with a large white corolla that is stained black. They bear long, green, rough pods which become brown when ripe. The pods contain large, irregularly flattened seeds. The plant is not very demanding, but it grows best in moist, limey soil rich in humus with a warm, sunny exposure. It is sown in February or March in rows with three to four seeds per seeding place. In very mild regions, it can be sown from October to February. Harvesting is generally done while the **broad bean** is still green; **broad beans**, raw or cooked, are consumed when young.

Young **broad beans** have a low nutritional value. However, they are rich in proteins (23%), magnesium, vitamin C and fiber. The plant is a diuretic and its high content of fiber facilitates digestion and helps fight intestinal spasms. The dried **beans** are rich in minerals and carbohydrates (55%). Because they contain more calories, they are more nutritious than the green beans. **Broad beans** are known to soothe pain and slow the activity of the nervous system.

XANTHOSOMA SAGITTIFOLIUM   ***Tania, Yautia***
Root and leaf vegetable
Family: Araceae
Origin: tropical America
Height: about 6.5 feet (2 m)
Flowering: spring
Properties: emollient, nutritious, mineralizing

Also known as **yautia** or **okumo** in Venezuela, the **tania** is a staple food in Central and South America. It contains calcium oxalate which is a highly toxic substance that is difficult to dissolve. The corns must, therefore, be thoroughly washed and cooked

before they are edible. Today the plant is cultivated worldwide.

Tania has tuberous rhizomes and very large, abundant, leaves with long petioles. Its stems, which can be over 3 feet (1 m) long, are triangular, in the form of an arrow or oval with a glossy topside and a lustrous underside. Flowers and fruit rarely develop. **Tania** requires a warm climate and damp, nourishing, deep soil. It is cultivated by replanting the tubers in the autumn. The harvesting of the shoots and young leaves takes place in the spring; the tubers are harvested at the end of the summer. Because the entire plant contains calcium oxalate, caution must be taken. Once the tubers are pulled out, they are left to dry in the sun for a day and placed in cool, dry and dark storage.

Tania contains a lot of starch, carbohydrates, amino acids, minerals (potassium and calcium), vitamins A and B as well as different fibers. The tubers stimulate digestion, alleviate inflammations, and prevent the absorption of fat and sugar in the intestine. They mineralize cartilage and strengthen the organism.

Once the calcium oxalate has been washed out, the tubers are cooked in water, steamed or fried. Peeled and mashed they make a delicious puree. Cut in pieces and cooked in the pressure cooker with herbs, they are used as an accompaniment for meat and fish. They go well in a ragout served with poultry. The starch of the tubers is used to prepare porridges, noodles, creams and cakes. The young flowers and the shoots are eaten cooked as green vegetables.

ZEA MAYS   **Corn**
Fruit vegetable
Family: Gramineae
Origin: Mexico, origin of the wild form unknown
Height: about 8 feet (2.50 m)
Flowering: spring
Properties: tranquilizer, analgesic, anti-cholesterol, diuretic

---

The tall, annual grass has a stout, erect, solid stem and large narrow leaves. Staminate or male flowers are borne on the tassel terminating the main axis of the stem, while the female flower is borne on the leaf axiles. Female flowers, which mature to become the ear, are spikes with a thickened axis, bearing paired spikelets normally producing seeds through self-pollination.

In the case of selected **corn** varieties kernels stand all around a woody central spike that is enclosed by modified leaves or husks. The leaves are large, lanceolate and narrow with wavy margins, spaced alternately on opposite sides of the stem. The roots are not anchored particularly deep in the soil.

Corn needs nourishing, deep, loose, moist soil with a sunny exposure. It is sown in rows from May to June once the earth has been warmed by the Sun. So that the plants grow strong, they must be frequently banked with earth. Regular and extensive watering is necessary. Harvesting is done according to the variety concerned. **Sweet corn** (*Zea mays var. saccharata*) which is consumed like a fresh vegetable, is harvested once the kernels are well formed, but still tender and juicy. **Cereal corn** is harvested mechanically early in the autumn when the shoots begin to wilt and the kernels are ripe.

Sweet corn is rich in carbohydrates, vitamin A, vitamins of the B group and vitamin C. Besides, it contains minerals, particularly magnesium, phosphorus and potassium. It is high in calories. **Cereal corn** contains 75% starch, 5% sugar, 7–9% lipids, and minerals. It is a very nourishing grain, but less balanced than **wheat**. Although it slows down the activity of the thyroid and regulates the metabolism, **corn** as basic food cannot replace **wheat** for it has an inferior nutritional value.

The germ contains, like that of sunflowers, an oil which reduces the levels of cholesterol. Its starch is easy to digest, especially for people with delicate and weak stomachs. Its spikelets contain salisylic acid, which has an analgesic and anti-inflammatory effect, and vitamin K, which is indispensable for blood clotting. It is both diuretic and soothing.

Corn leaves are used as livestock feed and the grains are used to feed fowl and swine. The stalks are made into paper and wallboard, while the cobs are used for fuel and in the preparation of industrial solvents.

Corn

Sweet corn can be eaten whole, raw or cooked in water, milk or steamed. It is a traditional accompaniment for grilled meat and fowl as well as for pork or lamb patties. The delicate kernels are the basic ingredient in many salads, meat and fish recipes. They can be used in stuffings and vegetable mixtures. Corn flour is used to make porridge, puddings, cakes, polenta, and biscuits. Mixed with wheat flour it is used to make a very heavy bread. Popcorn is obtained from a variety that has very small kernels; heated in oil, the kernels explode becoming puffy and soft. They are usually eaten salted or sweet. In Mexico fermented corn is used to make an alcoholic drink known as "chicha." When the young spikes are approximately 4 inches (10 cm) they are cut, pickled in vinegar and served as a savory snack. The can also be cooked in salted water like a vegetable and used in salads or served with exotic dishes. Corn semolina is an ingredient for cornflakes. Starch is also obtained from corn. It is used to bind sauces, and to prepare soups, fine pastries and milk puddings.

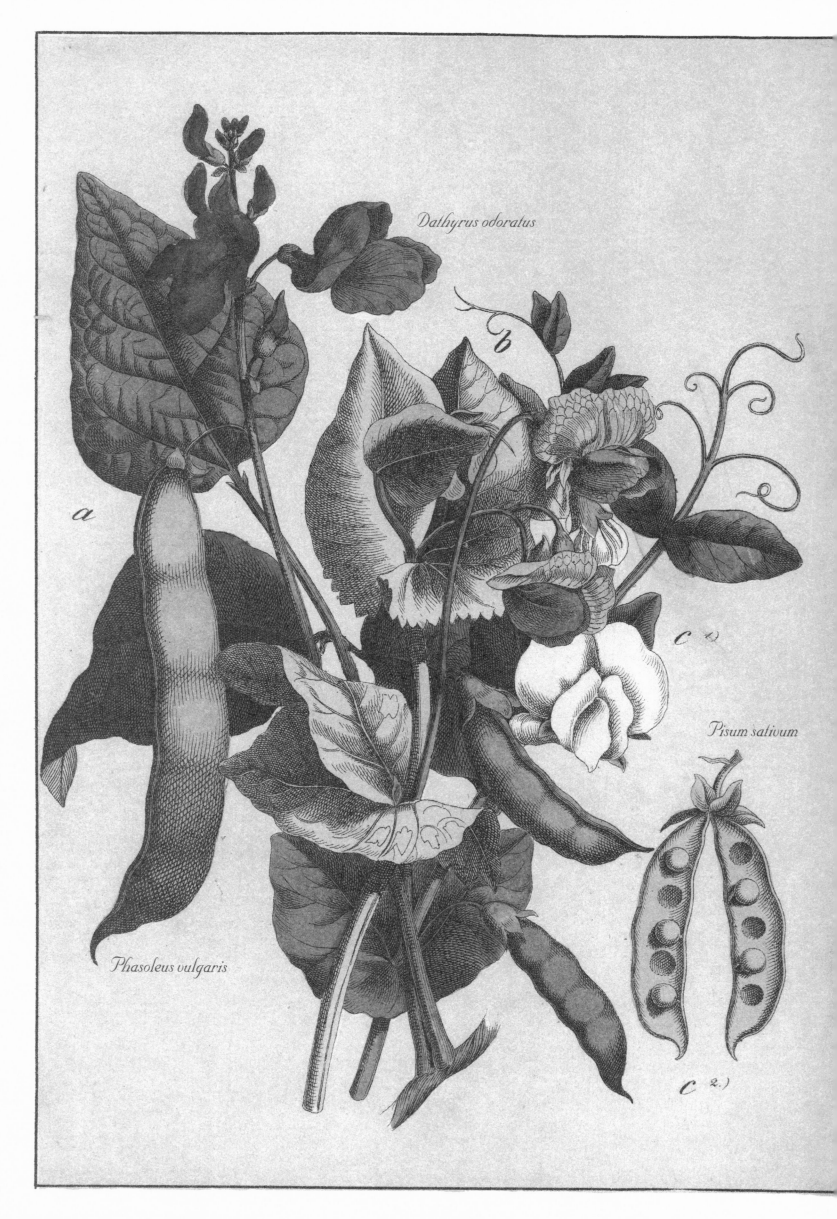

Dathyrus odoratus

b

c ♀

Pisum sativum

a

Phasoleus vulgaris

c 2.)

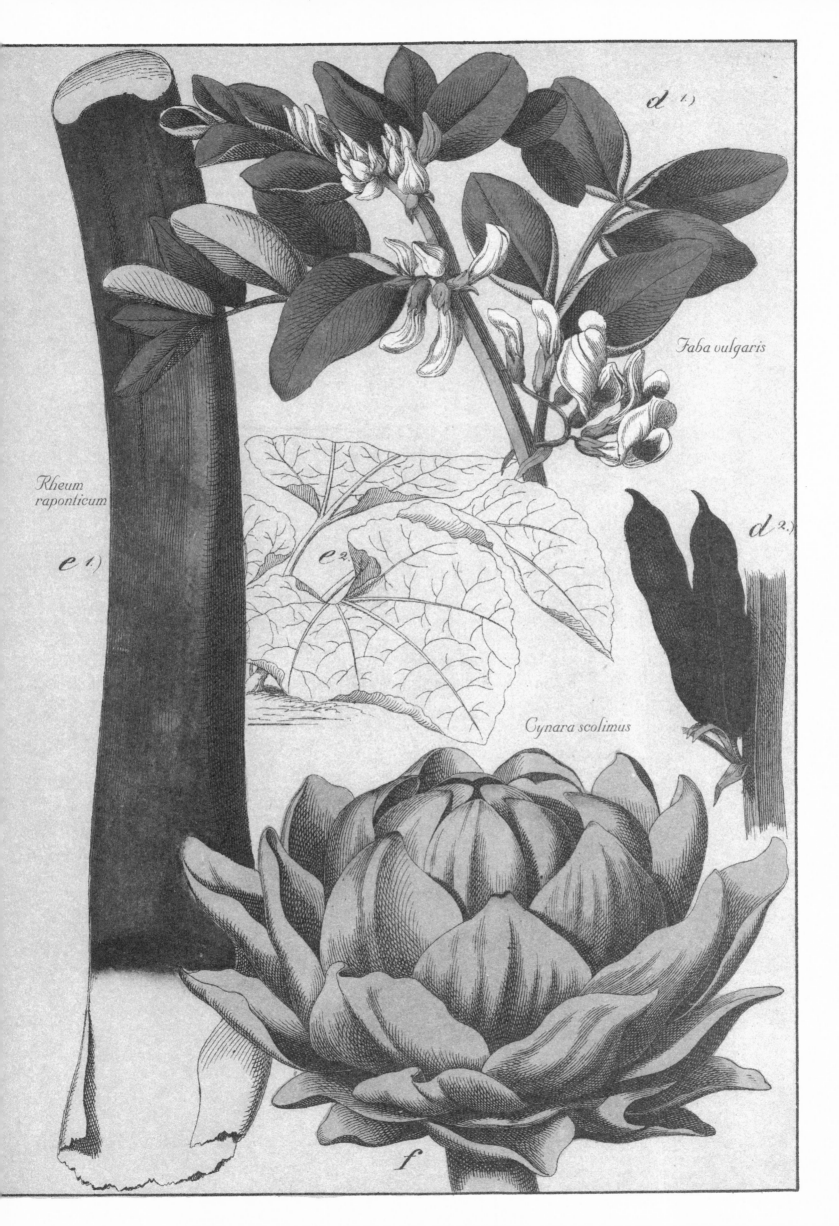

Faba vulgaris

Rheum raponticum

Cynara scolimus

d ¹⁾

d ²⁾

e ¹⁾

e ²⁾

f

123

Raphanus sativus

Apium graveslens

a. 1)

a. 3)

a. 2)

c

124

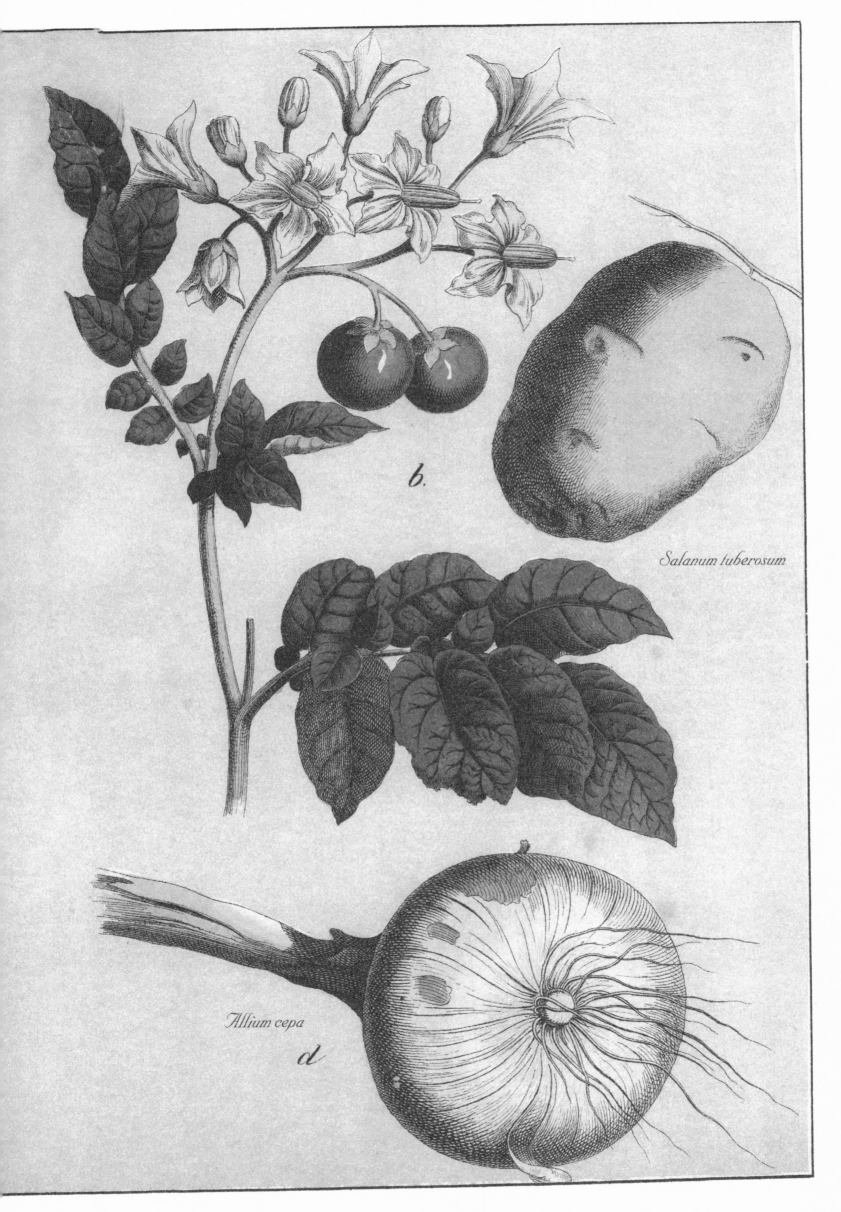

b.

Salanum tuberosum

Allium cepa

d

125

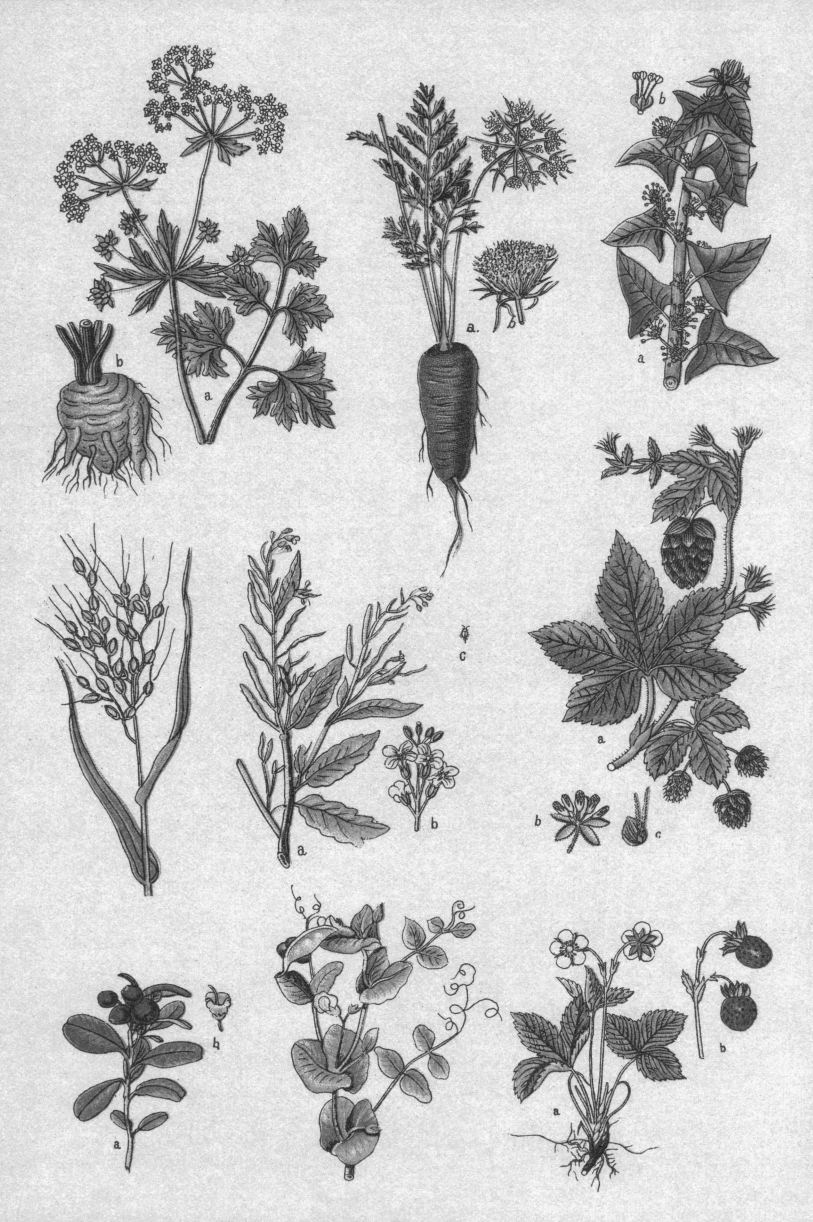

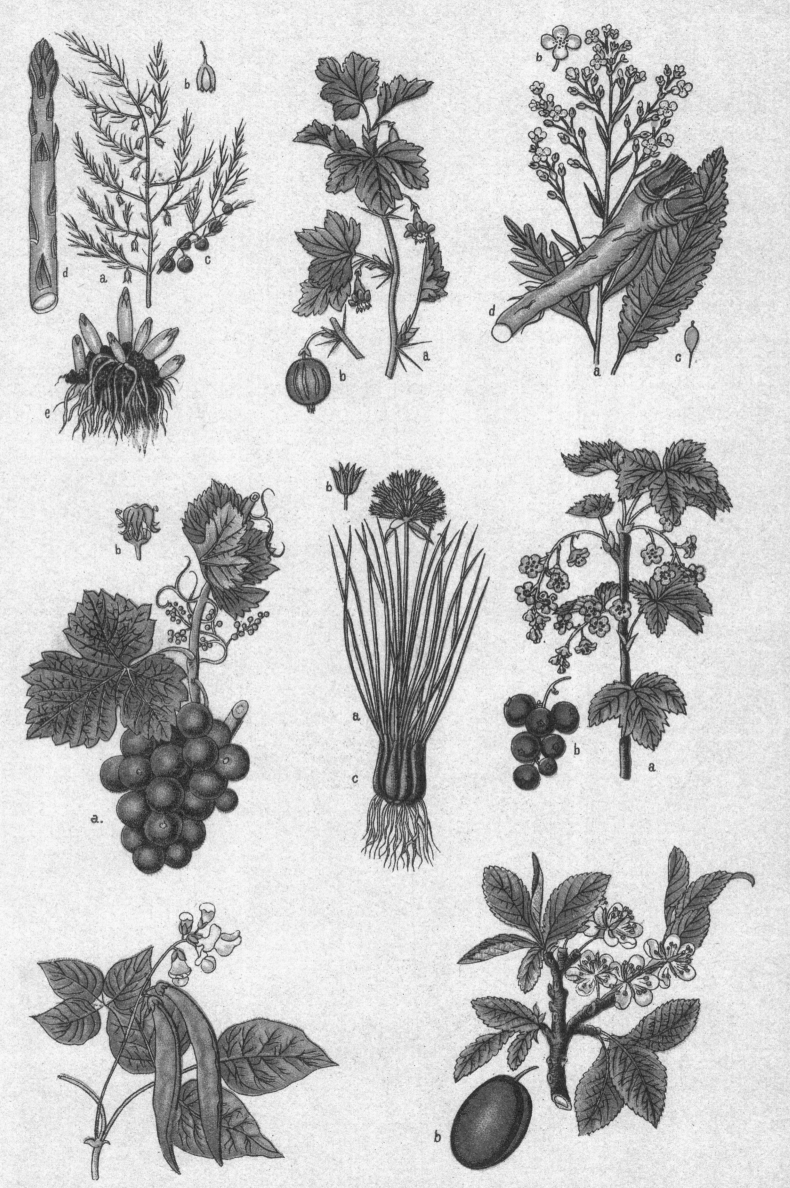

127

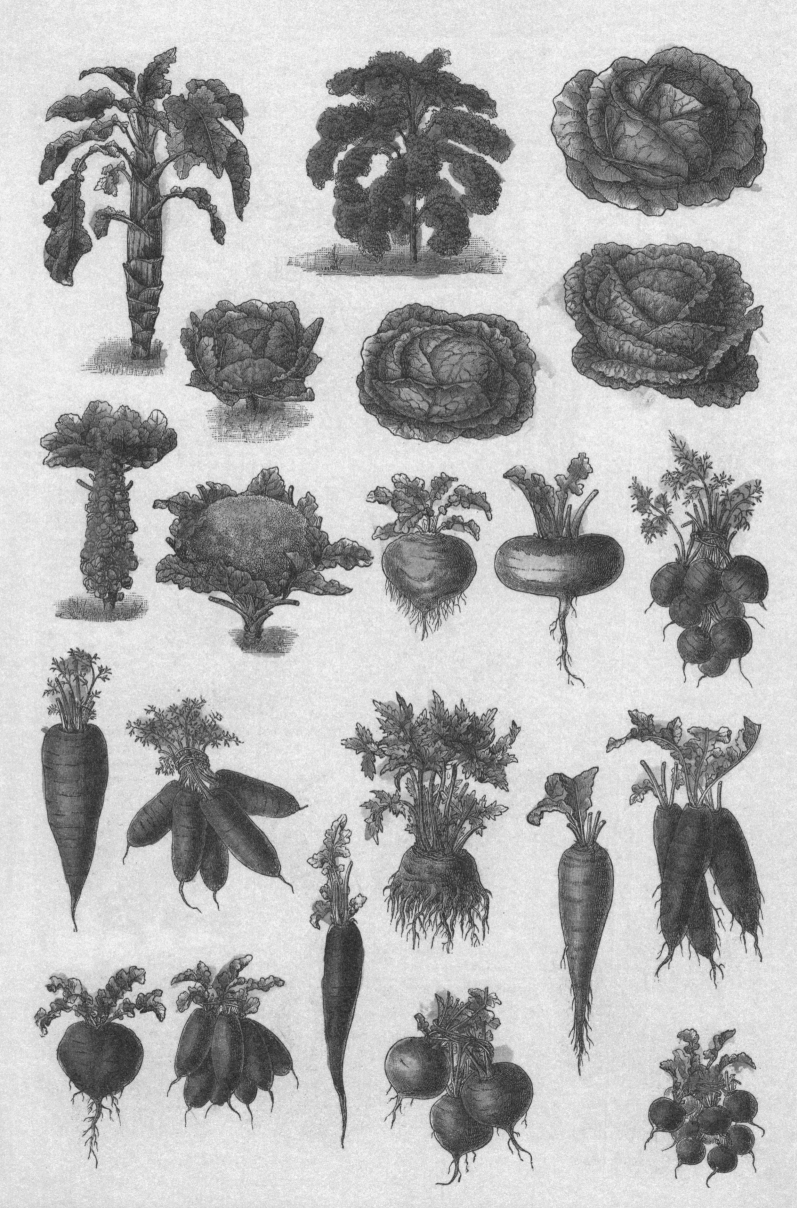

128

INDEX OF LATIN NAMES

AND OF ENGLISH NAMES

BIBLIOGRAPHY

Berry, Susan: Kitchen Harvest: A Cook's Guide to Growing Organic Fruits,
Vegetables, and Herbs, 2002

Brown, Lynda: Gardeners' World Vegetables for Small Gardens, 1994

Chandler, Lynda E.: Fruits and Vegetables, 2001

Heaton, Donald D.: A Produce Reference Guide to Fruits and Vegetables
from Around the World – Nature's Harvest, 1997

Katz, Pat: Parsley, Peppers, Potatoes & Peas: A Cook's Companion for Handling,
Using & Storing a Garden's Bounty, 2002

King, Darlene: Vegetables You Used to Hate!, 2000

Patenaude, Fredric: Sunfood Cuisine: A Practical Guide to Raw Vegetarian Cuisine, 2002

Robinson, Fay: Vegetables, Vegetables (Rookie Read-About Science), 1994

Robinson, Kathleen / Luckett, Pete: Vegetarian's A to Z Guide to Fruits & Vegetables, 1996

Shewfelt, Robert L.: Fruit and Vegetable Quality: An Integrated View, 2000

Smit, Tim / Macmillan Browse, Philip: The Heligan Vegetable Bible, 2000

Van Den Berg, Oona: The Exotic Fruit and Vegetable Handbook, 2001